Edited by
Jan Fook, Susan Hawthorne and Renate Klein

HorseDreams

The Meaning of Horses in Women's Lives

Spinifex Press Pty Ltd
504 Queensberry Street
North Melbourne, Vic. 3051
Australia
women@spinifexpress.com.au
http://www.spinifexpress.com.au

First published by Spinifex Press, 2004

Cover and book design by Deb Snibson, The Modern Art Production Group
Made and printed in Australia by McPherson's Printing Group

National Library of Australia
Cataloguing-in-Publication data:

HorseDreams : the meaning of horses in women's lives.

ISBN 1 876756 47 0

1. Horses - Social aspects. 2. Women and animals. I. Fook,
Janis. II. Hawthorne, Susan, 1951- . III. Klein, Renate.
IV. Title : HorseDreams : the meaning of horses in
women's lives.

636.10082

For Caroline Taylor,
and in memory of her horse Tehya

Contents

Acknowledgements vii

Preface viii

Section One   HorsePower   1

Seven Horses   Marge Piercy   2
Horse-riding Instructions from an Old Bushie, Or How Not To Fall Off a Horse   Munya Andrews   4
Calamity Jane—The Little Feminist Horse!   Caroline Taylor   8
Brumbies   Beatriz Copello   14
Pink Clover   Theo Wills-Johnson   16
Horse Diary   Finola Moorhead   20
Sounds of the Stables   Sarah Cowell   24
Of Power and Control   Wendy Ellerton   26
Born to Run   Janet Stumbo   28
Horse Byte   Rose Kizinska   32
The Homecoming of Bungala   Kiersten Coulter   34
Kimberley Moonbeam the Fourth   Melinda Tankard Reist   38
Don't Fence Me In   Chris Sitka   40
Over the Ravine   Sophie Barnet   42
Horse Dreams and Commonsense   Pam Bjork-Billings   46
La Marismeña Australiana   Kirrilly Thompson   48

Section Two   GirlDreams   51

Horses Schmorses   Ginger Ekselman   52
For Love, Trust and Nothing Else   Linley Maroney   56
For the Love of a Mare   Di Gatehouse   58
Clever Chap   Jan Williamson   62
Pedro   Deborah Wardle   64
Freedom is a Horse   Kirsten Bowers   68
Broken Memories   Lana Homes   70
Barbero's Story   Suzanne Coutanceau   72
My Horse's Heart   Caroline Taylor   74
A Horse Tale   Freya Berenyi   76
Tango   Marion Tyree   78
Pretty Girl   Anna Kay   80
Dedicated to Horses   Shelley Virduzzo   82
I Dream of Horses   Julie Copeland   84
What Is It About Little Girls and Horses?   Martha C. Sewell   88

Section Three   HorseMyths   91

At the Rim of the Plains   Jacqueline Crompton Ottaway   92
Shape-shifters   Sue Booker   94
Wild Wisdom   Karin Meissenburg   98
The Gift   Margôt Erikson   100
Hippocampus   June Kant   102
They Have My Heart, They Sing My Soul   Catherine Johns   106
The Woman on Horseback   Claire French   108
Equus   Angela Crocombe   112
I am a Sagittaria   Tatyana Mamanova   114
Stormy   Susan Wills   116
My Horse with a Golden Pole   Cheryl Osborne   118
The Last Melbourne Cup   Koa Whittingham   120

Section Four   NightMares   123

Black Horse   Eve   124
The Goddess Paddock   Lin Van Hek   126
A Holiday Romance   Denise Imwold   130
Night Journey   Marg Peck   132
For Drew   Niki van Buuren   134
Love is Caleb   Sandra Burr   136
My Friend. My Confidante. My Horse.   Schantelle Edgecumbe   140
The Beginning   Polly Klein   142
Champions   Brenda Coulter   144
The Horse Guard   Lyn McConchie   146
Fur Therapy   Lorelei Dowling   148
The RSPCA Horse   Coral Hull   150
Destiny   Kate Danby   152
Diary   Helen McLennan   154
Thanatos – Be Damned   Francesca Bass   158
Horsewoman   Pat Hodgell   160

Section Five   WorkHorses   165

Dress-up Donkeys   Donna Jackson   166
Bareback Rider   Amanda Owen   170
Cat Friday   Rebecca Gorman   172
A One Horse Tale   Sharman Horwood   176
Joyce Pilkington and Karumba Cassidy   Mary K. Hughes   178
How Many Times Do You Have to Fall?   Susan Hawthorne   180
The Vet Check   Linda Dicmanis   184
Lorna's Story   Lorna Oldaker and Maralann Damiano   186
Can You Feel It?   Alayne Renee Blickle   188
Joey   Anne Deal   190
The Black Horse   Jenny Barnes   192
Bay Rose: The Last of the Great Walers   Janne Ellen   196
Johnny Appleseed and Life on the Road   Zohl dé Ishtar   198

Section Six   InterBeing   203

Creatures   Ann Game   204
Dreaming of Pegasus, or Quin's Story   Lynda Birke   206
Horsefeathers   Beth Burrows   210
Talent   Elizabeth Campbell   212
The Smell of Love   Gwin Harris Steph   214
Change   Heather Cameron   216
The Tail of a Terrible Horse   Jill Mather   218
The Horse Whisperers   Doreen and Cathie Dunsford   220
Star   Louise Duval   222
I Remember, I Don't Remember   Margaret Carmichael Leonard   224
Lesson One: Thinking Outside the Square   Anna Bianchi   228
Barn Fire   Sally Armbrecht   232
You Ask Me About My Horse, You Ask Me About Myself   Alessina Brooks   234
The Orphan Foal   Helen McIntyre   238
A Vision of Horses and Mules   Marge Piercy   242

Permissions 244
Photographic Credits 244

Acknowledgements

HorseDreams is the third in our series of books compiling the stories of women and their companion animals. Once again it has been a huge delight to work on this volume. As with each of these productions, there are many women involved, and many different ideas represented.

First, as ever, Belinda Morris has done a wonderfully smooth job in co-ordinating the whole process of requesting and receiving contributions, filing and matching photographs, and generally liaising with contributors and editors. Her talents are an integral part of the project, and she has helped invaluably by streamlining the process. The books would not be the same without her. We also thank the other women at Spinifex Press: Maralann Damiano, Elana Markowitz and Jo O'Brien.

Copy-editor Barbara Burton deserves great thanks for all her patience and hard work, making such a diverse combination of pieces read so smoothly.

The cover and interior design is another triumph, and for this we thank Deb Snibson. The cover colours and photograph, we believe, convey the spirit of the horse which comes across between the covers. The combination of lime and misty chestnut speaks of both boldness and mystery… the essence of the horse can never be fully understood, or mastered, by humans.

Again, we want to thank each other for another joyful partnership and, of course, a very big thank you to all the contributors who shared with us these wonderful stories about the horses in their lives. Contributors Jenny Barnes, Suzanne Coutanceau and Lin Van Hek were also very generous in supplying extra photos for use throughout the book.

We extend a particular thanks to Christine Zmroczek for the title, and to those of our contributors who enlisted the contributions of other horse lovers. This project, like the others, has worked like a snowball to capture the imaginations of many different women from diverse backgrounds, around the globe. This would not be possible on such a large scale, without the enthusiastic participation of numerous horselovers who were previously unknown to us. It is been a privilege to read your stories, to glimpse a little of a distant life which meets our own in the love of these magnificent creatures.

Jan Fook
Susan Hawthorne
Renate Klein

Preface

Jan Fook, Susan Hawthorne and Renate Klein

What do horses mean to women? It's a question that has been asked for millennia: from amazons to Olympic horsewomen, from queens to jockeys, from girls who dream of riding a horse to grown women riding days on end in tests of endurance.

When we set out on this third journey into exploring the meaning of animals in women's lives, following on from dogs in *A Girl's Best Friend* and cats in *Cat Tales,* we wondered just what we would find.

One of the early themes to emerge was the importance of horses in the relationships between mothers and daughters. It is often the mother who first encourages the girl onto horseback; it is often the mother who teaches her daughter how to ride and how to speak the language of horse paraphernalia.

But not every daughter is lucky enough to have a mother who knows and cares about horses or can afford to have a horse in her life. Some girls learn to ride in spite of parental disapproval or sheer lack of means. There are girls who gaze longingly at the horse next door until they are given the opportunity. Some have cared for a horse and slowly developed a relationship that cannot be broken. For others, the horse as companion has been an important part of their growing up. It gives them the possibility of independence and solitude without actually being alone. It gives them mobility and a sense of power and freedom.

It is this aspect that begins the book. HorsePower explores what it means to be friends with these extraordinary creatures, frequently much larger than ourselves. The sense of height, the power of speed, the strength in horse muscles. It's no accident that horses are used as the metaphor for engine strength. The writers also explore what it means to feel free, to live with a sense that in company with a horse troubles can be overcome and places can be visited which are inaccessible by other means.

When we were considering titles for this book we kept returning to the idea of dreams. The sense that horses can fill an important space in the imagination and in one's life. We thought of Pegasus and of horses who have shown courage. We thought of all the literary horses from Black Beauty to Silver Brumbies and of heroines who rode horses into or out of danger. As girls we were all influenced by such stories, we dreamed that perhaps one day we too could have such adventures. Among the contributions we received were stories by girls telling us of their hopes, and stories by women for whom the dream of horses had sometimes turned into a reality, for some to the point of becoming professional riders. There are also stories by women who had never had the chance of riding when young but who later in life began to share their lives with horses. Some of our contributors have lived with and among horses all their lives.

The dreams girls have of horses are bolstered by the myths and legends told about horses, and this aspect informed a significant number of the stories in the book. Epona, the image which opens HorseMyths, is an ancient horse goddess rising from British soil. It was a white horse that Lady Godiva rode through the streets of Coventry. Was it perhaps Epona? Certainly it is Epona whose form is carved into the hillsides of England. The star sign Sagittarius is transformed here into Sagittaria and mythic horses of many cultures emerge from the mist whether they have magical qualities like the unicorn, the watery beauty of the seahorse, the fantasy element of the merry-go-round horse, or the possibility of winning the race that stops a nation, the Melbourne Cup.

Horses have real effects on women's lives. NightMares are both mares of the night who come to rescue us from some dire situation and those who become healing horses for both emotional and physical trauma. But nightmares are also the terrible occurrences that sometimes occur in our lives with horses and the terrible cruelty that some horses have experienced at human hands. The horse in many places carries the soul to the other world, assists the process of healing. In this section we are taken on a journey we hadn't really anticipated although we knew that animals are often involved in getting women through life's most difficult times.

Women and horses have also worked together and in this section we were able to explore the manifold ways in which horses have made it possible to make a living. WorkHorses are pretty tough; they have stamina and courage. Some horses have entertained us, others have drawn large weights or been ridden long distances on a daily basis. Horses also work when they participate in competition as racehorses, in ring events and even in circuses. Whatever their work, it has helped sustain human communities in many times and places.

Finally, we found that there was a special connection between horses and women in the bodily and emotional realms. Ann Game's piece gave us the title for this section, InterBeing. It is the way in which women and horses communicate whether as horse whisperers or through the bodily connection of riding a horse. It is the sometimes almost total identification of horse and woman.

A note is necessary about the occasional interruptions in *HorseDreams* by donkeys. We included donkeys in our call for contributions, and indeed they came. They have turned out to be the comedians of this book. The stories the donkeys and their women have to tell are as extraordinary as those told about horses. And we are grateful to them for making us laugh. As laughter has become an integral part of our selection process, it was great to have their spark and energy.

We hope these stories of horses and donkeys will carry you, the reader, to other realms, to other places and into a world transformed by the energies and strengths of horses.

Section One HorsePower

Seven Horses

Marge Piercy

When I was a pencil of a girl
I had seven horses, one
for each day of the week.

Thunder, Lightning, Sun
and Moon, East Wind
North Wind and Red Roses.

Only I could see them,
roan and black, grey,
palomino, dapple, white

and the strange one
the flying red horse
from the Mobil sign.

I rode them to school,
home, to the store.
I rode them down the slopes

of rocky night. In adolescence
I never mooned over horses.
Later, they were something cops

charged at us in demonstrations.
I'd sooner ride a cow.
No, it was not horseflesh

but power I craved
and speed. I longed to gallop
out of our tight mortgaged house

furnished with shouts and razors,
out of the smoke of frustrations
burning like old tyres.

I wanted to stick out my neck
and gallop at full tilt off
any map I had ever seen.

Marge Piercy is the author of sixteen
published novels, most recently The
Third Child. *Among her other books are*
Woman on the Edge of Time, Gone to
Soldiers, *and* The Longings of Women.
*She is also the author of sixteen
collections of poetry. Her recent memoir
is called* Sleeping with Cats. *She was
born in Detroit, Michigan and lives on
Cape Cod, far out to sea.*

Horse-riding Instructions from an Old Bushie Or How Not to Fall Off a Horse
Munya Andrews

This is the tale of a first time rider. It took place in Kalbarri in Western Australia in the not so long ago. The instructor was an Old Bushie whose riding philosophy was simple. 'There's no reason why anyone should fall off a horse,' he said to a group of tourists. 'No reason at all.' And then he proceeded to explain in simple terms why this could not and should not happen. With this philosophy shared and the barest riding instructions given, the instructor and riding group set off on course. One of those riders takes up the story as follows.

It was the first time I had ever ridden a horse. I was about nineteen or twenty years old. Ever since I was a little girl I had always wanted a horse as a pet but my family could not afford one. Now that I was an independent young adult, this meant that I could treat myself to one of my fantasies, that of learning to ride. On this occasion, I was accompanied by one of my closest school friends and her then boyfriend, now husband of twenty years or so. We did virtually everything together and so it seemed perfectly natural that we would be given horses that were known best friends. Taking off from immediately behind the instructor, we rode astride each other, two by two.

It was a perfect 'winter' day in Kalbarri, blue skies and moderate temperature. We were trotting along just fine until the instructor decided to put on a little pace. Before I knew it, my friend's horse just bolted out of the blue and took off. Being its best friend, this impromptu gallop immediately set off my horse, which decided to follow suit. All hell broke loose—just like the proverbial bull in a china shop, only, in this instance, it was a case of the bull on a galloping horse! As we both tore around a corner, my friend's horse threw her. Looking back, I could see that she was all right, although understandably upset, but I had to turn my attentions to what was unfolding before me. With my friend now dislodged, her horse was galloping freely. Not to be outdone, my horse raced neck-and-neck with its equine friend, like participants in the Melbourne Cup, storming down the main straight with the crowd cheering them on.

Fearful of being thrown, I clung desperately to my horse so that horse and rider were one. It seemed to know instinctively where it was going as it careered around corners, weaving in and out of the bushes. Ducking to avoid tree branches and shrubs, I must have looked like one of those riders in American Western movies with 'wild' Indians and cowboys doing special stunts and fancy equestrian manoeuvres. Or else a black female Roy Rogers riding on Trigger the horse, although in my case it must've been Trigger-happy.

I looked behind to see if some hero had decided to chase after me, take the reins and force the horse to stop, but there was no sign of the other riders or the instructor. We were completely alone, horse and I, after its friend had taken another path. As it raced on, I started to remember what the old bushman had told us—the part about

throwing my arms around the horse's neck, which I did. Yes, but what came next?

With my mind and heartbeat racing to the rhythm of the horse's hooves, I desperately racked my brain to recall the remainder of his instruction and then it came to me in a flash of lightning. Ah yes, the bit about throwing my right leg around the saddle and dismounting with both feet coming down so that I was in a virtual standing position. Then, using my arms around the horse's neck as a balancing prop from which to hang until both my feet touched the ground, I could release myself from the horse so that horse and rider could continue on their individual merry ways. This too reminded me once again of those Western movies where riders would freely swing their legs around, briefly dismount and launch themselves back up into their saddles as though they had landed on springboards that catapulted them into the air again.

Suddenly the true realities of the required manoeuvres became all too readily apparent. Not only did it seem an impossible task but a bloody stupid one at that. What is more, from my perspective, the ground looked as though it were at least six or seven feet below, which I am not. As I contemplated my options I pictured myself dangling precariously from this tall animal with my vertically-challenged body, legs and feet dangling, feeling about, trying pathetically to search for terra firma. Not a good look when you're twenty and trying to look sexy to impress the girls. Being concerned with appearances at that time and age, I decided that particular exit was not for me at all. Not only was it undignified, it now seemed quite dangerous. Nor did the idea of being thrown off the horse hold any appeal. As tough as I was, the idea of a broken limb or some other physical injury did not seem either desirable or heroic, not to mention the thought of possibly embarrassing myself.

These days, of course, I find myself beyond embarrassment given the countless number of mishaps and other calamities I have experienced throughout life. Like the time I once fell down a manhole in Perth in full view of urban observers… How the streetworkers laughed. So did I, in fits of laughter. There I was at the bottom of a six-foot hole in the ground with hamburger and bottle of Coke intact, until they eventually pulled me out! Or the time

when I was on a boat cruising the Fijiian Islands when I shamelessly asked a one-armed French tourist if he could take a picture of me. Of course, by the time I realised his physical predicament, and my own lack of sensitivity and tact, I was in far too deep to save face. Not that I should have worried, the picture turned out just fine after the poor man had graciously juggled my camera with his one arm and hand.

But I digress.

Meanwhile horse and rider were joined by an inexplicable sense of fate, of destiny. We communed at that moment, he and I, at first in silence until I heard myself speaking my thoughts out aloud. Tightening my vice around its neck, I heard myself say to equine: 'If I'm going down horse… you're coming with me.' I like to think the horse sized up the offer placed before it. That it deliberated upon the pros and cons of continuing in this mad, senseless gallop with inexperienced rider on its back before it came to a sudden, complete halt. It was then that I realised the full extent of its decision.

The strange sounds of it desperately gulping for air made me realise that, in my panicked state, I had almost strangled the poor animal to death, for the sounds it was making were those of a choked horse. It was truly one of those precious, comical moments, one of my finest theatrics and not an audience within a horse's whisper. No camera or video to record the event for posterity, just the horse and myself. Finally, in that moment, away from the pack of other riders and horses, we understood each other. And as I took control of the reins once more, he gently cantered back to base with the rider he could not throw.

__Munya Andrews__ has been riding horses for more than twenty years. She still does not own a horse as a pet, not because she can't afford one but because she doesn't want the responsibility that accompanies having a pet (or child or lover for that matter). She has never fallen off a horse in all those years (touch wood) but she has broken her leg in a motorbike accident. Some people mistakenly believe she has a 'death wish' as she continues to jump off cliffs and out of planes with parachutes and other paraphernalia attached such as long rubber bands, towels and Velcro. Her other passion is flying planes but that's another story (and another book).

Calamity Jane – The Little Feminist Horse!

Caroline Taylor

I saw you the morning of your birth, 12 October 1983. You were exquisite, stunning; you captivated me. And while all animals captivated me, something drew me to you —like two creature souls—you and I.

From the moment of your birth, you yourself felt different from other horses, I could tell. I lovingly watched you from afar, not wanting to disturb your baby-mother bond till you were weaned. Oh what a noise, what a performance when I weaned you. I wanted you to know that I would love you dearly—would always protect, and nurture and love you. My own bruised heart, from years of previous and still current child abuse sought always to love animals—and for them to love and nurture me. I know you sensed my pain, from the earliest days... And as frightened as I was of others—especially the perpetrator—you were not. Not ever.

You were Calamity Jane, and how quickly you bonded with me—even when you were naughty and tested me, even as a baby, I knew you loved me. You were very different with others, especially he who was hurting me still. One day you kicked him and two others—kicks directed straight at the groin—I was secretly delighted. Others could not handle you and told me you were mad, the same way they label women who are strong or different! You were both! You were my Calamity Jane.

I took you to horse shows and you were so stunning other people stopped to look and touch and even take photos—your brilliant white coat with leopard black spots and silver mane and tail. What a stunning Palouse! You would throw your head back in a way that shook your silvery mane and would prance so that others often

mistook you for a colt! (Typical to think that only males can move with such open pride!)

You won everything—and you knew you won each time. When judges presented you with the big sash and cup you would sometimes rear up to applause and strut your stuff. The secret joy you gave my bruised heart. I was abused and beaten, downtrodden and full of self-defeating thoughts and self-loathing but, when with my Calamity Jane, I felt strong and new. Whenever we were in the ring together, just the two of us on our own, I felt whole—for in your eyes I was complete.

Then I trained you to saddle myself! (I hate the masculine word of 'breaking' an animal and its emphasis on overcoming, overpowering, dominating.) Others laughed at first—I had left you too long to 'break' to saddle they said—she should have been 'broken' at two not four nearly five. I ignored them. We were soul mates and I knew you would trust me. I first sought your permission to sit on you bareback before introducing a saddle. Two hearts working as one... well, for a while.

Our first outing under saddle you just had to do an aerobic workout in the ring! Kicking up your heels and pig-rooting and leaping all over the place while everyone around us elegantly trotted and cantered around the ring. Not my Calamity Jane. I should have got a blue ribbon for staying on!

Disgraced we left the ring without a ribbon—my very first outing under saddle. The little horse who won everything at halter, including Royal Melbourne champions and national awards had put on the kind of display in the

saddle class best reserved for a rodeo. I was annoyed. You were unrepentant.

Over the next few weeks you decided to cheer me up by doing your aerobics at home rather than in the show-ring. At an A-class agricultural show you outshone every other competitor in our class. You won. We won. You did not put a foot, or hoof, wrong. Within a few months we were winning champions under saddle. Inside I quietly burst with pride. You gave me so much when I had so little in my life. You often gave me reason to keep on surviving and not to fulfil my other thoughts about leaving this earth.

Strong and haughty you let only me ride you. When men climbed upon you—bang! You threw them off! You were choosy and a feminist horse who would not be dominated by males—whether human or equine! People marvelled at our bond. I could do anything with you, take you anywhere. You were in parades and were never ruffled by anything. You had a particular 'squeal' that I knew only too well was your warning gesture to others who annoyed you—especially men! When one man tried to push you around because he thought you would be as good for him as you were for me, you rearranged his giblets in such a ladylike way! I got yelled at and bullied and threatened over it. They said you were a 'mad' horse and I was angry and offended inside but could not speak my mind—not then. I remember looking at you and I have no doubt you knew what was going on. When they had finished yelling at me I came to you and gently stroked and hugged you because I knew you loved me unconditionally, as I you.

I bathed you and massaged you, exercised you and made you special meals. You got injured once and they thought you would be permanently damaged but we worked wonders together and soon you were back showing off and winning everything. On those times you were not well I would sleep in the stable with you. I often travelled in the float with you—I loved it—to be with you and the others rather than with the humans in the truck. Never once did you ever harm me. You shared my soft drinks and loved eating oranges and cake, as well as carrots and apples! You learned how to listen for a gate latch not properly closed and would make your escape and make me chase you all over the property!

I often sought refuge in your stable and sometimes in the paddock. You never gave away my hiding spots. I know you knew of my sadness and saw often what was done to me. I would cry inconsolably as I kissed and stroked you. You in turn would gently put your soft muzzle to my cheeks and smell my tears.

Then it happened. April 1990. The nightmare I shan't forget and need a book to describe. I escaped barely with my life. I had to leave you behind. I tried to rescue you and the others but was battered and beaten. I came back to you some nights. I walked kilometres to get to you and lay in the grass, my arm outstretched through barbed wire to stroke and kiss beneath the stars—before walking the kilometres back to my hiding place, away from the humans.

Then, you were gone. All were gone. Some dead (murdered!), some sold. You were gone and I felt I would die. Police became involved in the criminal case of the abuse against me. I trusted no one but did beg a detective to find my beloved animals—especially you.

Unbeknown to me at the time, the policeman put in a herculian effort and found you interstate. He got a court order, telling the magistrate at the time he felt sure that my immediate survival on this earth depended upon being able to get back at least one of my animals—my precious Calamity Jane.

In July 1992, the police contacted me. They had found and taken possession of you. You would have to stay at a property belonging to one of the police officers but I could visit you as often as I liked. I could not believe it! It had been two-and-a-half years since I had seen you, touched you, kissed you, smelt you. The day they transported you to the policeman's house he said to me, 'She's just arrived; but it's no use coming out to see her. It will be dark by the time she gets here, the weather is terrible and I have no lighting in the paddock so you won't be able to find or see her.' I got in my car and drove to his home—it was a rainy and stormy night. The policeman took one look at me and said with gentle humour, 'Why am I not surprised you turned up anyway?' I walked into the pitch-black of the paddock. 'It's no use,' he said. 'It's too dark and windy; she'll be down the back of the paddock under shelter. Come back tomorrow.' It was cold and I was getting wet. I shouted your name into the wind. From the blackness I heard your familiar whinny, a loud and excited, desperate whinny! From this same blackness of wind and rain the white of your body emerged from the darkness. I screamed your name again as I ran forward to hug and kiss and caress you. You kept on whinnying, softly now, like a child finally finding the warmth, the love, the security it has missed and longed for. I cried and cried as I stood in the rain on that wintry night and held my precious Calamity.

It was as though the bond was never broken. In the daylight I examined you—and you me. They had chopped off your magnificent silver mane (like punishing the beautiful girl by attacking her feminine beauty). I read the signs upon your hooves that you had suffered ill-health in those two years. What had you been through and what had you seen? I came to you almost every day. We went riding together through the bush and you got to meet my new dog and together all three of us would go riding—Loci sitting on the front of the saddle, balancing like a little acrobat and loving every second.

The legal trials were over and it was time now, the policeman said, to have the courts recognise that you were my little horse, because the perpetrator and his supporters were trying to take you away from me. I felt sick about having to go back to court. The policeman got all the evidence to show that you and I were one—and have been since your birth.

The media heard about this unusual trial, fighting over a horse called Calamity Jane. I did not want the media to be there though and so the police threw them out on our behalf! A number of police attended as a mark of respect and, I guess, to support me should others from the opposing side attend. There was gentle laughter in the court when the magistrate, after hearing the evidence, asked me to stand and said, 'Well Caroline, I think you have been very brave and I am delighted to rule that Calamity Jane be released from police custody and returned to her rightful owner, you. I wish you all the very best in the future.'

I don't see myself as your owner—though that is how it is in law. We are each others' companion. I am in the privileged position of being your human guardian.

You, my precious Calamity, now live with me, my partner and our menagerie of animals on our rural property. You have your very own paddock and stable and a fashionable assortment of the very best winter, spring and summer rugs.

You got gravely ill in 2001 as a result of the ill-health you suffered during the two-and-a-half years we were apart. I slept in your stable each night and when things became critical you were hospitalised for five weeks. I visited you every day and stayed with you for various procedures. The vets have marvelled at your recovery and continue to marvel at your health when they make their regular visits to us. They say my dedication to you is one of the main reasons you have recovered and maintain such good health. Many other horse owners they say, would not go to those extremes with this kind of health problem and have the horse put down.

We are two and yet one and you will only leave me when you are a very old grand lady and you decide it is time to move to another form of being. We celebrate your birthday each year. Last 12 October you turned twenty! We had carrot cake that I baked and I relented and gave you a little soft drink! I gave you twenty kisses and one for good luck. You will be twenty-one this year—shall I give you the key to the stable?

I ride you occasionally, when I know you feel up to it. Visitors marvel at your nightly routine. I partially open the gate to your paddock, you get yourself out, run up the laneway between the paddocks and through another gate, around a corner and into the stable where you put yourself to bed!

I visit you at night still—like I always have. You are used to this and I know you have told the other animals that this is just Caroline, that is her way, she is more animal than human. I come to visit your paddock especially on starry nights, often with cup of tea in hand and portable CD player. I sing to you and dance around your paddock—especially beautiful when it is under a full moon. You watch and walk around me as I move and sometimes I playfully grab your tail and pretend you are my dance partner and I use your tail to help me waltz around: you love it.

You have loved me wholly. You were my first feminist role model before I met wonderful human feminist role models! You loved me in a way that enabled a hurting wild heart to feel free, to feel whole and loved within an environment where none of this was forthcoming from the human kind.

I love you my Calamity Jane. We have been together since the morning of your birth—twenty-one years this year. You nurtured a traumatised girl child/girl woman and, even when forcefully parted, we were brought back together and have been that way ever since. You know every ounce of my being. You still nuzzle me and from time to time, you still see me cry and you still insist on touching my tears with your muzzle. You love it when I lean upon you and stroke you and listen to the sound of your breathing. I smell your mane (it has grown back long and silvery!) and in 2000 I entered you just for fun at the Royal and again you won a blue ribbon! You are very much a part of why I am a survivor and you helped me to stay determined. You are every girl's equine role model and I could not have had a better companion to help me realise that a life can be made worthwhile—regardless of where one is made to start from!

Caroline Taylor is a passionate animal lover who lives with her partner and a menagerie of animals on their rural property. Caroline is passionate about animal welfare, human rights and children's welfare and is currently a Post-Doctoral Fellow.

Brumbies

Beatriz Copello

Brumbies galloping wild,
I saw them coming down a hill
their manes flowing in the wind
their muscle and flesh tense
their strong legs denting the soil.
I imagined beads of sweat
covering their hirsute flanks.
I imagined freedom in their eyes.
Innocent creatures unaware
that their hearts soon might be pierced.

Beatriz Copello, *a poet, fiction writer and playwright, has been published in Australia and overseas. Her poetry has appeared in* Southerly, Hobo, The Women's Book Review, *and many other journals and anthologies. She has won various prizes and was a recipient of an Australia Council Grant for Poetry in 1997. Recently she was awarded the degree of Doctor of Creative Arts (Creative Writing—University of Wollongong).*

Pink Clover

Theo Wills-Johnson

Two rituals were performed on our walk to the little bush school of my childhood. At the bottom of the hill we stopped and removed our sandals, hiding them under a bush. All the kids went barefoot and, even had we been aware of our parents' difficulty in ensuring we had proper footwear, it's unlikely conscience would have won over conformity. I fear, when we confessed in the last years of her life, Mother was considerably hurt by our ingratitude. Perhaps confession is not a beneficial indulgence.

The narrow bitumen road wound between enormous gum trees and paddocks, leading to our second ritual—feeding Lucky whilst dreaming of wondrous adventures in which we were brave and invincible. Lucky was a little gold-dappled bay mare, about 14 hands, around whom we wove a romance of having been sired by a wild Arab stallion said to have been seen in the district, and borne by a mare out along Hope Road.

Lucky belonged to old Stan Dixon who lived in a stone house topped with a battlemented turret which, so people said, had been built to repel marauders back when farmers first settled Bibra Lake—or was that another romantic invention of children with too much imagination? Stan had a cart horse, Roany, who did all the farm work, took produce to Fremantle and returned with stores. We liked Roany, she was a horse, after all, but it was Lucky, who did nothing but graze and look beautiful, who was able to come when called to eat the grass plucked from our side of the fence, treating it as some exotic delicacy when, in truth, it was the same as her paddock provided. After school Lucky, and those sandals, waited.

Five years, and countless wistful fence-side visits, and one evening Stan Dixon appeared at our home to see Dad. Stan had a problem. In very short order, Stan's problem became Dad's, because Dad really preferred mechanical horses. His youthful experience of farming with a team of six beautiful big work horses apparently mellowed slightly under the influence of young love. A very old photo shows Dad standing amongst the team with Mother, who

always loved horses, a tiny figure perched side-saddle on the bare back of the nearest one. But that was before drought and the war brought us to Bibra Lake.

Roany had had a foal. Stan had to put Roany back into work but he couldn't do that with a five-day-old foal at foot: it could be raised by bottle on cow's milk; those kids love horses. He wanted us to have the foal—and wily old Stan put this proposition with my sister and me quivering in the wings. Grave misgivings gave way to grudging consent harnessed to the dire warning that very few foals survive on a bottle.

My older brother's only contribution was christening her Clover and, like clover, she proved to be a survivor, going quickly from a bottle to drinking milk from a bucket. And like some clover, she bloomed pink. Clover had a black-grey mane and tail, and in winter grew a thick, rather fluffy, roan coat. As this was shed we would gather it, rolling it into balls—Clover balls—which survived for many years, turning up in odd places around the farm. By the end of spring her coat was gleaming pink which shone with silver in sunlight.

Clover was never formally broken in. Dad asked us to wait till he did it, but time was so slow in those days and, though Helen and I knew we were too heavy, our baby sister was the perfect size. Clover was backed before breakfast and in the snap of our fingers we had Jenny jumping her over boxes—bareback of course, because, apart from a piece of rope, we had no gear. Lacking a bridle made mouthing unnecessary.

After a lifetime of playing with horses, looking back I realise just how pragmatic Clover was. It would be impossible to count the number of people, mostly novices, who rode her and, though Clover would on occasion use their inexperience to her advantage—she favoured striding into the lake and lying down, saddle and protesting rider notwithstanding—she was never vicious or dangerous.

Sadly, her end was not as Helen had requested. Clover had been free-leased to a then well-known riding school on the condition that when they no longer wanted her or if there were any problems, Helen was to be advised immediately and would go and collect her. This was not done, and Clover passed out of our lives without any farewells. But I will always remember the pink horse with the silver shine and the girlhood dreams she inspired.

Theo Wills-Johnson left high school at fifteen and, intermittently, has been studying a smorgasbord of subjects ever since, including Equine Management. Her employment has been various, some paid, some voluntary: secretary, steno temp, credit manager, budget counsellor, court reporter, English tutor, RDA assistant. She shared the joy of riding with her three children—till they bought mechanical horses. Her riding—again all sorts: hunting, dressage, hacking, ODE, Bicentennial Cattle Drive, Bibbulmum Track Trek, Rabbit Proof Fence Ride—all for pleasure, itself the prize. Despite the name, yes, Theo is female!

Horse Diary

Finola Moorhead

I've come armed with swag and carriable camp in case I have to walk deep gullies and steep hills to find the horses. They were turned out on four thousand acres in the drought over winter. They could be anywhere. The swag cost me $250, which is a lot less than a caravan.

No one has seen them for six months.

I am not a horsewoman, I am an amazon and we ride now and then. Horses have always been in my life and my feelings are ambivalent. Although I went to gymkhanas and shows, pony club and hunts, although I've broken a Shetland colt and exercised a racehorse at dawn, done dressage and show-jumping, fallen off over a thousand times, ridden difficult mounts owned by others, fed, wormed, groomed, filed feet of, calmed, floated and paddocked horses, possessed jodhpurs, boots, saddlebags and chaps, spent money on vets, horses are not, for me, the centrepole of everyday, the source of conversation, the topic of books collected, magazines subscribed to, the aim and objective of life as they are for a horsewoman. But I love them, of course I do.

Friday. Jedda is in with the neighbour's children's horse. He wants to buy her. She is not for sale. She is not mine to sell. I need to find the others: the grey mare, the buckskin (or dun, if you like) and my Dancer. He is not gorgeous, like Jedda; he is a washy bay of 15 hands out of a quarterhorse mare by an Arab stallion. His mane falls on either side of his neck and sarcoids are in his system. They erupt through his skin like warts on a stem, like mushrooms. You would pass him over as a nag if you saw him with a mob, but he has a beauty which is beyond describing. He is a daydream; it is in his eyes.

The day is becoming dark.

A mouse has mothered young in the 44-gallon drum which holds the molasses-flavoured grain. The walls are sheer. I catch one glossy, fat baby and toss it into the bush.

Monday. Finally, sunshine. The mob appears on the opposite hillside: the grey mare, Jedda, the skeletal fellow and Dancer. 'Dancer, come on.' I call. 'Come on.'

A Stephen's Banded Snake (*Hoplocephalus stephensi*) is in the horse mix. Let's call her Stephanie. She has slung her muscles into a few easy Ss: her head is high, eyes glittering; the off-white labials and chin shields flash as she assumes a striking stance.

Now the drought has broken, every evening thunder and lightning, heavy rain and slashing wind. The roads impossible, impassable. The horses don't really need my feed, they're fine. The dun is old and unbroken. His bones stick out of his hide like an equine skeleton vacuum-packed in canvas. The two mares precede the geldings in all activities, including the hand-feeding even though they are the fattest.

I am only frightened of Stephanie in so far as she might damage my health. I am on my own and the road is a washout. When I see her there are no heart palpitations, no beads of sweat, no residual primitive fear—that fear of fear which pierces the adrenals and transforms one into superwoman. Nup, just oops. Excuse me, help yourself. They are your mice. Absolutely.

Actually I would like Jedda to be mine. She is totally black, about 14 hands, a registered Australian stockhorse and such a good doer that she was fat and glossy during the drought. Her feet are hard and she is young enough to become exactly the horse I want, the companion piece to Dancer, in my image of myself riding from Mt Buller to Cooktown, with hack and packhorse along the Great Australian Trail.

All daydreams come true, for everybody, but the flimsy stuff of fancy turns up in the rude three dimensions of reality, the minute of the breath, the hours of the work, the hard facts of actuality. I've seen the horses of adult women

trying to fulfil the imaginings of sub-teenage girls, and failing, becoming underutilised, neglected or overfed, badly ridden, stubborn, a burden; anthropomorphised into goddesses of nature with secrets in their noble, nose-dominated heads. In truth, for all its wonderful shape, the horse has a brain the size of a walnut. Its wisdom lies in gazing over fences to where the grass is greener and being satisfied for the time being with what is in front of its nose.

Thursday. I'm glad Stephanie has found the mice. Dancer comes when he is called. The grey mare continues eating. Jedda raises her head and watches him.

Friday. I call. The grey lets out a command. The horses gallop up my ridge.

Saturday. Dawn; from my bed I hear them grazing. We are in the midst of a cloud. Today I will bribe Jedda. Unlike Dancer who is permitted to go off without disturbing the herd, she is important to the grey mare, who carries on until the geldings follow. Although Dancer knows we will be back and the dun could have done without the extra physical effort, they all come with us. Jedda is willing, interested and, while the tack is on, she responds well.

Sunday. I catch the grey. One of the women's forgotten daydream-steeds, she has been in these hills for years. Wild and wise, cunning and cowering, she lets me lift her foot. For one second. Then flick-kicks me off her fetlock.

Dancer is my equine friend, the horse I dreamed of as a teenager. Then I had a fiery-red Arab who was difficult to catch, constantly trembling with the fear of things to shy at, to gallop away from, to bolt in blinding terror until exhausted. Mostly I stayed on.

Monday. Stephanie is still in the feed. Four lumps bulge in her lean form. Her forked tongue is lazy with its threats. Nonetheless, I'm not putting my arm in there. The grey mare thinks she has me trained. I respond to the thunder of hooves by promptly leaving my task and going to the stable. I put a headstall on her. Muck around with her stubbornness. She is sturdy. Not a tick, not a speck of Queensland itch or rain scald, neither as fat as Jedda nor as lanky as Dancer, she has the high tail carriage of an Arab. She is her own mare. Jedda won't be caught. Dancer just walks into my space, totally comfortable,

horsily affectionate. The buckskin is in heaven on earth. His eyes sleepy with the pleasure of lucerne chaff.

I am silenced

I am stilled

By watching the horses

The grey curls her neck around Jedda's; they kiss each other's manes. This doesn't seem to make Jedda happy; she goes down to Dancer. They do not caress. Perhaps she is monstering him. You wouldn't know with Dancer. Whatever is going on, the grey doesn't approve, so off she goes and the others must follow. I have never seen Dancer lay back his ears in anger, ever.

Thursday. Jewels of dampness on the leaves and seeds. My horse is at the door. Of course I ride him. Quietly we tread through the communities of plant life, vibrant rock surfaces and distant ranges thirstily absorbing the moisture of low lying clouds. Stephanie, skulking round the edge of the bin, shows me her aggressive tongue. Girl, you are becoming a problem.

Friday. Several days now I've been closed in by walls of cloud and the blanket sounds of cicadas and crickets. The grey mare materialises in the mists of high country bushland, sclerophyll ridges and rainforest gullies. Merging the daydream and reality into simply being, humbled by lack of knowledge, I experience a pure kind of joy: wonder.

Saturday. Two mice are actually playing with Stephanie, teasing her, burrowing into the fodder, tickling her from underneath, emerging to push her scales with their noses.

When I leave I'm sure the horses will be fine.

Finola Moorhead *Family legend has it that my great-uncle, an Olympic horseman, died by being kicked in the head by his favourite mare, walking into her stable at night. So I always talk to horses from about ten paces away. I have been riding since the age of three.*

Sounds of the Stables

Sarah Cowell

Horses trotting, Tails swatting
> These are the sounds of the stables.
Rails falling, Horses calling
> These are the sounds of the stables.
Doors closing, Horses dozing
> These are the sound of the stables.
Horses eating, Hooves beating
> These are the sounds of the stables.

__Sarah Cowell__ was born in and lives near Warrnambool, in south-western Victoria. She is a student in year four who loves to write stories and poems. Her poem reflects her passion which is horses, in particular her pony 'Mickey D'. Her inspiration comes from her mother who trains horses in the classical dressage tradition of the old masters.

Of Power and Control

Wendy Ellerton

After hours of searching I locate my horse and pony. They look skinny, their coats are dull and it is obvious they have worms. They are in the most unlikely paddock and I am not sure why. I'm not even sure I would call it a paddock; it is actually a vacant block of land. The vacant block has a loose makeshift fence, small patches of yellow grass and lots of gravel. It is situated in a bizarre location. The paddock is between two of the most expensive houses in Williamstown and it overlooks the water and city skyline. It is all very confusing. I can't work out why my horse and pony are here. I feel off balance, which makes me hesitant and timid around them. They sense my fear and, in turn, react by being unsure of me. I struggle to catch the first horse. I tie my unhealthy looking horse to a piece of twine attached to the fence. Once tied-up, he almost immediately pulls back and breaks the twine. I tie him to a new piece. He is agitated and steps about whilst I try to catch my pony.

It's strange how even the simplest task can feel impossible. Eventually I succeed and lead the horses towards the gate. It seems almost impossible to get them to walk in a straight line. Their pace is unpredictable, they walk a few steps and then dart into a trot, trapping me in between them. We are all frightened, I am not exactly sure of what.

As I lead them through the gate they almost run over me. One of the horses steps on my heel which pulls my boot half off my foot. I try to regain some composure before I continue to lead them out. I don't know what comes next; dreams always seem to stop just when you're about to get somewhere or, in this case, when you are in the middle of nowhere.

I awoke puzzled that morning by this dream and thought of a dream I had a few months earlier that also featured horses. That time the experience had been extremely different. There was no hesitation whilst we galloped through unfamiliar surroundings. A light breeze and the warm sun made the day feel absolutely perfect. I rode my horse with great ease and felt like I was flying. This was unusual, as in reality my horse was quite flighty and, mostly, he was a lot of hard work. However, in this dream I felt a great sense of power and satisfaction, and I was confident that I had total control. When I woke—I was away in Japan—I felt a total sense of control. It was extremely satisfying having been strong and independent in my dream. Lots of people dream of flying, but for me the power of freely galloping on a horse through the countryside seems a beautiful substitute.

The pieces of the puzzle suddenly fitted together and now it seems obvious. My dreams about horses were about control rather than horses. I don't remember what triggered the dream about my skinny horses that I found in the weirdest of locations. However, I do remember feeling a great sense of relief when I came to the realisation that my life was out of control but that I was about to fix the problem.

It makes me reflect on why young girls are so attracted to owning and riding horses when they are teenagers. Perhaps it is not so much about horses, but more about yearning for companionship, independence and, of course, about having control.

Wendy Ellerton *currently lives in Melbourne. She owned horses from the age of ten until she was seventeen. Currently she runs a design firm which specialises in graphic design, typography and typeface design.*

Born to Run Janet Stumbo

I hit the entrance onto the lot too fast and gritted my teeth as we bumped along the dirt track past the abandoned house. My army surplus jeep was so old it was a veteran of two wars. It had four-wheel-drive but no creature comforts—no doors, roof, radio, heater or even shock absorbers to speak of; just a bench seat on a little four-banger engine with a top speed of forty-seven miles an hour. I had been rewarded with the key yesterday when I turned fifteen-and-a-half and passed the exam for a California driver's permit.

When I slammed to a stop behind the derelict house, I was not enveloped in the usual cloud of dust. Last night's rain shower had settled all the dust in the valley. My thoroughbred gelding was standing, his head out as far as he could reach it, neck pressed up against the top rail of the 10 x 10 foot corral Dad had built for him. My heart ached at the sight of the big thoroughbred in such a tiny prison.

Horses are born to run, just as birds are born to fly, and humans to think. Thoroughbreds are born and trained to want to run faster and faster. His confinement was the only thing keeping this magnificent animal alive but how was he to know that? The ways of men must be a perpetual mystery to creatures with no understanding of fractures, Jockey Club papers, breeding potential and all that motivates humans to treat them as we do.

Or et Argent—Gold and Silver in French, and Or for short—had broken down in his last major race with a fractured medial sesamoid. He was such a generous spirited horse that his human connections could not bring themselves to put him down. Since my determination to go to vet school was already legend at Hemet High, he came to be mine when I agreed to do whatever was necessary for him over the long period of 'absolute bed rest' his recuperation would demand. There was, of course, no guarantee that he would ever become sound enough even to ride. But then he was my problem. Although I gave my word that I would never try to return him to racing, his Jockey Club papers had been destroyed at that time.

Or stood perfectly still, both ears pointed directly at me, both soft brown eyes focused on me as if I were his entire world and everything in it. Not an eyelash batted; not a nostril quivered. Or et Argent this morning was a classical statue poured of neither gold nor silver. Lustrous he was, tinged by the earliest sunlight to a fiery bronze. Perfect and still, but for the blemish of the bandage wrapped around his near side fetlock. Checking that bandage was the reason for my daily visits.

Never a demonstrative soul, Or was silent as the sunbeams that bathed him, singing out no greeting, not even a shrill whinny. I wasted no time collecting my feelings. I knew he wouldn't stand still for long and, technically speaking, he was still under doctor's orders of bed rest. I hurtled out of the jeep with a fistful of carrots.

'It's just me, Or! I know you're surprised to see me in the morning, but I got a job yesterday at the vet's I told you about, so from now on I have to go down there right after school every day. I'm really going to have to move it to fit you in before my first class starts at seven-thirty.' I was up the side of the corral and perched on the top rail in a heartbeat, swinging one leg over and wrapping my legs securely around the rails.

In spite of these precautions, the horse nearly knocked me off to get to those carrots. He devoured the two I held out to him, then hit me in the chest with his nose trying to ferret out the sugar cubes I usually carried for him in my breast pockets. 'Hey! Give me a break you maniac!' I scolded him. 'It's not winter any more, you know. I can get carrots now it's spring. Carrots are better for you.' His chin rested momentarily on my thigh and I lay my cheek against his face. My heart was full to bursting with great news so it was hard to sound cross with him. I reached out to his broad face and rubbed that special spot between his eyes, while my voice fell into more soothing lower tones.

'Get back now, Or. Remember that vet and his x-ray machine last week? No, I don't suppose you do. Well, Dr Moon found that we have healed your fractured leg.' I glanced down at the last bandage I had so painstakingly wrapped around his near fetlock. 'Your leg is almost as good as new. So I'm going to break you out of here.'

I jumped off the fence, landing nimbly on his near-side and knelt to the work at hand. Carefully unwrapping the bandage, I kept up the constant chatter that, years later in vet school, I would come to call 'horse talk'. Or stretched his neck over me and helped himself to the last carrot I had tucked into my back pocket.

Horses don't understand English but they like to know where you are in the space around them. And, like all animals, they do respond to the tone of your voice, so I struggled to keep mine calm and unhurried. Or stood patiently, accustomed to this frequent chore. I felt lightly over the surface of the back of his fetlock joint, with fingertips that had become sensitive with practice: first the inside which I could not see, then the back, then the outside which my fingers could see better than my eyes and, finally, down the edges of the great flexor tendon which ran down the back of his leg and over the sesamoids.

The leg was unblemished; I could feel no swelling anywhere, and a hard push over the actual site of the fracture elicited no response. I was not hurting him! I straightened up and reached to scratch him high on his neck. 'Just a minute big guy, wait till you see what I've got for you.' It was getting harder for me to keep the excitement out of my voice as I slipped out through the lower rails and fetched the bridle left behind in the jeep.

'How would you like to go for a real walk?' I was smiling so broadly that my face hurt. Or stamped at me behind the rails; I couldn't keep the smile out of my voice. I was delighted to notice he stamped again and again with his unbandaged foot, which meant it did not hurt. I caught my breath, as I bent over to again slip through the rails. I glanced at my watch. Oh, hell, it was going to be tight for me to make it to school on time.

I clambered up the rails to be tall enough to fit the bridle over his ears and ease the unfamiliar bit over his teeth. It was the first time he had tasted a bit in his mouth for a long, long time. Even so, he remembered what a bridle was for. He shook his head and rattled the bit joyously against his teeth. I only just heard it over the pounding beat of my heart. I led him out and alongside the corral. 'Whoa! big guy,' I soothed.

Up the rails again I went, then he snorted in surprise as I landed on his back. He had stayed as lean as when he was racing, so I easily wrapped my legs over his ribs to retain my seat. It was probably the first time in his life that anyone had climbed onto him without a saddle and he propped both front legs in surprise. I gentled him with my hands and voice, 'It's okay, Or. I can't ride in a saddle anymore with my athlete's knees. This is how I'm going to have to ride you, if I'm to ride you at all.'

The horse took an uncertain step away from the corral when I urged him forward. I sat steady and solid, my hands very light on the reins, feeling him relax under my clenched knees. We turned at the fence to ride alongside. It was a lovely, warm spring morning. I was aware of nothing but twelve hundred pounds of power between my knees and of the beat of my heart, faster and faster. I had no difficulty keeping him in check as we walked toward the farthest corner of the paddock. We turned around when we reached it. 'What do you say we try out that new leg?' I asked.

My knees and heels told him to get a move on and he gratefully broke into an unhurried trot. My heart beating in time to his hoof beats, I urged him on. His canter was unbelievably smooth, easy to ride. 'More, Or, give me some more.' The whisper was ripped off my lips as my hands told the reins. His stride lengthened. I could feel each pent-up muscle stretch. My hands easy on the reins, I bent low and his stirring black mane whipped my face. I narrowed my eyes to slits, able to see nothing but sunlight. The racehorse knew, instinctively, that he was free at last.

Bursting out of the starting gate that was no longer a part of his life, he went faster and faster. I bent lower, almost double, and clung with every muscle in my legs—tight as they had ever been. I was flying with my magnificent horse, the blur beneath us no longer the ground. I didn't make it to school at all that day. It is not every day you ride a flying horse. It is not every day you meet your future and it swallows you whole.

Janet Stumbo *was born and raised in rural California. She migrated to Australia in 1974 and later graduated from Melbourne University with Honors in Veterinary Science. She worked as a veterinarian in New South Wales until severely injured and disabled in a car accident. Now she works as a writer and public speaker. She has no spare time.*

Horse Byte

Rose Kizinska

NB A byte is composed of eight bits.

Brumby Business

If he could've shrunk significantly and grown wings, he would have glided through my open bedroom window at night and then shrunk me too and taken me away. But Wild King was still my benevolent Pegasus, even without the wings. Branded with an anchor on his thigh, when the visiting sniggering drunken sailor jumped on him, my trusty steed reared and the sailor did fly. My horse galloped over to me then and we took off for the day; jumping over logs, wading through the creek, through fields and untended orchards we flew. 'Good boy King. You showed him. Good boy.' Wild King took me away from it all, at least on the weekends, away from the wrath of the father.

Equine Equity

For this kindness, I decided I owed the equine species a great debt. The Dandenong Stock Yard was the only equitable place of repayment. 'Can I ride your horse in the ring for you? I'll make sure she doesn't get a whipping in there.' I had spent a considerable amount of time at stock auctions screaming out for the sadistic horse handler to stop whipping and taunting the creatures of such beauty and grace. Some Fridays I would have to wag school for this. I became a regular stock market crasher and quite adept at ensuring that I didn't raise my hand at the wrong moment. If I were old enough to hold a credit card though, my equine debt would have been significantly higher.

Horse in 'burbs

Wild King came home to the 'burbs with me one day in a float. The traffic was silent that evening. I dared myself to ride him around the block and revelled in the different sounding clip clop he made on the pavement. We were suburban kids but the horses lived in a paddock in the country and so usually walked on grass or occasionally on pebbled roads. In Springvale he made the clip clop of the milkman of my youth. I never woke early enough to catch a ride on the back of the milk carriage although my sister swears she'd been on a few.

Let Go Inferno

Pegasus was the thundering horse of Jove who carried lightning bolts for Zeus. These bolts are regularly thrown around the Australian sky with impunity. During the Ash Wednesday bush fires, smoke billowed all the way over my high school, some thirty kilometres away, dropping flame-licked glowing gum leaves like dying fireflies. My only fear that day, when the father drove out to check up on them, was that Wild King and the others were harmed. If the horses survived and father didn't, how happy I would be. I couldn't manage to muster up any repentant feelings or thoughts when the other kids said, 'But he's still your father.' If Wild King were my father, him I would respect. Am I perhaps Medusa, snake-headed mother of Pegasus? An ever-fuming head ablaze with anger, rarely doused. It was Wild King who sheltered me as I lay on his chest in the hay-bale-storage tin shed, throughout the whole fearful night when the father kidnapped my siblings and I, in a lame attempt to turn us away from our mother.

Equine Enchantment

I kept bits of hoof, tail, mane and horseshoes stored away in my clothes cupboard as if each piece of my Wild King was precious and sacred. As if in someone else's hands these pieces could be used to perform voodoo and the spirit of my King would be stolen forever. When I ran away from my family home I had to leave Wild King and all of my talismans. In the inner city, horses are far away, except for the ones you may meet at a demo, with the police astride. Carousels attempted to fill the void. They were nice but just too plastic and always returning to where you began. I then collected all things zebra. But nothing matched the memory of the flared smokey nostrils of King, sprinting freely, curve-necked and tail high in the air.

Equestrian Leather
The smell of leather, boot polish, saddle soap, horse sweat and fresh cut hay; sense and scents of the ideal weekend.

Equine Sensory Perception
A horse senses your moods. Smells your fear. Feels you quiver. Is remorseful for throwing you off its back when it sees a hissing snake or when an iron horse passes by it for the first time. It returns to you, shaking and sorry. Wild King always did.

Star Signs
Mr Ed, Francis the talking mule and Pie from National Velvet are all thundering across the sky together. Wild King may never have made a television appearance but I'm sure he is up there with them too, undoubtedly leading the pack, lightning fast, bolting.

Rose Kizinska *is a writer and lapsed horse rider. It had been several years since her last horse session. She recently took her niece on her first trail ride for her tenth birthday and was delighted when she turned around and yelled out, 'Aunty Rose, I'm flying. This is the best.' Consequently, her niece has converted to an equestrienne. Rose misses the joy of girly horse talk and laments never having had the fancy Western saddle she possessed only in dreams.*

The Homecoming of Bungala Kiersten Coulter

'Bungala,' according to one of the Aboriginal/English dictionaries, undoubtedly interpreted by a whitefella, means 'happy meeting place beside quiet waters'. It seemed a good name for a wild horse from Anna Creek Station in Northern Australia. Starved to nothing but a skeleton, scarred from beatings and rough handling on a long road and rail journey to the dusty Adelaide sale and slaughter yards, Bungala was a proud and terrified mare, ferociously trying to protect her three-month-old filly foal. The foal resembled a child from a developing nation in the middle of drought. Swollen dropped belly and bones, eyes wide with fright, thirst and hunger. Bungala was a chestnut mare with a large white blaze and three knee-high socks. About 15 hands, she was nothing to look at in that state. My attention was taken by the foal. She was the same colour, dark brown to black, and similar markings, white blaze and three instead of four white socks, just like Brandy who died weeks earlier in my arms. I was alone as I watched him writhe in pain until he finally died. At thirteen I was grieving my young horse's loss from colic. I enthusiastically pointed out the foal to my mother but commented that she unfortunately came with 'that old mare'.

When Bungala and the foal were shunted into the sale ring, she stood regal and defiant. The heavy swinging wooden gate was closed without care, bludgeoning the foal in the face and trapping her by the neck between the gate and the side of the enclosed sale ring. She struggled drawing the gate tighter around her neck and nearly decapitated herself. Bungala screamed. My mother and I stood up and also screamed out loud for the gate to be opened and for them to be sold together. The gate swung open and the foal joined her mother. Even in that condition, there was something special about 'that old mare'. I had no idea what it meant to have a completely wild and untamed horse, whose only contact with humans had been the brutal round-up and gruesome trip down from the north; a journey many of the horses did not survive. Witnessing the carnage, horrific injuries and damage and breathing the smell of fear from these animals put my mother and I into an altered state of consciousness and distress. Before we knew it my mother had put up her hand, the auctioneers hammer had fallen, and she had paid $120 for them both. Most of the horses were bought by doggers. Out of spite they had tried to outbid her but given in when the price was too high. My mother was determined. What inhumanity that the horses were not shot on site and shipped in refrigerated trucks! The men around the sale ring looked

at my mother with incredulity and disdain. Quite simply they thought she was an idiot.

My mother and I were shaking as we watched Bungala and foal skittle from the cruel prodding and leave the sale ring. We went out to the yards and looked at them. What now? We not only had to find a way of getting them home, but we had to tell my father. It wasn't going to be easy. The drive back home to the Adelaide hills was over an hour. That day all four of us, my brother, parents and myself returned to the sale yards with a hired open double horse float.

The few stock hands that were still left at the yards were now convinced they had never seen anything like it. They hung around to watch for the highlight of the day's amusement. Not only were the two horses wild, but their treatment had made them defensive and ferocious. The foal was skittish and free with her heels. Bungala was calculating and prepared to attack, striking with front legs and hooves, teeth bared like a snarling dog with mouth wide open ready to grab at anything. She charged and kicked and struck and threatened tirelessly—for hours. It was dangerous to be anywhere near her. No one dared get on ground level. We scuttled around the walls of the sale yard, up out of the horses' reach above their heads, the float backed into the yard gateway with the tailgate down and gates jammed into either side of the float. We put food in the float and coaxed and encouraged, yelled and screamed. A few times one or other horse would get close, even onto the tailgate, only to whip around and take off again.

The sideshow had got repetitive and boring and the onlookers had left. My brother Peter had been in an accident two years previously. He was still trying to piece a life together following his acquired brain injury. Legally blind and partially paralysed, he had learned to crack a stock whip as part of his rehabilitation. His accident had changed our lives forever. We had lost most of our friends. His behaviour was difficult, his needs were great. They always would be. At that time I resented him and took in my parents' grief as they watched him. After hours of dust and stench and frustration, and on the verge of conceding this was a futile exercise, Peter spontaneously got down, some distance from, but behind the horses. He cracked the stock whip—just once. The horses jerked to attention. He cracked it again and they moved towards the float. Two more cracks and they were in the float, tailgate fastened. It was a language they understood. Peter was the hero.

They could easily have panicked, reared, somersaulted and kicked their way out of the open float—and we knew it. We travelled up Main North Road in Adelaide (a main highway) with my father driving and my mother and I illegally perched on each mudguard of the float, holding our hands out over the horses, peering down at them. It was a demented attempt to deter the horses from trying to jump out of the float. But they didn't move. Their heads were down, their noses almost on the floor. A police car pulled up behind us at a set of red lights. We tried to explain the situation. They were amused and with a smile pointed out that they thought our position on the mudguard was precarious and certainly illegal. We dashed into the car and kept driving, all the way up the main South Eastern Freeway, in silence. Bungala was home.

A few weeks later I took myself to a weekend horse-breaking school. The Jeffrey Method is a way of handling and breaking in wild horses gently and with respect. As a petite thirteen year old I came home convinced I could saddle break Bungala myself. Only recently, some thirty years later, my father told me how proud he was of me going off to that course and coming home and following through with it. Bungala and I worked together, quietly, gently and patiently. From that time she has remained a proud, thoughtful, stubborn mare who has been totally delightful.

When she was carrying her second to last foal (Bungala Boi) my parents finally divorced. My mother bought twenty acres further into the hills with a truly beautiful large dam on it. She built the house overlooking the dam. We called the property Bungala. Bungala the horse, now in her thirty-third year, owns this magic place, living there with Boi and my mother now in her seventies. It has indeed been 'a happy meeting place beside quiet waters'.

__Kiersten Coulter__ is a Criminologist and PhD candidate at the University of Melbourne. She lives on the outskirts of Melbourne with her partner Di, her dog Zorya, and agisted not far away, is her thoroughbred mare Holly. The pleasure she gets from a horse's presence, from just hanging out together, is a pure meditation.

Kimberley Moonbeam the Fourth

Melinda Tankard Reist

Surely every young girl should be given the chance to learn to ride on a horse called Kimberley Moonbeam the Fourth. That was the name of the Welsh Mountain pony who taught me to ride, though mostly we called her Kim.

I had loved horses for as long as I could remember. This love was fed by my father's stories of his Shetland pony Topsy. Topsy had been given to my grandfather by his father. Dad rode her to school every day and when Topsy had a foal they were even allowed into the house. She lived till her 30s. Dad also spoke with affection of the family Clydesdale, Roanie, who worked the family property in rural Victoria and I could picture this magnificent white and pink creature tilling the soil which had sustained five generations of Tankards. My horse love developed with a picture book of sweet-faced Shetlands, palominos, piebalds, Spanish dancing horses, dressage horses and English hacks; novels like *My Friend Flicka*, *Thunderhead*, *Green Grass of Wyoming*, and *Summer at World's End* about children who had run away from their cruel home to live on an abandoned farm and care for horses they rescued from the knackery; and the Marlboro Man horses in my grandmother's *Women's Weeklies*, treasured finds for my scrap book.

Kim belonged to Lee. Well, she got him from a bloke in Donald for a lend—a lend that lasted years. I met Lee through a friend of my mother. They were racing people. Lee was about eleven, I was a year older. I rode my bike to their place. When we met it was like resuming an old friendship. She was tall and weedy, her defining feature the mass of blonde hair which fell all the way down her back. Lee introduced me to a world of racehorses: Rapeed, Naretha, Argos, Maranina. I still have hair from their tails in a matchbox.

Kim was a bag of bones when Lee got her but she soon fattened up. It was only later we realised that it was more than good chaff and molasses—not to mention candy canes, lollies and the sweet biscuits she so enjoyed—that caused her to swell so rapidly.

Kim loved to 'ride work' with the racehorses. She didn't seem to realise she was a third their size. Lee would take Kim out on the circuit with strapper Jan and one of the racehorses; they'd come back, take out another horse, and Kim would go back again with them. She never seemed to tire.

But one day Kim seemed particularly stubborn. We could not get her to move in the yard and we were keen to ride. Lee wanted to work on my cantering technique. The afternoon was planned. Despite much kicking and harsh words, she stood firm. Something was wrong but we were too foolish to realise.

The next morning, Lee found a white colt with a black head and white blaze, fully formed but stillborn, in the paddock. We were devastated.

Time passed then one magical day my dad gave me Rajah, a 14 hands-high three-quarter thoroughbred chestnut gelding we found in the newspaper. Dad got me a new saddle, orange saddle blanket, blue-and-yellow-striped girth, a woven two-toned leather bridle, brushes and saddle soap. He made a tack shed out of an old water tank where we kept lucerne hay and chaff and all the horse gear.

In the summer Lee and Kim would meet us at six a.m. and we'd take off through the scrub along the Murray river, galloping madly, jumping fallen gum trees. We'd leap off our horses into the river in our underwear then dry off in the sun while our horses munched grass on the river bank. Then back home where we hosed the sweat and foam from our mounts and refreshed ourselves with homemade iced coffee full of sugar and icecream. Our horses were freedom for us, young girls disappearing all day and nobody ever worried.

I rang Lee last week. It was the first time we'd spoken in twenty years. She'd become a jockey, riding at Flemington in Melbourne, interstate and overseas. She'd strapped for Ark Regal who won $600,000 then flopped at stud. A two-year-old, 17 hands-high colt reared on Lee in the starting gates at Flemington. Another horse she was riding crashed through the running rails. These accidents left her with fourteen broken bones, a twice-broken nose which was now caved in, a punctured lung, a plate in her cheekbone to hold her face together, a stuffed shoulder and a scar under her left eye. I could not imagine her face so damaged.

'I had to learn how to get on a horse again,' she told me. 'I knew there was no way I was staying on the ground cleaning out stalls...' They're an addiction, race horses. But Lee's suffering went much deeper than physical injury caused by horses. Twin baby boys, born too early, buried too soon.

I thought of the dead foal. For so many years I felt responsible for his death. 'Lee, it was our fault Kim's foal died. I've never forgotten and we were to blame that her lovely colt lay dead. She was pregnant and we rode her anyway.'

'No,' said Lee. 'We did not know she was pregnant. No one knew. We wouldn't have ridden her if we'd have known the foal was due. The foal was out of season... there was something wrong.'

'But I thought...'

'No Mel. We didn't know.'

Kim lived to a good age. A three-year-old child was riding on her back not long before she died.

Melinda Tankard Reist is a Canberra-based writer and researcher. Her early writing days included a brief stint on the Melbourne Herald's *racing guide. Melinda is author of* Giving Sorrow Words: Women's Stories of Grief after Abortion. *She is teaching her daughters to ride.*

Don't Fence Me In Chris Sitka

I used to ride Chukulpa naked. I could do that. We lived on wimmin's land. Both of us galloping naked. Me without clothes. She without saddle, bridle or reins. It was wild bush. A place to experience unknown freedoms as a woman, as a lesbian; on the run from patriarchy. People thought we were desperados. They called us feral, long before that became a fashion. We thought we were gloriously free, the lead mares.

We chose to share this freedom with the horses. Like us they were free to roam the unfenced hills and valleys. They formed their own packs amongst the herd of thirty to forty. We didn't put bits into their mouths to control them. We were developing communal co-operation to stem the rampaging evil of hierarchical power. Even saddles were considered too stiff and weighty. Made, as they are, from dead things.

Chukulpa was an ordinary kind of horse to look at. A simple bay. No markings. Short (14 hands). Stocky. Once one of the young girls asked, as we were walking around the Crown Land, 'If the Queen came for a visit would you let her ride your horse?' 'She wouldn't be interested,' I replied. 'The Queen only rides fine bred horses. Not plain, bay hacks.'

Chukulpa, though, was perfect for me. I'd had enough of falling off horses. She was steady, calm and reliable. Yet when I wanted to run with the wind she was up for it, without insisting on bolting for home like most of the others. She was round enough that I could tuck my legs behind her shoulders to stop me falling off as we pounded down the steep hills. That was when riding naked was an advantage. We'd both sweat and the sweat would stick us together. Sweet-smelling adhesive. Stopped me sliding off her rump on the up-hill slopes too.

She was never fazed by the kangaroos or wallabies which often leapt onto the track in front of a galloping horse. Lead mare of her pack, grand dame, phlegmatic, self-possessed she was not easy to ruffle. Where others would shy and rear she would give but a disdainful snort. 'Hmmp, bouncing kangaroo, how boring. Takes more than that to deflect me from the rhythm of my stride.' She had an easy trot too. One fit to sit without stirrups.

Once, on a wildly windy day, picking our way along a narrow trail on the edge of a precipice, a big branch fell right across her withers, barely missing me. She simply stood quietly there while I pushed it off us, then walked on. If her hooves snared in hidden wire she just stopped while I slid off and pulled the wire away.

Her steady nature meant I could leap onto her back with a single bound, stand up, ride backwards, perform tricks. I gave lessons to beginners, pony rides for little girls and carried toddlers through the scrub and over creeks and rivers... All these beneficiaries of her tolerance became her adoring fans. She was popular. Not only amongst women. She had horsey fans too.

Even after we built one small holding paddock by the feed shed, Koota, a temperamental grey Arab, would jump the fence and race whinnying with agitated complaint if we tried to leave her behind. She would then walk in front and thrust her rear end in Chukulpa's face. Lifting her tail.

Being a Taurus, I am suited to a horse like Chukulpa. We are creatures of habit. Many would be bored, but I liked it that there was a mutual agreement about where we usually trotted, where we cantered, where we pulled up. Those rides were predictable. I could dream off. I didn't have to watch for the bounders and blunders. I could survey the landscape. I could ride without using the reins. We co-operated with each other. When she came to her favourite patches of grass I would just sit on her back as she grazed. Entranced, I would go into horse mode. Free meditation classes. If I thought at all, I thought 'Wouldn't it be great if we could live off grass and water. We would be free from the materialism of capitalism.'

Knowing I could trust her also meant I could have adventures. Ride off into unknown parts. Climb distant ridges and gaze at new views and find abandoned copper mines and unexplored, maze-like valleys. Crazed by the headiness of my freedom I didn't care that I hadn't told anyone where I was going. I didn't know myself where, until we got there. She could always lead me home.

Sadly I'm in the city now. Chukulpa disappeared into the bush from where her free roaming spirit still leads me home.

Chris Sitka *is lesbian feminist writer, researcher and creative thinker. When she is not being an intellectual activist in the big bad city she still loves to bash around the bush and sleep under the stars in her swag. Her osteopath has made a lot of money out of the consequences of her earlier years of miscreant riding. This does not deter her from her new project of moving to the country and getting another horse to amble about on.*

Over the Ravine

Sophie Barnet

Soon, through the gaps in the houses, Pip could see glimpses of sharp sandstone cliffs. It was the first sense she had that they were following a major ridge, like a spine, over the mountains. Soon they would descend into the endless valleys and start looking for the cattle. The tarmac eventually gave way to ground that was rocky and hard. The horses picked their way carefully, occasionally tripping on sharp rocks. Bird song floated up from the valley. A quick flutter of wings, like a camera shutter and a wattlebird swooped overhead. Stunted ghost gums, stout and strong, gave way to small strands of scrawny looking acacias bearing thorns. Although individually they appeared stunted and misshapen, they had a sweeping beauty covering the whole end point of the plateau. There were also tall reedy grasses and plump bushes with pine-like leaves reaching straight up. In between these, as if purely for contrast, were the serrated starry leaves of the bottlebrush, bursting with bright orange cones. The air was soft on Pip's face but she knew, by the way the bushes and shrubs gripped the earth, that the place saw high winds and piercing cold.

Dismounting, they tethered the horses to a visitors sign and walked across the rock. The ground dropped away spectacularly to reveal a huge canyon valley enclosed by sheer sandstone cliffs. No matter how many times Pip saw this view (and it was commonplace along the ridge) the thrill it sent through her body never dulled. It was a slow healing straight to the heart. A cool drink on a warm day that seeped into every vein and subtle nerve. Pip stood and breathed out, unaware that she had needed to but nevertheless relieved. The air did something good to her. But then, when Pip looked out at the seemingly endless expanse of wilderness, it turned her inside out. She felt keenly that she did not belong down there in the bush and, due to her ignorance, feared she would not know how to survive should something go wrong. This was an irrational fear but one that presented itself to Pip as she stood at the edge of her known world. She sensed the bush was a hostile force, a secretive circle containing knowledge and places that would not open themselves to her.

Grace stood next to Pip looking out into the valley where more cliffs butted up opposite. To the north, mountains and sweeping valleys could be seen, carrying an endless flow of trees to the horizon. From here each valley looked the same to Pip.

There was the faint swish of cars from the highway as people passed hurriedly up and down the mountains. The bush to Pip was simultaneously a place of magnificent splendour and a place that needed to be endured. A gust of wind swirled upward and a shadow darkened Grace's face as though she too, held memories that were painful to let go.

'It's amazing, isn't it?' Grace's face told Pip she saw something very different, her eyes looking outwardly everywhere but still at the same thing. 'You know,' she continued, 'Everything is collapsing back into the valley floor. The rivers, wind, rain and frost are slowly eroding the rock away.' A hawk hovered way out, over the middle of the valley. 'We're nothing but specks on their time line.' Grace turned to Pip.

'Why would you want to go to the city when you have this at your doorstep?'

Pip knew Grace didn't expect her to answer but she did anyway.

'To get away from the property. I don't belong there.'

'Where will you go?'

'To the city.' Pip answered, unwaveringly.

'You sound sure about that.' Grace said, setting her hat further back on her head.

Grace was straining her eyes to the horizon, scanning the valley floor where there was a gentle undulation of tree-covered hills. The trees, Pip noticed, looked like mere shrubs although she knew them to be fully grown eucalypts of some thirty metres or more. There was an orange track that scarred some of the hills at the bottom of the valley, disappearing between the folds and reappearing on the next hill.

'Will we take that track?' Pip asked, pointing at it. Grace shook her head.

'No, it'll be easier if we go off the north end here and take the old jump back pass down into the valley.'

Pip hoped Grace couldn't see the apprehension blooming in the red of her cheeks. Still looking at the view she asked, trying to sound casual, 'It'll be pretty steep?'

Grace curbed a smile, 'It's steep but it's the quickest way down unless you want to ride another day up to Karanja then another day back along the valley floor to reach that river.' There wasn't a choice.

Where they had tied the horses a small group of children had gathered. Pip and Grace disentangled themselves from pleas for a ride and headed for the pass at the end of the escarpment. The track was overgrown and barely visible. The branches of the eucalypts all the way down the side of the gully were twisted, fish supple, their leaves swimming in the gentle breeze. Grace went first for she knew the way and Pip followed behind, leading Lucky.

'Just follow me,' Grace yelled back as she began sliding over rocks and between trees, scarcely enough room for her legs. Pip hovered on the edge, unsure about the angle of the descent. Visibility did not extend past the first steep incline; it could be a sheer, gravelly cliff face for all Grace knew. Vida hesitated, reluctant, despite the disappearing tail of his new-found friend willingly crashing through the scrub. Pip knew that if she didn't push Vida on, and force him to follow Grace down, it would be too late and she would lose the way because there wasn't an obvious or marked path.

Rocks and flints leapt out from the horses' hooves and the hill rolled back as though it was the lid on a sardine can. The air rang with the clipping noise of horseshoes on stone. Pip had her heart in her mouth; she lost sight of the lip of the escarpment and where she had come from. The crystal blue sky seemed to reach out for her, instead of the other way around. She concentrated on the weight of her feet against the stirrups as the horse puffed, slid and strained below her. She could afford no other thoughts beside the motion of the climb. The trees grew sideways out of the hill and birds flew up in great flapping bursts. They passed some rock overhangs, one of which Vida spooked at violently and, for one moment, Pip saw herself snowballing down the hill. But she sunk her weight back against the warm comfort of her saddle and concentrated on Burd's strong haunches in front.

Once they were at the bottom, Pip caught her breath. The world around her was like none she had ever seen before. The ground was pattern swirled with clumped grasses growing between rocks; purple, brown and copper green. There were rough iron barks gathered closely around, as though there was much to hide. Scrubby, low to the ground, drought-tolerant and tough. There was a feeling that someone was watching her, although not from any fixed vantage point. It was as though the air itself was heavy with an awareness of who and what went through it. Pip felt uneasy. It was a growing sense of claustrophobia she could not shake. She wanted the security of a cleared site with a house, electricity and other people.

They stopped briefly to give the horses a rest but soon resumed their crashing through the rocky bush country. They found a skinny track made by either cattle or wild horses and followed it until they reached open country. Before them was a sloping woodland expanse. Pip brought the horses to a halt, and Grace spoke, almost to her self.

'I love it here, no clocks, no radio songs, no trains, no people to upset your dreams.' Grace seemed to belong to the bush, her face was alive.

Before Pip knew it, Grace had pushed Burd on and leapt away, charging down the valley as though riding for her life, laughing and whooping. Pip followed close after her, Lucky in tow, Vida's ears back, intent on catching up. The wind ripped through Pip's heart.

The horses slowed up at the bottom, where a stream ran. Pip's face felt flushed, 'Do you think it's possible to belong to a certain place?' Pip asked Grace, wondering what Grace would call the emotion Pip had seen in her face.

'Yes and no.' Grace answered

'That's a cop out, not an answer.'

'It's true though.'

'All I know is that I don't belong at the farm.'

'No?'

'No.'

'When does the harvest begin? How can you tell the early stages of a cow with bloat? When was the last time you were off a horse for more than a week?'

Pip was quiet, knowing Grace was trying to show her she was somehow part of the place.

'And it's not your home?' Grace finished.

Although Pip had lived there longer than she had not, she still longed for the place where she would feel herself. She did not know where that was, she just knew it wasn't the place she was in.

'They don't understand me there. They think I have strange habits. They say if I'm reading it's a waste of time.'

'But they love you all the same.'

Pip had to admit that she had never felt unloved, just misunderstood. Grace straightened her hat and said, 'Everyone dreams of a place where they will be fully understood and truly happy. So what do people do? They leave and find somewhere they think they'll be happy. But when they arrive they realise it wasn't the place they were looking for after all, and they start looking for something or someone else. Everyone wants to belong somewhere, it comes from a deep yearning. Longing is a condition of the human heart. No matter how old you get, you are never immune to that yearning feeling of wanting to go home. And you know where that home is?' Grace looked at Pip, 'It's here,' Grace hit her chest with the flat of her hand, 'it's in here and the sooner you learn that, the better off you are.'

They were walking the horses slowly, side by side, and Grace turned to look straight ahead as Pip thought her words over. Pip found them hard to take in. Could it be possible she was already in the place she belonged, but didn't realise it? This was a shocking thought. It sparked off an avalanche of doubt in Pip's chest. She had always thought belonging was a fixed attribute connected to each person, and that there was a place that existed in the world where they fitted in, like a piece of puzzle finding its niche. But if belonging was an attitude you could choose... Pip felt as though she was a cartoon character who had run out of ground, having failed to realise it was running in mid-air over a ravine.

Sophie Barnet grew up, and still lives, in the Blue Mountains, in New South Wales. She has always written and ridden. In her spare time she likes to garden, knit and bushwalk. She has just finished a Masters in Creative Writing at the University of Western Sydney.

Horse Dreams and Commonsense
Pam Bjork-Billings

I am the little girl who was never allowed to have a pony. Growing up on a small farm in a small town in 1950s and 1960s Australia, horses were all around me. Dad said that I would grow out of 'it'. A pony would eat too much grass, grass that we needed for the cows.

Luckily, even then, they began to be both the best teachers and the bringers of the truest friendships. Then I learnt that you don't accept the father's decision. The kids next door had ponies and they didn't always want to ride them. I was happy to help. The other kid from down the road, who had the show horse that she had to exercise every night, was more than happy to trot down the road and let me ride the horse, while she sat on our shed roof eating fruit. These were the beginnings of a passion born in me that has never faded.

The next important lesson was that if you want something enough, you will have it. Timmy lived over the road. Timmy was a 15 hands brown thoroughbred ex-racehorse; a real character. Timmy loved people but he liked to play. He especially liked to play with his owner who was not a good rider and was easily dumped by Timmy. I loved feeding Timmy, petting him over the fence, dreaming that when I finally got a horse it would be one just like him.

I kept finding people who would let me ride their horses and couldn't believe my luck when Merryn lent me Mystic, her beautiful grey, to ride in the school holidays. What manners he had. What a delight. Lesson from Mystic—the harmony that comes from respectful co-operation.

After going to riding schools at weekends all through Teachers' College, I ran into Timmy's owner and asked after the horse. Poor Timmy was being wasted in the paddock, not being ridden. He was offered to me to ride anytime I wanted. He was mine! Not only did I have a horse but it was the very one that I had desired and mooned over as a child. There was no stopping us. Timmy tried his famous shy, but I managed to stay there, kicked him in the ribs and flew off down the road.

Next lesson—if you think you can do something, you can. Riding club and eventing we went. Timmy was aged twenty by then, and had not been out of his paddock for ten years. Nothing fazed him: trail rides, competitions, shows, jumping; we did everything. It was while I was bowling along the country roads on Timmy that I met Joyce, coming the other way on her little chestnut. Years of friendship and hundreds of happy hours on horseback were spent with Joyce and Giovanni.

And so it has gone for the next thirty years. After Timmy came Strider Macsen or 'Mad Max'. As my instructor said at the time—the best horse I would ever have. A gangly youngster that moved like poetry, with a presence that turned heads. He made me feel like the queen of the world. Every time I took him out, good riders would approach me and ask could they buy him, or whether I would lease him to them so they could bring him on for me. Trouble was he knew he was fabulous and would buck like a gymnast when he felt like getting me off. I was sure he was too much for me, too good for me. But my wonderful instructor Gill would not hear of me getting rid of him. Lesson from Max—I deserve the best and it will come to me. After Max broke his leg I experienced the most intense grief at his untimely death.

But then came Fagan; chestnut and sweet. Found for me by Cathy. Lesson from Fagan— don't give up. I became pregnant a year after getting him and common sense, finances and time constraints indicated that I really should give up for a bit. But when have our horse dreams had anything to do with commonsense? Isn't that the point?

Commonsense has no place in our horse dreams. It is not just that we learn our most important lessons from horses and meet our truest friends. It is the place of magic, mystery and an indescribable connection with the primal and intuitive.

Now I have Jay Dee, a 16 hands brown thoroughbred gentleman. We found Anne and Casey to ride with to the beach, to the bush, and Gill and Hobbit to go to dressage competitions.

The meaning of horses in my life? Joyous unfettered physical freedom, and a host of wonderful women friends who understand me, support me and travel with me through my horse dreams.

Pam Bjork-Billings lives at Connewarre near Geelong with her horse, pony, dog, cats, goats, ducks, chooks, husband Michael, and children Seth and Aphra. To finance her riding she works at Deakin University as manager of the Equal Opportunity Program. She is also studying for a masters degree by research on the topic of women jockeys.

La Marismeña Australiana

Kirrilly Thompson

Kirrilly Thompson lives in Adelaide, South
Australia. She and her equestrian partner,
Chelsea, have been together for eight years.
During this time they have competed up to
elementary level dressage and at the Adelaide
Royal Show in breed and saddle-horse classes.
Kirrilly is in the final stages of a doctorate in
Anthropology at the University of Adelaide,
focussing on the cultural significance of horses.

48

In Andalusia, each year on 26 June, bands of semi-wild marsh horses are driven fifteen kilometres from El Rocio to the neighbouring town of Almonte, where they are given their annual once-over. The event is called La Saca de Las Yeguas, the removal of the mares. It takes its name from the female collective rather than the male. The young are branded, wormed and trimmed and horses of all ages are bought and sold. Three days later, the remaining horses are driven back through the cobbled streets of Almonte to the marshes, where their survival is in the hands of the elements and the Holy Virgin. This return is called El Regreso. It takes only four or five hours, which is half the time it takes to drive the horses away from their homelands. In 2001 a stranger offered me a ride on his horse named Marismeño, 'he of the marshes'. We left the stock yards at about seven a.m. The horses were excited and my new friend asked, 'You do like to gallop don't you?' I had ridden only a handful of times in the past ten months and I started to worry that more than my pride might be dented by the end of the day! I uttered a very unconvincing, 'Si'! It was too late to back out now.

A long wooden pole was thrust into my right hand, to sling over my shoulder and hold out behind me should any of the marsh mares try to break away from the herd of fifty and beat me home. I was the only woman among the group of half-a-dozen stockmen. Some ignored me, others laughed at my rising trot and gloves (stock horses are only required to walk and canter, for rider comfort) and one asked me if I would prefer to travel in the car. This was mostly due to a cramp in my side which was not long after diagnosed as a kidney stone! I was a few feet taller than the owner of my horse and had not adjusted his stirrup length. My knee joints were on fire. I had been given orders to stay behind the group but my horse had other plans. I couldn't hold the gelding and spent the ride in front of the group but constantly looking back to check if I was going in the right direction. My left arm ached from holding back such a strong horse with both reins in that hand; elbow in front of my hip and my thumb facing to the right. That night it couldn't even hold an icecream cone at the local fair without shaking! My right arm ached from swinging out the wooden pole behind me to keep the following herd tightly together.

I pressed on and was soon distracted by the trickling river beds and fields of sunflowers that we rode through. I began to live in the moment and feel like I was a participant and not a tourist—despite the bright red cap my friend insisted I wear to keep the sun out of my eyes and the equally gaudy yellow polo shirt, both colours considered unlucky and rarely worn by horse riders and bullfighters.

Part way through the ride, I heard a rider behind me call out 'La Marismeña Australiana' in the seemingly random but precise flamenco tone in which 'Ole' is spontaneously exclaimed in a bar. The experience couldn't have been better from then on. I had been given the nickname of the Australian Marsh Girl while riding in Australia's antipode. I was an oxymoron on horseback! I could well be the only Australian to have taken part in El Regreso and I am definitely one of the few women. It was the proudest moment in my life—but it was that sense of pride that comes from achieving something so personal that it doesn't matter that no one was there to share it with me. No one who could have cared was there to see and I couldn't have cared if they did or not. That was the moment of my life in which I most fully lived. I can relive it when I'm in the saddle and I close my eyes and hear the hoof beat of fifty horses behind me.

I arrived in El Rocio five hours after settling into the sheepskin-lined cowboy saddle when I had said, 'No thanks, the stirrups are fine...' My companions and I spread out and galloped freely over dry mud flats to drive the mares and their foals far into the scorched marshlands. I breathed an excitement that was equal parts adrenalin at the speed of the little horse, mixed with fear that the uneven ground would make the next precarious footfall my last. After the ride, I was walking like an eighty-year-old woman and the kidney stone had ricocheted around my side like a broken spur rowel. But I was happy—satisfied that in the moment of becoming a Marismeña Australiana I also became aware that I was a woman, an Australian and a rider. There is truth in 'being one' with a horse whilst riding school figures and movements in an arena for the appreciation of a judge—but there is another truth in 'being one' with a horse in the countryside, intuitively negotiating terrain and the movements of the galloping herd that follows for the appreciation of no one but self.

Section Two GirlDreams

Horses Schmorses

Ginger Ekselman

Sally started it. She has been wearing leggings and riding boots to school. Zoe wears her riding boots too. Sally has a bright blue jumper with black horses on it and a bright red one the same and leggings that match. Zoe's leggings are thick and beige. Every weekend they go to the Collingwood Children's Farm and ride horses. You just have to do one hour's work on the farm first and then you get a riding lesson for free.

Me and Gina decide we will go too. We don't have riding boots, just gumboots that are hard to get on and off. Because we are new we are in the beginners class, not the class with the big kids like Sally and Zoe (even though I am two weeks older than Sally). Because we are new we don't know which jobs are the best. So we end up cleaning out the chooks' pen. It's disgusting. There's lots of chicken shit everywhere and spiders and a dead baby chicken and an old egg that some boy smashes on the ground so we all have to run away.

Sometimes when you are really lucky you get the job of feeding the baby sheep or calves. They drink out of bottles. You have to make sure the milk isn't too hot. These are the best jobs, but you can't do them in winter because there's no babies then.

Mostly me and Gina end up cleaning out the pigs' pens. You think pigs are small and cute and pink like in *Charlotte's Web* but they're not. They are huge. They come up to your chest almost. And they are spotty and black and white and very hairy and coarse. You have to wash them as well. You do it with the hose. You have to get out of the pen to do that because sometimes the pigs run. They don't smell that bad though, and they only get dirty when their pen is dirty. It's not their fault. It is very muddy. You can see how deep the mud is by seeing how far it goes up your gumboots. Me and Gina kind of like this job.

Because we are new we don't know which horses are the best. You have to go out in the field and catch one. They go crazy and start running around and around in circles, you have to wait until they stop. We are always the last ones to catch a horse because we get scared, so we always end up with Sally, the black Shetland pony.

Her name is Sally, just like Sally's name. She is small and black and fluffy. She is very cute. At first we don't know why the others don't want her. Then we find out. Sally hates kids. If you say she is cute she will bite you. You have to be careful. When you brush her she tries to kick you. She pretends she is gentle to lure you in and then she kicks you when you are in the stable with her. When you try to put on her saddle she puffs up her tummy so you put it on too loose. When you get on her it slips and you fall off. She can hold her tummy puffy for a very long time. She waits until you are in the yard doing the lesson.

Sally hates being ridden. She stands completely still like a rock. You kick in your heels like you're meant to. Everyone else in the class walks around you while Sally is like a statue. Then she lets more tummy puff out and you fall off again. Lucky she is so short.

Me and Gina, we decide we don't like horses that much. Sometimes we just clean out the pigs and then we hide in the tree house near their pen. The pigs are looking good because we clean them every week now. One day while we are hiding a famous politician comes to look at the farm. His name is Paul Keating. We watch him. He has newspaper people and photographers and everything. He stops in front of the pigs. He likes them best too. He turns around and stands in front of the photographer looking very proud. The photographer takes his photo. We are very proud our pigs will be in the newspaper but we hope he doesn't pretend it was him that cleaned them so well like that.

Ginger Ekselman is a Melbourne-based writer. She runs two community writing groups and also works with young people at a secondary school. She has completed a Diploma in Professional Writing and Editing and has been writing short stories since before she could write and had to dictate them to her mum. Her sister has a horse but Ginger doesn't know him that well.

For Love, Trust and Nothing Else

Linley Maroney

There's something universal about the love of horses. It doesn't matter where we go, or whether we're with complete strangers, but the second we spot 'one of our own' the conversation will be guaranteed to run something like this.

'Oh, you ride do you! What discipline are you?'

'I'm training my youngster up to do show-jumping. You?'

'I've got a school Master and we're currently competing in Elementary. Where do you keep your horse?'

And away it goes, the tones becoming higher and more excited; an instant bond formed. It doesn't matter if this person just rear-ended my car. Suddenly, they speak my language.

I've been absolutely crazy about horses since I was ten. My family couldn't afford to buy me a horse so I had to make do with trail rides. This went on until the age of fifteen. By that time I was well established in all the basic gaits of trail riding: walk, jog and bolt. It may not have taught me much, but I learned to hang on like a burr in a horse's mane. Around this time, we moved house a short distance and to my great delight, our new neighbours were 'horse people'. Whether they did it to stop me hanging off their front fence, or if they genuinely took pity on me, I'll never be sure. But they gave me my first horse. And what a horse!

Jatz was all of 12.2 hands-high and built like a barrel on very fast legs. He was half-Arabian and half-Welsh Mountain pony, which in every day terms meant he was crazy and he had the stamina to be crazy all day. He was dappled grey and so intelligent it was dangerous. Talk about love at first sight! My parents conceded and bought

me a saddle and put up the ten dollars a week it was going to cost for him to live in a paddock down the street. Life couldn't have been more perfect. I quickly became acquainted with the other horse girls in the area and we could be seen on any given weekend, tearing up the local area like an out-of-control lynch mob. There was nothing Jatz and I wouldn't try. I remember a number of occasions where a few of us rode into town and rode our horses through the McDonalds drive-thru. We also rode through the park in the centre of town but they threw us out after we started jumping the fence in and out of the cricket field.

I had Jatz for three fantastic years before I gave him back to my wonderfully tolerant neighbours. I still miss him at times. I'll never forget the time I raced a car with him… Or the time I was riding through a quarry and raced a truck.

It makes my hair stand on end to think about the insane things we used to do. I'm not sure about the scientific explanation for this but, as I've gotten older, the ground has gotten harder. I don't seem to spring back like a tennis ball when I bite the dust these days. Perhaps one too many falls off Jatz is the reason. In any case, I don't take the risks I used to. I moved on from Jatz to another leased horse, then another. Each one slightly madder than the one before. Somewhere along the line I actually learned a thing or two about riding and equitation. And somewhere just after that I realised that if I really wanted to be a good rider, I had to quit with the hand-me-downs and get my own hand-picked horse. One that would complement me in every way. One that would be as one with me as we galloped the plains into the sunset.

Instead, I bought Gidget. I thought that after Jatz, Nikki and Laddie, I was more than ready for anything a young horse could do to me. Not so. One thing all riders come to understand very quickly is that we know nothing. This horse was in the process of being broken in when I bought her. She had just turned three and looked so out of proportion I wondered what I'd seen in her. She kicked, she bit, she struck at everything within range and she had a penchant for standing on her hind legs. I quickly saw I was out of my depth, and was about to have a dangerous horse on my hands, so I found a highly recommended trainer and, three weeks later, she was at least controllable.

From that day forward, it has been an amazing journey. Turns out Gidget does complement me, after all. We're both stubborn, we're both lazy, we both do crazy spontaneous things and we both enjoy the ride. It's so damn hard to get Gidget to do the right thing but, when she finally does it, she does it brilliantly and I can't put into words how worthwhile all those long hours are. From our six dressage tests, we have five ribbons; two of them are blue. They are among my proudest moments. We're now focusing on learning how to jump and in so many ways it's like starting from scratch. But we've passed the refusals and we've passed the hooning and as long as we keep taking the small steps forward we'll be okay. It's not about how fast we get there. It's not even about getting there. It's about her being my trusted companion along the way. My heart swells when Gidget finds herself in a frightening situation and her black ears flick straight back to me, waiting for me to tell her it's all right. A hand on the neck, a quiet word and she'll willingly take my word for it that I won't let her get hurt. I've put blood, sweat and tears into building that trust and I wouldn't break it for the world. Sure, we have our bad days—make that terrible days—but ten of those are overcome by the one day when I seem to be inside her head and we get everything right without even feeling like we really tried that hard. I live for the smile that touches my face as I drop the reins on her neck and point her towards her paddock, telling her she's the best.

Linley Maroney *is a data network technician living in the beautiful Hawkesbury, north-west of Sydney. Working to support her horse addiction, she is training her young mare to become a show jumper. Outside of riding, she is an accomplished pianist and aspiring author.*

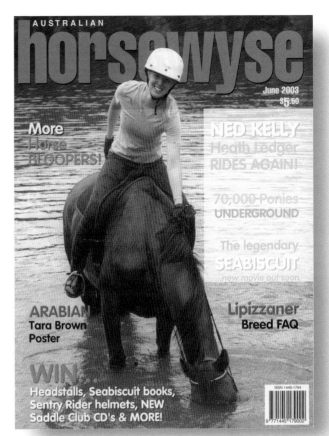

For the Love of a Mare

Di Gatehouse

The way of the horse world in the wild is matriarchal. The pecking order is decided more by negotiation than fisty cuffs. It was a matriarch of grand proportions that first captured my heart, even though my first greeting would have been at her knee height.

Sally was a Clydesdale mare heading for her dotage and she and her son Patch were legacies of the petrol-rationing era of the Second World War and the years immediately following.

They did most of the haulage work around a rich pastured property near Launching Place east of Melbourne. In the farmyard old trucks and a tractor stood where they had stopped, monuments to another time. The whole property was a monument to a bygone era of comfortable country guest houses where city families went to take in a bit of farm life or chase elusive trout in the river that ran through the area.

I remember the wide verandahs of a house with a name that sounded like Go Honnie, countless empty rooms and the old guests' lounge with its limp lace curtains, large club chairs, long couches, the out-of-tune piano and a wind-up gramophone. Lack of suitable needles rendered silent the pile of 78 r.p.m. records in its cabinet. At the front of the house was a tennis court with a sagging ragged net and lumpy surface that didn't deter my elder brother and friends from at least trying to play. Life revolved around the kitchen and the huge wood-burning stove beside which my Aunt Jean seemed to be permanently stuck. There were a lot of mouths to feed plenty of food and it was here that I learnt milk came from cows and not bottles.

Most of my days were spent with Uncle Billy behind Sally and Patch, and they mostly pulled a wooden contraption on sleds across the wet paddocks and, much to my delight, sometimes through the river. I watched in awe as the two Clydesdales dug in with their massive hind legs to pull us up the river bank and the hill to home. At some stage I must have plucked up the courage to ask Uncle Billy if I could ride one of the horses—after all, our family friend Anna who was always around, rode horses. I can remember quite clearly being told I would have to ride Sally because Patch was known to buck. Patch was eight and Sally was an age I just could not even relate to.

The day came when Uncle Billy tied Sally's halter rope so that I had two reins and told me I didn't need a bit in her mouth. After lifting me up onto her broad back we set off down the long tree-lined dirt driveway to the front gate. By the return journey I had

gained enough confidence to stop hanging onto her mane for security, learnt to balance, even though my little stick-like legs were poking out at right angles to my body, sit up straight and hold the rope reins just as Uncle Billy had shown me. I was on top of the world literally, I could see over the front gate and suddenly my elder brother and his mates looked decidedly insignificant.

Riding Sally came at a price. I had to help brush her and considering I could only get my arm half-way up her ample sides, it proved difficult. Most of my efforts were confined to her legs and vast underbelly. She was so patient, standing stock still, her only movement being to lower her head for the two-armed bear hugs that she was frequently given.

There were many holidays at the wonderful old farm and, as I grew older and stronger, I became more confident with 'my horse'. I learnt that by taking her up against the haystack I could easily scramble aboard. Dismounting was also easy provided there was enough hay to cushion my landing. Sally patiently carted me around the farmyard and up and down that driveway for as long as she wanted, never at any stage putting her small charge in danger and never raising anything more than a firm walk.

It was Sally who gave me my first lesson in negotiation. I had become confident with her to the extent that the Warburton Highway, along which few cars travelled in those days, started to look tempting. How I got the gate open I don't remember but what I do remember was that there was an invisible line there across which Sally would not go. No amount of bouncing my short legs off her side would convince and neither did the twig plucked off a nearby tree to use as a whip. Yelling proved totally useless for she had the answer. Swinging around, and at a slightly faster walk than usual, I was returned to the haystack where she just munched away until I conceded defeat. Uncle Billy just said she was looking after me but I never asked that great dame to take me out of bounds again.

Di Gatehouse has worked as a specialist women's sports writer for the Melbourne Sun, *and works as a contributing writer for the* Sunday Herald-Sun *and the* Age. *She has contributed to magazines such as* Hoofs and Horns *and to a number of books. She is also a horse breeder.*

Clever Chap

Jan Williamson

I wanted a pony. Then I envied my boss his donkey. When I heard 'Know anyone who wants a donkey? Free to a good home.' Me? Please! He was a colt, a Jesus-donkey from a family, kept to run with bulls. As a hobbledehoy, for a peppermint he was anybody's. Almost! He wouldn't answer to just anything, so I tried a 'Rumpelstiltskin!' Not 'Jack!' And 'Robert' he scorned. But when I called 'Hieronymous?' he pranced, he skittered, he cosied up… from then on, he was 'My Ronnie Mouse'.

He needed a soul mate, so did I.

He lived beside the house. He soon learned not to nip me; and I, instead of twisting his velvet nostrils, caressed them, breathed onto them, smooched them, while I pulled his long, furry ears. He came galloping when he saw me.

Time to use a halter, and a leading rein. At first the idea didn't grab him! I manoeuvred and coaxed, he twisted away. I got cunning; he got stubborn. I persevered… until the phone rang. I dropped the halter on the car bonnet and went to answer. When I came back, he had the halter on the ground, working his nose into it. We co-operated. We succeeded. We went for a walk.

It wasn't always that simple, you understand. I learned patience with (and laughed during—you should have seen him, on his back, feet in air) his chosen 'bath'—a roll in the middle of the gravel road: his feet wore down nicely, his teeth kept in condition munching the delicacies there; roundweeds growing in the sand. And the long acre held thistles, flowers the best bit! We couldn't get past those. So we helped the farmer.

Round the paddocks at home he followed me.

Watching me with interest, down by the bonfire, collecting his 'apples' into a plastic bag to feed the rhubarb. Stepping daintily round nests of plovers' eggs by the reeds. Racing round the paddocks with boys on bikes. Or, when bored, performing the gentleman's part in a cunning fox-trot with the heifer, Cal-fie; ballroom-dancing her backwards, cheek to cheek. He stood outside the fence, munching weeds as I threw them, or, when I was gardening close enough, he'd take a lock of my hair between his lips, and pull it gently as I bent. He even, by flattening his ears, snaking his neck, baring his teeth and with one stamp of his hoof, sent the great grey hunting cat hurtling backwards into the blackberry.

He was a guard too, greater than the geese of Rome! His claim to fame was the dry evening at the drinking trough, when he was fidgeting, braying urgently. 'What's he up to?' I wondered and went to see. Good thing too. The ball-cock was broken by steers, and water was streaming out, a rivulet in the dust. Quick phone call, fix-it farmer and compliment, 'Cunning chap, that donkey! Saved me a lot of work, and water.'

Sometimes they came in… he and Cal-fie, to my garden; they didn't eat much, they fertilised the lawn, before sunrise. She went out easily: he wanted to come in and join me for breakfast. At dusk he'd have joined me on the front deck, had the tall steps been wide enough—instead, he stood with his nose through the guard-rails, jaw resting on the floor! Soulful eyes and lovely lashes he had.

Sometimes he escaped from the paddock. An urgent demand one late evening sent me after clothes, shoes, halter, peppermints… 'Mum, your donkey's down the road. He won't come home so we've parked the car and they're standing guard so he can't reach the main road.' I parked my car blocking the road this end; I trudged along wielding torch, carrying halter, fingering the peppermints, praying silently and singing out of key his favourite song: 'You're my lovely little petunia in…'

The clatter of hooves, the gleam of red eyes in the growing dark… there he was, mouthing for his peppermint, huffing at my shoulder, walking daintily tethered on his imaginary 'piece of string'. Dear Ronnie. Then he was ready to ride and to drive. But I couldn't keep him. Now I take peppermints, or mint, and I visit. Sometimes. We get up-close but not too personal.

When I lie in my bath, gazing out the long window, I can imagine him, standing on the hillock under the gnarled old pear tree. Or, I see the worn old totara board where he rested his strong jaw, having a good scratch. Sometimes I expect to see him come from the camouflage of the old macrocarpa stumps, galloping, ears flat, neat feet sliding and teeth bared, 'Where's my peppermint?'

Dear Hieronymous, clever chap, I miss you.

Jan Williamson is a New Zealand superannuitant who in childhood aimed to have a pony and ride a hilly two hundred acres as her Dad's landgirl. He died though, and the family moved to town. She taught; married and bore three children; became a city secretary. She has 'retired' to country life in a converted woolshed.

Pedro

Deborah Wardle

In my childhood memories, Pedro shines. My recollections of five or so years of adventures with that rapscallion pony illustrate how he both reflected and formed certain aspects of my developing character. Recalling going with Dad as a six-year-old to buy a pony from the local knackery and Pedro's subsequent local fame as a mighty kids' pony casts a light on some great growing up years. I now appreciate the many things that Pedro fostered in me and taught me.

A scruffy brown-and-white pony stood at the back of the small slushy yard at Berrisfield abattoirs, the old sleeper railing fence tall behind his muddy withers. He looked pretty thin, and grubby; a long forelock half-hid his face. He looked at us intently in that first moment. I couldn't reach his teeth to check his age, and it was too muddy to pick up his feet, so I just checked out his eyes. They glinted. Dad didn't know too much about horses. The dirty white patch over the pony's neck and back where the saddle goes made me think of Indians' ponies; a piebald. Beneath the mud he'd have four white socks. Black mane and tail were matted into dirty ringlets. He stood about 13.2 hands-high. He looked a wiry, belligerent fellow at that moment. The smell was acrid, stale mud and animal fear. I remember looking at Dad and saying something like, 'he looks okay'. Somehow he came home to stay.

We'd head off every afternoon after school, galloping around the suburban blocks and patches of bush land around Cardiff, a western suburb of Newcastle. I always felt safe on Pedro. I had images of Hopalong Cassidy.

Pedro soon learnt the standard routes and would save that extra bit of energy for pulling, bit in his teeth, on the homeward leg. The shopkeepers on the main road home would bellow out after us as we galloped under the shop awnings, clattering straight past the shop doors. We would gallop on, oblivious to the potential disaster. Somehow we never collected a grocery-laden customer.

Pedro was a plucky character, who didn't like men. He would try to bite the old blacksmith Vic, as he bent over to shoe him. I'd scold the impudent equine, pulling his head around, away from Vic's behind. He was sometimes hard to catch in the paddock and would charge at his would-be captors, teeth bared and ears laid back. I would yell at him and swing the bridle at him as he thundered past. He soon stopped doing it to me. He became a sort of one-girl pony. I loved that about him.

I'd clip his mane and wash and trim his shaggy fetlocks for special Pony Club events. He never seemed to mind me climbing amongst his feet, scraping bot fly eggs off his nobbly knees. He'd polish up pretty well for show days, hooves blackened and his coat brushed to a shine.

We both shared a passion for jumping. On bush rides I'd find any log I could to hurtle over. At Pony Club Sundays, I would dig up courage to approach the ringmaster to ask could I please go in the under-nine show-jumping. There was no jumping for the under-sevens. He would mostly say yes. I would have a surge of nervous excitement as Pedro and I would fly around the course. This for me was the start of many years of show-jumping on many fine horses. Pedro initiated me to the joys of soaring through the air, on the back of a horse. The golden rule was that if you fell off you had to get straight back on. You just had to break the bubble of fear and keep going. What a great lesson that has been in life.

We would sometimes ride our ponies to school and leave them in a paddock over the road from the convent. Sweaty, horse-hairy legs under our green-checked school uniform always seemed sort of special to me. A sort of Annie Oakley feeling I guess.

Maybe it was his name, with shades of Patagonian wind-swept plains and gauchos with long black moustaches, but Pedro sort of reminded me of wild cowboys, trouble-making, risk-taking, but oh so loveable, rascals. He had a lazy habit of half-cantering, half-trotting. It must have been the slouchy cowboy in him.

Pedro was a warm and tough friend and I loved him intensely. I remember the soft fur on his nose. He taught me about courage and tenacity and the value of sheer gutsy effort. I remember the glint in his eye as I caught him, the munching of his teeth as I sat beside him in his stable, the smell of his sweaty coat. It was agony for me to pass him on to my little sister when I was ready for a bigger horse. The ignominy of her successes after all my hard work stung my eleven-year-old heart.

Many years later Pedro died of old age, in retirement on a large wheat farm, chasing mares, rounding up his herd. Instant, it was probably a heart attack. He still had a glint in his eye to the end.

Deborah Wardle (born 1957) lives in Castlemaine, central Victoria, where she built her first mud brick home. Deborah studied and worked in Women's Studies and management and is now managing the Castlemaine Steiner School. She has a twelve year old son there. Deborah still keeps a horse, the third generation of mares, the great grand daughter of the thoroughbred mare she show jumped at Sydney Royal Show in 1972. She still breeds an occasional foal, just to keep her hand in.

Freedom is a Horse

Kirsten Bowers

Horses provided me with a life apart: dreaming of horses, reading and writing about horses, drawing horses, immersing myself in their wonderful smell, their being, and finally, the zenith, riding horses. Horses (two in particular), provided me with my first path to freedom, a life apart, an escape from a domineering abusive father.

Horses taught me about power, so different from the corrupt power I had known until that point, the power of the thick-buckled strap wielded by him and its attendant atmosphere, slick/thick with terror. Horses were immensely powerful and could be dangerous, but it was the bond of trust willingly entered into by each that made the difference.

I was typically 'horsey' as a child and teenager—couldn't get enough of them, but what a wonderful obsession! I couldn't ride regularly until I was in my teen years, saving all my pocket money and earning all I could through doing chores. Every Saturday, Mum would take me to our local riding school where there were three-hour-long bush rides—those hours provided me with my first taste of unmitigated joy. Slowly I learnt to ride, confidence and skill developing with each week. I can't remember those 'early horses' now, their names, what colours they were, their temperaments.

Albi, a beautiful white albino pony is where memory really starts. How I loved his delicate pink-rimmed eyes, with beautiful white lashes! Others thought he was a freak but, to me, he was special, his nature gentle and trusting. I started riding him regularly. He was swift for his size, and I was at the stage in my riding where I wanted to go very fast. The complete exhilaration of a flat-out gallop was in my blood (it's never really left)—the power of these amazing creatures, muscles bunched, legs pounding,

literally flying. (He could never catch me on my magic white pony.) When I was good enough, I started riding Albi bareback. No saddle for me; I wanted to be as close as I possibly could to him. I loved the way my jeans would be caked with his horsehair and sweat at the end of the day, loved the smell. I loved jumping off him and having to swing back on without the aid of stirrups… so natural, so easy. And, at the end of the day, quiet time spent with Albi, grooming him down.

Well, a couple of years later I was growing and it was time to move on up. Albi led me on to my next great love: Gyro, 15 hands-high or thereabouts, also white, although he had brown spots flecked throughout his coat. I had had a passion to ride Gyro for some time. He was the riding school's 'best' horse, only ridden by the owners or one of the more experienced riders. He had this amazing 'rocking horse' canter; he could canter on the spot, he was so graceful. I just had to connect with him.

I had gotten to know well Bill, one of the riding school owners, by this stage. I was able to start riding Gyro regularly. I'd been helping out for some time, saddling up the horses, checking that riders had the correct stirrup length, doing whatever I could, because I wanted to learn as much as I could about these magnificent creatures and, along the way, I was also learning about myself. My confidence was growing and it was safe to trust.

By the time I was fifteen, I was fully immersed in my chosen horse dream. Bill had taken me under his wing and wanted me to start competing in shows. Not dressage or jumping but the adrenalin pumping gymkhana events— barrel racing, bending, flag-and-rescue races. For these events you needed a fast, agile horse that could turn on a dime. Gyro was perfect. He was taken out of the paddocks

with the other horses, stabled and fed on a special diet to bring him into peak condition. It was my job to train him. Heaven! Now, instead of just riding on Saturdays, I was riding nearly every day of the week. I'd ride my 'normal' bike to school, three miles and back home. Then I'd jump on my racing bike and ride the six miles to the riding school.

Now it was just me and Gyro on the bush trails, practising in the paddock, developing and cementing our relationship with each other. That horse definitely pierced my soul. Gyro was sensitive. He had been badly treated when he was young, and never fully trusted men so, generally, I was the only one who could catch him when he was in training, separate from the other horses. There was definitely an unconscious connection here with my own history; two wounded spirits coming together, helping to heal one another.

We made a great team, Gyro and I, and won a lot of events together. But while I still recall those times, what really touches me is the quieter moments; just the two of us miles from anywhere, a shared pleasure, riding to be free.

Kirsten Bowers is forty-two years old, lives in Thornbury and works part time in administration. Her other great love is martial arts, especially kung fu. She lives with a wonderful man, Moxi the cat, and Cub, a Belgian Shepherd.

Broken Memories

Lana Homes

I walk among the broken fences in my heart. I open my eyes and find myself thrust sharply back into reality. I stand in the paddock where I remember feeling happy… laughing… running my fingers through Silver's soft fur. It seems so long ago that I felt so happy. Now there is bareness… nothing… the black sand of the empty paddock. I feel sadness remembering my beloved pony who was so unfairly taken from me. I wish I could talk to Silver and find some comfort in her kind eyes. I wish I could say goodbye. Ever since I got the phone call. My pony is dead. I will never get to see her again. I sit on the fallen tree by the fence. A flood of memories come rushing back to me…

We got Silver when I was eight… a furry white teddy bear. She was a Welsh pony and looked every bit the part. She had the feathers, the fur, the fat, and the big kind eyes that all Welsh ponies seem to have. My previous pony had been a bit wild, and I had lost a lot of confidence with my riding, but Silver was so placid and gentle that I slowly started regaining that confidence. She became my best friend. After a bad day at school, I used to go and talk to her for hours. I knew she understood me…

We used to just go on trail rides at first. She would plod along beside Mum, always looking after me. Then we went to Pony Club. We did jumping and games and flatwork… we had a ball! My only complaint was that sometimes I used to get frustrated by Silver's laziness when doing games.

And so it continued for a few years: going to Pony Club, doing a show here and there, a couple of one day events. And it got to the stage where I had outgrown Silver… not in my size, but in my experience. I wanted a pony that would jump higher and go faster. That's when I got Eli, another Welsh pony. He was a bit smaller than Silver, and finer… but he still had the feathers, the fur, the fat, and the big kind eyes.

Eli was definitely faster than Silver, and more jumpy. I had to work hard to ride him well. He had big movement for a little pony, which I found hard to get used to after Silver's smooth and lazy trot. I used to go to Silver when it was all getting too much with Eli.

I started doing some more shows with Eli and, to my surprise, we were actually successful. Eli turned out to be a great little show pony, winning many champions for me, including the Royal Show. Because of this, and because I still wasn't very confident with jumping, I started to specialise in showing, and started doing a bit of dressage, in which we were also successful.

I still used to go and talk to Silver all the time. She kind of turned into the companion pony, as she was getting a bit too old and stiff to do much riding. If any of my friends came over who couldn't ride, we put them on Silver, knowing that they'd be safe and that Silver would look after them as well, as she had looked after me so many years before. Even the dog liked to ride Silver occasionally!

Eventually I physically outgrew Eli and, though it was torture to part with him, we sold him to a nice home in the country, where he was very much loved. He's still there. We bought and sold a couple of other horses, which were all beautiful and special, but I shared the strongest bond with Silver and Eli. Several years later, when I was seventeen, and finishing high school, we ended up with a horse called Zani, as well as Silver still in the paddock.

The time came for me to go university. I was really enjoying my course, but finding that I didn't have much time for the horses any more due to the travelling. It took me an hour-and-a-half just to get to university from Bullsbrook, so we decided to move closer. At first, we were looking at horse properties, but we ended up with a nice little house in a suburb about fifteen minutes from university. Of course, this meant we had to sell the horses.

It was horrible having to part with Silver, who had been my friend for all those years, who I'd been able to see any time I wanted to, who I could talk to when things were rough. I knew I'd never be able to do that again. Selling Zani was hard, too, but Silver and I had been together since I was eight years old. We gave her to a lovely family from Pony Club, who wanted her for their two-year-old boy. It was about six months later that I got a phone call from them to say she had died.

———

I'm crying again. I always seem to be crying now. Nobody understands. Nobody knows how I'm feeling… what a crushing sadness I now feel. How my life will never be the same without Silver. I sit on the fallen tree beside the fence, the salty tears streaming down my cheeks. I'm watching the emptiness of the paddock around me, wanting to say goodbye.

Lana Homes is twenty years old and grew up in Bullsbrook, Western Australia. She works as a receptionist and in her spare time enjoys riding horses and dancing. Lana would like eventually to own a horse again but in the meantime takes lessons at Tallarook Park Riding School.

Barbero's Story Suzanne Coutanceau

January 1985

The Age classifieds: 'For sale—11yo 15.2hh chestnut thoroughbred gelding, ex-racehorse, needs loving home. $200.'

Barbero: born 1974, dam Toy Show, sire Frascati. Raced well (too early, of course); injuries stopped his racing career at age four. Small for a racehorse; damaged hock and pastern, slight limp on off-fore from arthritic knee. Hooves too soft from steroid dosing; cruel, cruel pinfire scars on forelegs. Rich chestnut, tiny white new-moon star in middle of forehead, white bobbysox on hindlegs. A bit skinny. Eats a lot—making up for being starved in a paddock for years with no food after he was abandoned by the racing stable. Teeth worn down from chewing trees and fenceposts, and picking at non-existent blades of grass and getting dirt instead. How could such a lovely horse be treated so badly, and yet still be so kind?

March 1985

Dear Pat,

That day, when I came to look at Barbero, owning a horse was still only a dream, something I'd always wanted ever since I could remember. But as soon as I saw Barbero, I knew he was perfect. I know you wanted to keep him but circumstances prevented it. I know you had such a hard time when your house burned down. You hoped Barbero would compensate your daughter for losing everything, and give her something to love and be responsible for. It's a pity it didn't work out. Thank you for trusting me with Barbero, I promise I'll take good care of him.

Sincerely, Suzie.

1985–1995

Bero was agisted close to my home in outer eastern Melbourne along with Alice, my sister Annie's stockhorse. They were exactly the same age and size, and became fast friends. We rode together most of the time: fourteen kilometres of Koonung Creek track where the Eastern Freeway is today; occasionally traversing down to the Yarra River at Warrandyte; in the summer holidays, taking kids and horses camping in the bush north of Melbourne.

Bero was a pleasure to ride; trustworthy, calm and unflappable, unless riding fast with others. Then the competitive instinct would take over and result in a dance or a gallop! On our own, we would potter happily along the dirt roads listening to the birds, watching the clouds, communing, thinking the same thoughts, reins hooked over saddlehorn, totally relaxed. My escape.

Beautiful clear kind brown eyes, long eyelashes, glorious honest face. Glowing golden chestnut coat, fine soft mane and tail. Deep chest, huge shoulders, long elegant neck.

In 1987, Annie and I moved Bero and Alice out to the Dandenong Ranges where they ran free with a small herd of horses on a big old farm in the hills. Bero and Alice were always together, usually a little apart from the others.

A funny thing happened one day. I arrived at the paddock but couldn't see Bero anywhere, which was most unusual. So, with a sigh, I picked up his halter and his favourite food (carrots) and traipsed off over the hills in the rain to the far corner of the farm, thinking he must be with the herd; I could just spy them in the distance. Calling his name occasionally, I walked on, slipping and sliding on the steep muddy track wondering where he could be. Reaching the herd, I couldn't see him anywhere. Now what? I turned around to retrace my steps and collided with his nose! He'd quietly tiptoed after me the whole way, sound muffled by the rain, with a quizzical look on his beautiful face!

Gentle nature, comes when called. Loves attention. Clumsy with his feet—broke my sister's toe once. Dislikes men intensely. Won't have anything to do with them, laying back his ears and snorting. A legacy of the cruel atrocities of his racing days?

May 1995

My daughter Mel, a dizzy horse-lover like me, discovered Pony Club. She went along, borrowing other people's ponies (Bero was way too big and strong for her to ride), until one day: Mum, you know Diamond Sal? She's for sale. Can we buy her? Please, please, please?

———————

Dear Cheryl,

It is with great regret that I'm giving Barbero away to you because I cannot afford to maintain two horses. My only consolation is that I know you'll look after him. Bero and I have been companions for over ten years. It is very hard to part with him. As I said to you when you came and visited, Bero is the kindest of horses, and it is my wish that he live out the rest of his life in comfort and with someone who loves him. As he's getting old now, he'll make a perfect stable companion for your little mare. Please kiss him every now and then for me.

Sincerely, Suzie.

Suzanne Coutanceau *was born and bred in the city. Always a bushy at heart, she 'discovered' horses at a very early age but, as a youngster, had to be content with horsey books. Daughter Mel inherited Suzie's love of horses, and they both enjoyed years of Pony Club with three lovely equines—Diamond Sal, Bluey and Glenn. Suzie now owns a young Arab pony who is destined for leisurely ambles down bushy or beachy tracks, riding side-by-side with her horsey partner Chris, also a bushy (but a real one).*

My Horse's Heart

Caroline Taylor

I was dressed in my most expensive dress and favourite, treacherous heels. It was a freezing night and my heart was broken. I knew I couldn't go inside to my silent bedroom so I stumbled out to the paddock, shivering and gasping as the tears threatened to overwhelm me. I didn't even need to call out to Ali, my red-headed Anglo-Arabian mare, before she raised her head and nickered curiously. I watched as she picked her way over to me in the moonlight. She betrayed no particular surprise at this midnight visit, just pricked her ears, hopeful… perhaps it was feeding time already? As always, even through my tears, she looked achingly beautiful—her white blaze and socks glowed pale blue in the night and she held her tail high, like a dainty lady picking up her skirts. She stopped and breathed into my neck, then stood still as I leaned into her mane and sobbed… adding to the tears that had soaked into her neck over many years. This time though, she refrained from rolling her eyes and fidgeting. Nor did she nudge my pockets impatiently, wanting a bribe for her comfort. She knew this was not just a bad day at work and these were not simply tears of frustration. I wound my fingers into her flaxen mane and, gulping into her dusty coat, I wondered if she understood more than I did.

Ali has always been a perceptive creature and she displays all the keen intelligence (and much of the high-spirited scattiness!) of the breed. I bought her as a yearling, after falling in love with her exuberance and character. We both learned together, as I had never had an unbroken horse before, and it was a very proud moment when I watched the trainer settle into her saddle for the first time. My little girl was growing up! She wasn't so impressed, however, and seemed amazed that she was actually expected to move with someone on her back. She preferred to stand stock-still and pretend she couldn't hear his patient clucking for her to go forward. But she soon conceded that this was a little boring, and deigned to walk on.

Since then, Ali has approached every outing as an adventure. There is always something amazing or fascinating around the corner and she dances enthusiastically onwards, ears so far forward they almost touch, eyes huge and nostrils flaring. You always feel you are going somewhere great when you are on her, as if the desert blood of her noble ancestors is rushing through her veins. She doesn't tolerate complacency on the part of her rider, and if her mind is left inactive for too long, her imagination takes over. Harmless rocks become possible assailants and rustles in the trees herald imminent attacks; her evasive action is swift and dramatic. Meanwhile, traditional horse bogeys like noisy trucks or vicious dogs are dismissed with barely an ear flick.

Ali's sense of humour and constant demands for attention ensure that she is never ignored or neglected. When her water trough is empty she plants both front feet in it and bangs indignantly and constantly until the situation is rectified (even if she herself has removed the plug, after days of trying, with her face up to her eyes in the water). Ali knows exactly how to distract me from any self-absorption, by pulling her rug off the fence, or grabbing the grooming kit and flinging it to the ground, while my back is turned. She chases dogs foolish enough to enter her paddock, but runs from stray plastic bags that blow in. She neighs when the lights go off in the evening and no one has come out to visit her. She loves the feel of the cool sheets from the clothesline against her skin, and is the reason for many loads of washing having to be redone.

In many ways she is everything I'm not. She is brash and confident and utterly convinced of her own beauty. At the risk of attributing too much understanding to an animal who is, after all, highly suspicious of rubbish bins (making bin-day rides perilous!), the occasional knowing look convinces me of her mute wisdom. And, while the Biblical horses in Job have their 'necks clothed in thunder', my horse's neck is clothed in my secrets and tears, my endearments and private jokes… and sometimes my freshly washed sheets.

That night I left the paddock knowing that, at the very least, my most abandoned moment of grief had been witnessed only by a trustworthy soul. Hers was the one gaze I could meet after such an outpouring. As a confidante, Ali is matchless—although proud, she does not know how to scorn; although sensitive, she is not embarrassed by emotional excess. Her wordless comfort met my wordless pain and her own heart was instrumental in the long process of curing my broken one.

Caroline Taylor has been afflicted with the horse-bug all of her life and her parents finally succumbed to the pressure and bought her a pony at age twelve. Since then she has owned and leased a succession of horses, and managed never to sell any of them, or grow out of them in favour of boys, as her parents feared (although she sometimes wishes she had left boys right alone and stuck purely to horses!). She is twenty-seven, has a degree in communications, and works as a technical writer to support Ali.

A Horse Tale

Freya Berenyi

I'm Mary and I'm a horse. I was bred in Merrijig by Mick Kelly who ran a trail-riding business. He was hard on us horses, all whips and spurs, and we had to put up with people who couldn't ride bouncing around on our backs. A good thing about being a trail horse is the bush. It's a fantastic place, logs to jump, green grass, birds calling and wild animals.

My first memory was of being branded. I was wrestled to the ground and tied down. A white hot iron was pressed into my shoulder. Pain shot through my body and a girl's voice said, 'Does it hurt Daddy?' A man's voice replied, 'She can't feel a thing love.' I thought, 'I wish you could feel this.'

Then there was the day of the river accident. A group of horses were herding cattle. We turned a bend and came to the Delatite River. I don't mind water but as soon as my hooves touched this time I knew something was wrong. My friend Mystery knew it too. I could sense her uncertainty. We hesitated but the men whipped us on, the dogs yapped at our heels. As we plunged in deeper I could feel the sand disappearing under me. Suddenly Mystery was caught on a submerged log and her rider didn't know what to do. She was floundering in the muddy water and disappearing below the surface. She gave a desperate lunge and miraculously pulled herself out. We were all exhausted and bleeding. Mystery has deep scars and no horse who was there has ever felt the same about being in water again.

For some time after this incident fewer people came trail riding. Mick was always in a bad mood. Floats would appear and my friends would be loaded and taken off, never returning. It was upsetting to see them go. Even Mystery went.

One day Mick came home looking very happy and he called to his wife Trudy, 'I sold Mary Lou at last, to a mate at the TAB. Got a good price for her but I lied a bit about her age.'

The following afternoon I was led out of my paddock and forced into a float. I had never been in a float before but I had heard terrible stories about them. I was painfully swung from side-to-side each time they turned a corner. Eventually the tailgate was lowered and I shot out backwards. I was in an unfamiliar place and the ground was still moving under me. A strange man led me to a paddock. I whinnied frantically and to my surprise it was answered. Charging down the hill came four horses. A chestnut mare, a golden mare and a handsome grey gelding. They were to be my friends for many years.

Freya Berenyi (aged eleven) is a keen Pony Club competitor. One day, she had almost completed the perfect cross country round when her horse, Mary, refused the final jump, a water jump. To console herself she created her story to try to understand Mary's shock refusal.

Tango

Marion Tyree

To this day, I remember vividly a little poem, written for me by my mother, tied to the halter of my first very own pony.

I am a little pony
Tango is my name
I'm red and white in colour
With a long black tail and mane
We'll ride the fields of clover
In sunshine and in rain
The logs we'll jump right over
And sometimes all the drains.

We lived on a sheep station in the high mountain country in New Zealand. I had been riding since I was three, learning on a huge old racehorse called Darkie who would put his head down so we could hop on behind his ears, putting his head up as we slid down onto his back. He was much loved as all four children had learnt to ride on him. I was the youngest.

From Darkie I progressed to my sister's hand-me-downs—two small Shetland ponies that had minds of their own: Beautiful, and Whiskey, a black pony who, due to my constant kicking to make him move faster, spent his time trying to get me off his back. My pleas to my parents for a new pony had fallen on deaf ears. I was alone at home, too young to go to boarding school where my siblings were. Correspondence school was not enough to keep me busy. Riding around the farm with my father was my favourite pastime, and this was hampered because Whiskey's legs were too short to keep up with Dad's large horse.

On my eighth birthday Mother suggested that we go to the shearing shed to take morning tea to my father. Our house was on a ridge of the hill with a long winding drive curving down past the shearing shed and sheep yards to the main road. My mother made scones and pikelets and the tea went into a billy of hot water. I carried the scones in a small wicker basket lined with a checked tea towel. Underfoot the drive was crunchy with frost and the puddles still had not thawed their covering of ice which made a crunching noise against my gumboots. The drive was lined with laburnum and rowan trees. Their limbs bare of leaves, remnants of the red and black berries of autumn hanging from the branches. The bulbs had yet to raise their green leaves and the agapanthus were stoic against the feeble winter sun. At the front gate was a large horse truck. I thought my father had a delivery of cattle. Mother said that we should have a look to see what was going on. My father was standing talking to the driver. The back of the truck was down and from inside I could hear the sound of stamping.

There he was. A wonderful pony, his ears pointed forward, his large soft brown eyes looking at me. Tied to his halter by a red ribbon was a piece of paper with the poem written on it. His coat gleamed bright chestnut overlaid with large white patches. Just like the Indian ponies from the cowboy movies. I walked up the ramp towards him and he snickered at me with a soft sound. As I reached up with my hand his soft breath flickered across

my palm and his head moved down to smell me.

I think it was for both of us love at first touch. I fell in love at that moment. I do not think I have ever had such a moment again.

For the next eight years our lives were intertwined. We did everything together. From morning to night he was near me—grazing on the lawn while I did my lessons, galloping down the road for home when we heard the sound of the cowbell ringing to call us to dinner or to come home. I would lean forward close to his neck like a jockey as we rushed past the shadowy trees. Riding bareback my legs would clasp his sides like those American Indian riders. He was a source of endless

presents: a saddle, horsecovers, brushes, currycombs, bridle, numerous books on horses and their riders. Pat Smythe was one of our favourites, Foxhunter our hero. Tango listened to my dreams and failures. I would bury my head into his neck and I can still remember his comforting warm horsey smell. He was my rock, my platform on which I stood to reach the pears and apples in the orchard. He was part of me. We went with my father, easily keeping up with the long strides of his large thoroughbred. We raced up the valleys to herd the cattle or picked up orphaned lambs to place in a sack hanging from the back of the saddle. We were perfectly happy. He welcomed me in the mornings with a moist kiss and I hugged him.

Although I looked forward to boarding school I dreaded leaving Tango. But he was there when I came home waiting for me, his ears pricked, his soft brown eyes watching me as I ran to give him a hug.

Marion Tyree *is a writer and horticulturalist. Her love of books comes from the early years in the New Zealand high country. Her childhood favourites remain Mary Grant Bruce's* Billabong *series and* Black Beauty. *She still loves to ride whenever time permits. Marion lives in Sydney with her husband Chris, Bruiser the Jack Russell and Lily a beautiful grey-and-white cat.*

Pretty Girl Anna Kay

I used to climb the post-and-rail fence and sit on the top strut, kicking my legs backwards and forwards and taking large bites out of an apple. I'd watch my grandfather in the middle of the yard, the lead rope long and slack with Dolly—his prize, the apple of his eye, my pretty girl and my grandfather's girly girl—trotting in circles around him. After, I'd feed Dolly my apple core and her lips would make a soft open and close on my flat hand, like feathers tickling my palm.

Dolly was gigantic. She had great hooves the size of dinner plates; a thick brown tail that flish-swished flies away; teeth which looked huge and skeletal, vaguely prehistoric. When she had the bit in her mouth, her lips sometimes curled down at the corners and looked disapproving.

Every weekend, my grandfather and I would drive down to the trotting track. There was a football oval in the centre and a dry bush incline around the edges. The dirt track was white dust, its surface uneven, as if giant fingernails had raked the top into a series of crooked lines. At the end of summer, yellow wattle flowers fell from the trees, landing on the dry earth, like piebald patches of sifted, bright-yellow icing sugar.

Sometimes I'd crouch down in the dust and with a twig draw the outline of a horse pulling a sulky with me sitting in it. I'd draw families of horses; the mother and father with long, flowing manes, standing in fields of tall grass; foals with knobbly knees and wobbly legs. Other times I'd sit on the cool earth in the shade of the stable wall and unpack the special shoebox which contained my model horses. I'd make fences out of broken sticks, a circular trotting-track from a jam-jar lid. When I looked up in the distance I'd see the glaring white dust track and my grandfather, sitting low in the sulky, working his girly girl around and around.

I longed to be in the hessian sack seat, 'tsst-tssting' like my grandfather, feeling the creak of the leather harness as we circled the track with the reins in my hands, listening to the steady sound of Dolly's hooves as they hit the ground and left a trail of half-moon prints in the gravel.

After was best.

My grandfather would remove Dolly's harness and the leather would be clouded with white salty patterns of horse-sweat. He'd slide her bridle off and pass it to me and I'd carefully lay it over the fence-rail. He'd knot an old rope halter around Dolly's head and sometimes he'd pass me the lead rope and I'd take her, her head hung low, and we'd walk lazily to the corrals. We'd hose her down, my grandfather making broad sweeping motions with a currycomb so the water fell off in sharp lines. In the afternoon, Dolly would dry shiny brown in the sun.

'The safest way to tie a horse to a post,' he said. He showed me over and over. 'Keep your fingers out of the loops; let the rope go slack. You never know when a horse might play up and pull back. Not that she'd ever do that.' I'd look at Dolly. Her forelock was kinked; her eyes were brown and intelligent. 'Good girly girl. Thatta girl,' my grandfather used to say as he smoothed his hand down her neck.

While my grandfather was talking with the men, I'd fuss with Dolly's mane, sectioning it into rows of plaits, combing it over to the right so that it slowly folded back over to the left as if pulled by invisible strings. I'd trace the diamond of white between her large brown eyes while her nose was buried in the feed bucket. Her eyes reflected the trees, the sky; when she put her head down low, I saw myself in them. I'd run my hand along the underside of her neck, where the skin was looser and where she felt softer, until I reached the irregular swirls of fur on her chest. Sometimes, I'd rest my shoulder on her side, so my head was level with the tops of her legs and I'd whisper to her. 'You're my pretty girl and one day we'll go away together. We'll sleep in barns and I'll steal you apples from apple trees.' Then I'd stir melted molasses through her feed. I'd lean against the fencepost watching Dolly, her nose buried in the bucket, chewing her feed, her jaw crunching like she was grinding a mouth full of stones.

One day, my grandfather sat me on his lap in the sulky and put the reins in my hands. Dolly was full of the early morning, strutting with her front hooves and stamping the ground, pulling her head forward. 'Pretend there's a bird, a baby bird, cupped inside each of your hands,' he said. I looped the reins through my fingers, put the strip of leather in my palms, and kept a space for the baby bird, for its tiny puffed chest and throat and beating heart. Dolly snorted air through her nostrils, the metal bit and the harness clinked around.

One day, if I wait, I'll get to sit here on my own, I thought.

I held this invisible bird.

Anna Kay *has published fiction in various anthologies and journals.*
Her work has also been adapted for theatre and radio. She lives in Paris.

Dedicated to Horses

Shelley Virduzzo

Horsey… That's what I am. Everyone says it! I am the horse-craziest kid in my school. I have driven my friends batty because horses are all I think about, dream about and talk about. Well, I have made them like horses too. I'm not sure how I did it. Some people tease me about loving horses. But I know that my love for horses will never ever go away, no matter how much people tease me.

My auntie had a very sweet, affectionate and clumsy gelding called Sundance. He was too clumsy to ride because he kept tripping over his own feet so he was really a pet. When he was a colt, he and his dam were mistreated when they were agisted on a property somewhere. His mother was very sick and they were both not looked after very well. My auntie's sister-in-law rescued Sundance and he was given to my auntie. Any chance I got I went to see him and his mates. The first time I met Sundance I was three months old and Mum took me to the paddock to introduce me. He nuzzled my stomach, I giggled, and there started a beautiful friendship. I think because of him I love horses so much and horse-loving comes from my mum's side of the family. Sadly, Sundance passed away of old age. We had a little funeral for him.

Next I made friends with a chestnut Shetland pony called Oscar. My auntie, mum and I feel like painting his little hooves with nail polish. He is so cute. I sometimes ride him. But my mum has to lead me around because he has never had a bit in his mouth before. My auntie's friend agisted him and her horse Madison over at my auntie's house. That's how we met. Oscar's owner said that I can do anything I want with him. So now I groom and ride him.

I have been to three different riding schools. I am only going once a month because my family can't really afford it. I am grateful that I go once a month because some kids don't even get to go. The first riding school I went to stopped doing riding lessons. The next one I went to was too expensive and my mum said that we will try to find a cheaper riding school. Eventually my mum did find a cheaper riding school called Melbourne Indoor Equestrian Centre. So now I am happily riding there and intending to stick with it.

I guess that I admire horses so much because of their beauty, grace and elegance. With the fighting stallions and the playful foals. Watching their movements is just so calming. I love watching their antics when they are clowning around with each other. It takes my breath away when I watch a horse galloping just for the sheer joy of being alive.

Shelley Virduzzo is an eleven-year-old Australian primary school student in grade six, who loves horses and other animals. In her spare time she likes to ride horses, watch The Saddle Club, *go to her auntie Jean's house, draw horses, hang out with friends, read horse stories, write horse stories, study horses, hang out with horses and ponies, spend time with her cat Sasha, and train her budgie Violet.*

I Dream of Horses

Julie Copeland

When was the first dream? The first horse? Aged three, sitting in the gutter outside our shop at the top of Alma Road, up from St Kilda Junction, watching and waiting for the baker's horse, Ginger. A chestnut, of course. My little finger's still crooked, because one morning, through no fault of his own, the patient cart horse bit through it, along with the apple pieces my mother always gave me to hand him.

Just two years ago, I lost the top of my middle finger in Greece, snapped off by a hungry horse, as I poked grass to him through a wire fence, an accident which, given the village's inadequate medical facilities, generated quite a Greek crisis.

My strongest adult dream is of another chestnut—not Ginger, because this is a mare with a foal gazing at me across a stream, not a distressingly distant divide, because her gaze is one of reconciliation, fulfilment, peace.

The other real chestnut in my life was named The Gent, a 17 hands racehorse I rode to victory a couple of times at race meetings in Wentworth, New South Wales. At that time, as a fifteen-year-old girl, I rode in what were called 'Ladies Bracelets'—country races for female jockeys only. Nothing much has changed.

I was madly in love with The Gent, but I had trouble controlling the handsome thoroughbred, who bolted with me regularly, as he knew only walking and galloping.

When we moved from Wentworth across the border, I rode The Gent the thirty miles to Mildura and, after we had walked decorously for some miles, I vividly recall defying the horse-trainer's orders, leaning low on the horse's neck and letting him stretch out and run along a track by the river for what seemed like forever—glorious!—pulling up panting and sweating... and then the panic that I'd ruined him, destroyed him, as we limped into town an hour later.

Although I had some of my most thrilling moments with The Gent, and spent a lot of time gazing adoringly at him, my father was right: for a girl, a large, highly-strung thoroughbred was no fun.

Enter my bay stock pony Bambi who, although he was no beauty, could, and would do everything and we became inseparable; out all day, trotting across the dry flat claypan, tearing through the saltbush, jumping logs, swimming in the river.

At the annual show, we entered every novelty riding event, and the pony races.

Despite the enjoyment I had from a much-loved succession of horses and ponies, accidents and broken bones—there was always the endless yearning for the dream horse.

In fiction, there was The Golden Sovereign, a spectacular palomino stallion, and The Mandrake, the perfect bay. Black Beauty was unbearably sad (I still can't read or hear of animals

suffering). In film, there was National Velvet, Flicka and her son, Thunderhead, the white stallion—and later, my favourite Australian filmstar, Phar Lap.

Sometimes they actually appeared, in all their heart-stopping beauty; I even got to briefly ride one or two dream horses, owned by wealthier families than ours. Once I was loaned a champion grey gelding to compete for Best Girl Rider at the Mildura Show, and I only had to arrange myself on top of this perfectly trained grey rocking horse to effortlessly win the blue ribbon.

Wherever we lived, my younger sister and I fell in love with horses and dragged them home, all shapes and sizes, from everywhere.

It was Shetland ponies for my sister who, when she was very small, had a terrible fall off my first horse, and never quite recovered her nerve.

I spotted Satan in the Dandenong Horse Sales, a large, stunning, jet-black thoroughbred, sired by a famous steeplechaser. I had to have him. My grandfather bid and got him for a very reasonable price. But the charismatic beauty turned out to be a killer, who even my powerfully built father couldn't handle.

I only drew horses. And despite not having done so for decades, on a recent holiday in Italy, I spent happy mornings on the terrace drawing horses with an eleven-year-old, horse-mad friend, Sophie, and was immensely flattered when she pronounced me the very best drawer of horses ever!

Sadly, although I believe the best way to view the world is from astride a horse, there is no horse in my life now. But their superior beauty still obsesses me. I respond to every image of a horse, watch bad movies on television which feature horses; in the city I stop, notice, every police horse, carriage horse, speak to them, smell them, touch them when I can.

And they're always, always there in my best dreams.

Julie Copeland *is one of Australia's most significant radio broadcasters and producers. She has worked in political and arts journalism for more than thirty years and is currently the producer and presenter of ABC Radio National's weekly arts program,* Sunday Morning. *She initiated, produced and presented landmark programs including* First Edition, The Europeans *and* The Coming Out Show. *Julie loves horses, reading, painting and arguing about the arts and politics.*

What Is It About Little Girls and Horses?
Martha C. Sewell

So high up. So fat around. Feet not reaching the stirrups. Holding on for dear life to the saddlehorn. Pretty frilly dress. Tailored little coat. Shiny Mary Janes with little white anklets. Round and round a circled enclosure. Sunday morning in the park with pony.

Not a particularly auspicious start to my love affair with horses. Nor was the next encounter I remember. In a big pasture at a riding stable. Riding around with a group of horses and ponies. Trotting—hey, this is fun! If a bit teeth-chattering. Uh-oh. We're beginning to run. Faster and faster—down a hill the size of Mount Rushmore. Pony comes to a dead stop at the bottom of the hill. I do not. Vaguely remember my dad dashing across the field. Dim memory of the group leader saying, 'She better get right back on or she'll always be afraid.' Not this daddy's girl!

But as the years went by, something in me would not let go. Even when my best friend and I began to go regularly to the local stable I would awake on riding day sick to my stomach and hold on to the saddlehorn with such vigour that blisters formed. Then one day it happened: the blister broke; I could no longer hold on. The horse began to canter. Wonder of wonders, I not only stayed on, I began to feel the rhythm. I felt the horse and the wind and noticed a thousand pound animal responding to me.

City girl with country dreams. Why couldn't we live on a farm? Or better yet—a ranch! Somewhere I had read that Dale Evans and Roy Rogers had a huge family of adopted children and they all lived on this terrific ranch with horses as far as the eye could see. Why couldn't I be adopted! Instead I was an only child in a boring family that lived on a boring street in a boring city.

Constant pleadings for a horse brought no response. When I graduated from eighth grade, my mother indicated that I was going to get a gift that I had long been wanting and that would last me for years. For weeks I anticipated. How would they present it to me? What would I name it? Where would I keep it? On graduation day, a big, wrapped box was put in front of me. Seemed a bit small for a saddle. Some other kind of tack, perhaps? Tore it open. A typewriter! For high school, my mother said. It will last you for years.

In high school, I finally did get my horse. A little bay mare that was my life until I went to college. Followed by other horses in other places at other times. But there is no love like your first love. And no dreams like little girl dreams of ponies ungranted.

Martha C. Sewell *An Air Force brat, I was born in San Francisco and lived in Germany, but spent most of my growing years in Omaha, Nebraska. But not on a farm! So close and yet so far. My career has been in museums and exhibition development. Now, I work in Washington, DC and live in the wilds of the Virginia suburbs.*

Section Three HorseMyths

At the Rim of the Plains

Jacqueline Crompton Ottaway

Milena stands on
volcanic land
rough and   wild
she watches the horses
listens for her special Comet
her fire in the sky.

'Gun down the horses,' says her father,
'chase them into the canyons.'

Milena shares a bond with Flaming Star
she loves the horses
they are the *kaitiaki* of the land
protectors of the northern boundary
she hates her father
she hates the army.

'Kaimanawa,' she whispers,
'Eat the wind
the brave will eat the wind
their cries will echo to the edge of the world.'

Only the brave will survive.

kaitiaki means 'spiritual guardian'. These wild horses form the Maori hapu (extended family groupings) of Ngati Tama Whiti of the tribe Tuwharetoa and each hapu has four kaitiaki. These kaitiaki protect the four corners of their boundaries and the wild Kaimanawa horses protect the northern boundary of this area for this tribe.

Jacqueline Crompton Ottaway *grew up dreaming that she might become an accomplished equestrian but when she met a boating enthusiast she spent her spare weekends exploring Auckland's Hauraki Gulf instead. She has had stories, poems and articles published in New Zealand and overseas and currently she is considering a novel about the wild Kaimanawa horses of New Zealand.*

Shape-shifters

Sue Booker

I learned to ride on a horse called Flight.
Aged ten, I didn't know that ancient tribes
had worshipped horses as I did, or that
shamans rode spirit horses in their ecstatic
flight to other worlds. Nor did I dream that
a shamanic vocation awaited me.

Before Flight taught me to ride, I drew
ordinary horses, copied from books my
parents bought me, instead of the horse I
kept requesting. But after Flight's owners
sold their stables and left for the country,
my realistically drawn horses began to
shape-shift. The foreheads of some grew a
spiralling horn that distinguished them as
unicorns. Rare or non-existent, the way I'd
begun to feel.

As puberty transformed me, the riders I
drew transformed too. Instead of jodhpurs
or long dark hair like the girl star of
National Velvet, they wore armour and
bore lances, like knights of old. They
traversed futuristic landscapes, for I had
yet to meet one. Though helmets hid their
faces, they were male. They symbolised
who I wanted to be: invulnerable, in
control, and riding away.

Other males became fused with their
steeds as I raided the zodiac for
talismans. My centaurs needed no armour;
horsepower made them robust. Other
horses sprouted wings, inspired by
Pegasus. Thirty years later, I'd read of his
mythical birth, from the blood of the
Gorgon, Medusa.

A mysterious first-person narrator hijacked
my third-person novel last year. Her
obsession with snakes soon gave her
away. To research my new character, I
delved into ancient myth and found that,
before the patriarchal ancient Greeks
hijacked Medusa, a matriarchy had
worshipped her, the Libyan Amazons, who
reputedly tamed and bred horses first. The
ancient Greeks credited the goddess
Athene, Medusa's enemy, with taming
horses first. Yet older sources suggest that
she and Medusa had once been united as
aspects of the Triple Goddess.

Born of a murdered Medusa, spawn of my
dying dreams, Pegasus leapt from my pen
as I longed to fly free of my mother's
petrified gaze. She dared not trust me to
go to school dances, let alone care for a
horse, and no knight in shining armour
confronted the monster I perceived her to
be. My father had worked as a horse-
breaker before the Second World War, and
I doubt that he saw as much magic in
horses as I did.

My parents were growing long in the tooth as they raised me. Their old-fashioned rules, combined with the surveillance an only child can inspire, ensured that I felt fenced in while my peers ran free. Instead of blonde or red-haired, my role models were silvery or palomino, with names like Thowra or Flicka.

Plain old brown Flight fell short of my fantasies. While her name expressed to perfection my desire, the ageing mare's contrariness rivalled that of my parents. Only under duress would she deign to trot, and never to canter. She couldn't teach me to fall because she lacked the spirit to throw me, and she walked too sedately to ever stumble. Yet she initiated me into the nature of death.

One day I returned from a ride on a spry, young gelding with whom I'd been entrusted as I'd gained experience—the horse that had taught me to fall—to find Flight lying on her side in her stall. Flies encrusted vacant eyes, which an hour ago had been merely dejected. For all her resistance, she'd borne me over many trails. Now, only a colic-bloated carcass remained. Flight had departed the world I knew.

I wanted to depart it too. At school, isolation crushed me.

The year I left school, a new planet was discovered. Named Chiron, after a mythical centaur healer, it would mean much to me fourteen years later. As an astrologer specialising in vocational guidance, I'd observed that Chiron stood out in the horoscopes of outsiders, mavericks, and shamans—hybrids born to bridge different worlds.

Why does my dictionary define a centaur as a monster? It seems that failure to conform to the straight and narrow can offend. Diagnosed with a spinal deformity in the year of Chiron's discovery, I felt monstrously bent. Before the corrective surgery I was urged to undergo, I was warned not to ride again, to reduce risk of falling. Since then, I've ridden through the hills above Christchurch and around the Giza plateau on horseback, ridden a camel up Mt Sinai, and fallen off a few bikes.

Today, horses grace tarot cards I've designed, bearing goddess-worshipping knights that were banished from decks in the Middle Ages. Mares and foals emblazon Irish linen tea towels from my mother. Thirty years on, she hasn't forgotten. And when I walk south along the coast, I come to a field where horses graze. Then time warps and I fall into a trance.

Sue Booker is a visual artist, astrologer and writer with a background in the performing and psychic healing arts. Her commitment to full-time writing has been supported by four professional mentorships in the last four years.

Wild Wisdom

Karin Meissenburg

I know my way through the forest. *I know where the best grass is. I know where the soil smells delicious and tastes good. From my mother I learned to sense the rabbit holes in the ground, to avoid treacherous terrain, to be respectful to the nature beings. We belong to an ancient and wild tribe of horses who freely roamed the earth between sea and mountains. Now two-legged creatures have confined us to a woodland near Duelmen in a country they name Germany. That's what they call us, Duelmener.*

I know when I meet understanding two-legged beings. They tune into our language of the heart. And we can make sense of their sounds. Most of the two-legged ones I meet inflict pain to heart and body. Wild horses need to be tamed, I hear. They lack any clue about life, the joy and delight of being, free movement, deep musings.

Soon I'll go to greener pastures where no whips will ever spoil the bliss of light-drenched morning dew. 'Quicky!' That's the voice of the one who trusts me. She'll find me lying not far from the open stable. I cannot lift my head. It is too heavy. She cradles it in her lap. I no longer struggle for air. It is too painful. Day after day for the last two years it has been like this.

'Quicky! Don't leave me now. I can't sustain another loss after my lover has passed on.' I beg you to stay, to get up, to be. We remain on the tough grass for hours. Breathing in, breathing out. Breathe, my friend. Breathe! I need you. Now. Breathe in gently. Let it flow like your spirit takes wing when you fly over meadows, hooves barely touching the ground. I can feel the warmth of your breath on my hand. Long moments of silent communication.

Finally, a deep sigh, then Quicky stands, shakes himself. A deep sigh, I also stand overwhelmed with gratitude. The thyme the land yields for him alleviates his breathing difficulties. We walk through the woods. Equals. Six legs moving. From Quicky I learn about being a creature of the wild. To follow inner promptings (not outer proddings); to savour the morning; to take obstacles only if absolutely necessary, by-passing them is easier; to remain in a state of relaxed, yet acute awareness; to be sure about each step one takes however fast; and if in doubt stop immediately (even if this means that someone somersaults over your head).

I receive practical advice as well. Like, eat while the eating is good. It is the number one rule. You eat as much as you can get; don't believe you are a squirrel which stores nuts away. Especially in autumn. Get rid of two-legged contraptions in the form of fences. Find the weakest post, lean against it, rock it, break it down, run. The hoof prints give away their technique (horses do have techniques, ESP, and they do co-operate with each other). Today, I see Quicky and his mate coming back: two barrel-shaped horses ambling towards me. Their huge bellies bear witness to a satisfying feed of corn from a field a mile away that we passed a few weeks ago. I invite them in through the door as the fence is now repaired. They grin and walk to their evening ration of oats in the open stable.

For over three decades now Quicky has been a soul-companion—no longer existing in his physical form, yet always here when I need him. Recently, I was sad because my friend's dog Corrie died. Walking along the Stromness shore, listening to the thundering waves, I suddenly felt the soft warmth of a horse's nostrils in the palm of my hand. A surge of comfort and quiet assurance: *I'll look after Corrie.*

I know that one radiant day I'll be met with delight by a horse who knows.

Karin Meissenburg *has worked for more than twenty years as a translator, editor and facilitator in Germany, the Orkney Islands and Aotearoa. She is director of Global Dialogues, an international translating, editing and publishing consultancy company. She is author of a wide range of publications among them* The Dynamic Web: Tuning Into Contextual Logic. *For further information see www.dunsfordpublishing.com*

The Gift

Margôt Erikson

Lilly is in his territory, she is within the mists. She senses rather than sees his presence and she knows she is being watched. Her skin electrifies. Twigs crack, brittle in the undergrowth. He moves about. The wind is rising; it keens, it laments. Towering black pines tremble and sway and Lilly is afraid. Then the wind dies and the night is silent in its hush once more. 'It is time to be seen,' the Spirit World whispers and the mists retreat. Moonbeams soft, are gentle on equine back. The world is muted in shades of grey. With heartbeat pummelling, Lilly holds her breath as he gallops toward her, he halts with rigid legs. His ears are back. He snorts, dark eyes arrogant and proud. His muscled body is scarred, testament to battles past. Eyes roll, but Lilly stands her ground.

This is not what he expects. This mortal child shows no fear. He draws himself up to his full height. Then, with a shuddering sigh, Lilly whispers, 'You're the grey stallion, the Moon Stallion. You're in Great, Great Granny Lucy's photo.' She drinks in his explosive strength, a morepork cries. Startled, Lilly realises she is within kicking distance. She turns side on, eyes averted but ever watching. 'It's okay boy, I'll back off. I won't hurt you.' She keeps her voice low, deceptively calm. He must not smell fear in her sweat. She walks unhurriedly away. She is a threat no longer and he is intrigued. He is motionless except for his alert twitching ears. Muscles loosen as he watches the child of generations after.

He lifts his head to the indigo sky and curls back his lips; he breathes her scent. Lilly jars over rutted earth. She stumbles and the stallion's large eye begins to soften. He wants to get closer, he chooses to follow, his head lowered slightly. He smells an apple, fragrant red in her pocket. Feeling his warm breath, Lilly stops. The stallion

mirrors her. She continues and he is with her. Lilly changes direction, not allowing herself to look back. He shadows her. He is ready.

Lilly turns to him with excited eyes. She blows gently down through her nose. He understands her greeting. With wide, quivering nostrils he copies her. Scents mingle and trust begins. Soon, his dark, soft muzzle sniffs at her pocket. Lilly delights in his gentle nibbling. 'That's Harry's apple. Do you want it?' He rumbles softly. Molasses sweetens the air, as she wipes the bits of chaff and feed off the apple. The spirit horse grows impatient, he nudges, he pushes. 'No, not yet. You have to wait,' yet he hears the smile in her voice and he knows that she is kind.

Lilly slices the apple on thin fence wire. Juice drips. The Moon Stallion waits for her hand to open, for her palm to be flat, upturned. Cracked lips nibble, then with teeth uneven, he relishes its freshness. 'Is that good?' The lilting young voice is soft, ears twitch and Lilly dries her hands on faded blue jeans.

She runs her eye slowly over him. He is quiet. Her hand is deliberate, he knows it is coming yet he stands utterly still. He waits. He wants this earthly touch. 'How's my beautiful boy?' He listens to her soft murmurings. Lilly strokes him, firm in her gentleness, his skin ripples. She grooms him with her bare hands, again and again, the oil rising in his coat. She buries herself in his earthy smell. Their breath hovers, white in the chill of night air and clouds wash the moon. Velvet blackness cushions and protects. Leaves rustle and pine smells sweet. The silvered strands are lifted, untamed and long with time. Lilly slides her hand under his mane and is grateful for its

warmth. She smoothes his forelock and exposes expressive, intelligent eyes. He gazes at her and she is lost to him. He looks deep within this mortal child and sees only goodness.

Lilly scratches his neck the way her thoroughbred, Harry, likes and the Arab shifts his weight. He leans against her. She braces her muscles, she will not break the contact. Then with voice barely audible, she sings to him and his lashes drift lazily as he savours the sound. His head droops, he is weary. Minutes pass. Then he rests his head on her arm. Lilly feels her throat tighten. This connection is of his choosing, is of his will. Stinging tears flush her cheeks and she tastes salt on her lips. He is giving his love, but time is short, there are drifts of dense grey.

Their moment to treasure is almost gone. She touches him, she whispers and she tries to make it last. 'Thank you, Moon Stallion, for choosing me. I know you belong to Granny Lucy's time, but I do love you; I really do. Please don't forget.' Tears stream as she strokes the time weathered cheek, one final time. Together, they are complete.

Margôt Erikson *is currently working on a novel for teenagers. Moon Stallion explores the relationship between humans and horses, the sharing of unspoken minds and their connection with the earth. Her daughter's treasured thoroughbred, Harry, weaves his magic throughout. Margôt tutors in Creative Writing and Phonics, from her dining room table, in Auckland, New Zealand.*

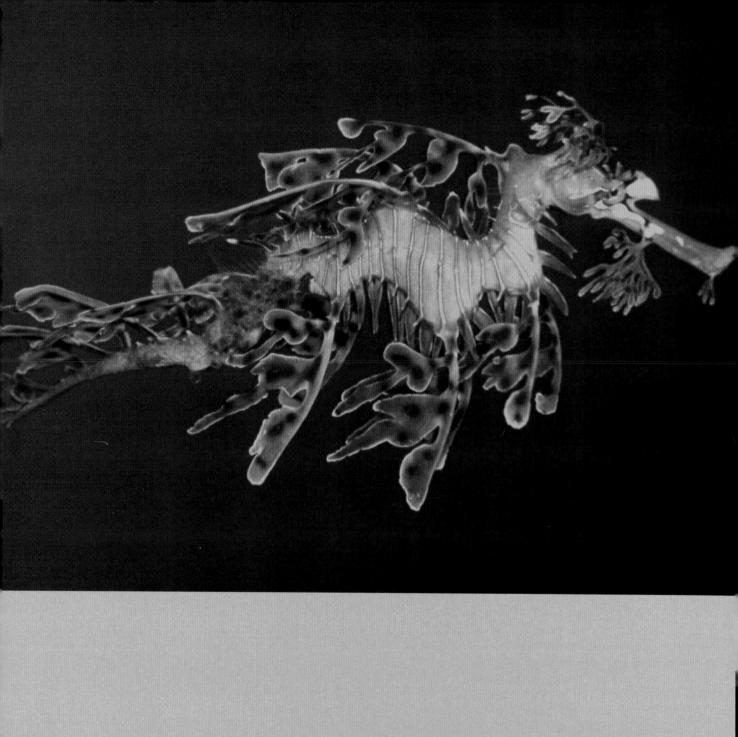

Hippocampus

June Kant

Far from shore, adrift in a limbo of bauble-bodied sargassum weed,
allowing my senses to slip below the empty vastness of life's surface,
I searched for solace and found you there, soul mate, small sea mare.

Understanding every nuance of your need,
I saw you stalk the willing steed of your desire,
felt the percussion of sensuous signals that lured him to your side.
Voyeur, I watched your interminable wooing dance
then abruptly held my breath—your pas de deux was halted
as in a trembling nuptial embrace you gave your all.
With rare grace, he accepted the myriad brick-red spawn
relinquished in the heat of hippocampus passion but,
still swooning with sensations, you paused to wonder
at this encounter's worth—and found it wanting.
Craving more of life than mere maternity, like me,
you spurned your sated mate and drifted further, fetter-free.

Ramrod erect, your stallion lover rolled wild eyes,
flushed angry flaming red to think you'd dare!
Nostrils flaring, girding bony cuirass firmer
he made to follow in your wake, then faltered—
responsibility overrode his lust. Was he an equine knight
whose honour must be saved or a pawn, impregnated,
reluctantly entrusted to propagate the species?
Pot-bellied with brood chamber, chagrin reined in,
he watched as carelessly you left, somersaulted
through the aquascape, never looked back, never halted.

So now you're single. You flaunt your freedom, flirt silkweed mane
and skitter through a shaft of light, descend a fireman's pole
of eelgrass, elegantly curlicued about its slender girth.
You flutter yellow fanlike fins to taunt your lovers, preen—
and exit if possessive passions threaten to wax keen.

Yet, could some instinct claim you when you swan this way again
and find him frantic, darting after nimble foals?
Will you, remorseful, go to join their prancing throng,
allow transparent perfect miniatures to lure, arouse
maternal zeal with hearts that beat so vulnerably?
Will you succumb, deny the basic nature of your need
and stay? Or will you again move on, refusing to pay heed?

Such is our quandary: trailing filaments of fuchsia and vermilion,
camouflage scarves of purple and gay aureolin,
sashaying through drifts of daphnia and iridescent krill
we claim joy, blindly leaping, swirling, pretending—until,
exhausted, we fall prey to desperate hungers, deeper needs,
unable to reconcile our reasons with our selfish deeds.

The sea's ellipse becomes a crystal ball, revealing
to my reluctant eyes our entwined fates foretold:
for you the merciless crush of pharmaceutical pestle,
your bones stamped fine and steeped in honeyed wine
while, compounding the irony of life's injustice,
my fate decrees that I ingest your sweet remains,
a remedy for searing flushes—an ancient, decadent cure
to prolong fertility, the blessing that I steadfastly abjure.

June Kant *After many years emulating
Ulysses on an extended voyage across
oceans, June made landfall in Brisbane in
2000. In the past three years she has won
eight awards for her short fiction which has
been published in* LiNQ, *and aired nationally.
Her ship's cat appeared in Spinifex Press's*
Cat Tales—the Meaning of Cats in Women's
Lives *and her play* Vintage 65 *won the 2003
Todhunter Literary Award. It won't be another
Odyssey but there is also a novel washing
around in the bilges...*

They Have My Heart, They Sing My Soul

Catherine Johns

'She's given her heart to the horse, she'll never love a man like that. She's a gonner, she'll never love another like she loves horses!' I heard the words the old man spoke to my father as I patted the big horse and drank in the beauty, the touch and the smell. I was in love. Fifty something years later I am still in love. I will always be in love with horses.

'They must be Gods,' said May Sarton, the writer, when she first encountered the big heavy farm horses. They are Gods. Amazing, beautiful, strong, courageous, loving and they smell wonderful! They let us humans treat them the way we do for if they didn't there is no way we could do the things we humans do to them. We are puny against them, they are magnificent against us.

Of course, far too many people still use brutality to 'master' and 'train' a horse. This just breaks the spirit, and is a deep unkindness perpetrated on such a wonderful being. I recognised what a horse was when I was nearly two years of age. I 'saw' my first horse at a racetrack and I was besotted. When living with my nana in South Australia, in suburban Adelaide, I was in horse heaven. I spent all day waiting for the Clydesdales to arrive. The milkman, the breadman, the rabbitman and the bottle-oh. Those giants with the big clop and the feathered feet. As soon as I could, I began escaping from the confines of the house and backyard and went searching for those horses.

They were stabled and paddocked only a few blocks from where my nana lived. She couldn't keep me at home. In exasperation she had to let me go and spend my day with the horses. She placed a dog collar around my neck; the tag told my name and her phone number. She didn't want people to think I was lost!

When I went to live with my father we travelled for a time by horse and cart. He finally sold both to buy alcohol. I wouldn't speak to him for weeks. We had to walk!

We are Romani. Many of you call us Gypsies. He taught me Romani ways of being in the world. He taught me what I still believe, that we humans are only caretakers in this world: caretakers of the earth and all the non-humans. The animals, the birds, those that swim and those that crawl; all life is under our care. He encouraged me in my love of the animals. I am from the Welsh and Irish Gypsy people, those of the horse and dog.

I went to my first school by horse. I spent more time out of school riding than locked in by four walls and too many rules. I was a 'truant' and by twelve had my own horse. By fourteen I was working as a jillaroo on an outback sheep station. At sixteen I was working in Whyalla and riding track work and driving pacers and trotting horses. One morning on the race course a 17 hands horse bolted on me. It was a wild ride, ending with the horse falling and catapulting me into a brick wall. I died in that accident and spirit sent me back. I opened my eyes in hospital to be told that I was a quadriplegic, that I would never walk again. Each hand and arm took two-and-a-half hours under open x-ray to reset. In less than a year I was walking; five years later I was riding again. The doctors call it a miracle. I didn't and don't. I needed to walk to ride to live. But the accident ended my wild riding and my love of jumping.

Espirit is still with me. I saw her conceived and she was born into my arms; at twenty-seven she is a liver chestnut beautiful Crabbett Arabian. Ebony is my harness horse. Saved from being butchered when she was four, she is now eleven and so perfect in traffic and on the road that she is a true gift. She has been in some very sticky spots and has always proved very solid. Humans in cars can be so very stupid! Ebony was 'broken in' at six months, raced when she was a year old and at the 'knackers' by four. Orlando is my baby at eighteen months, but what a huge baby! He is an Appaloosa Percheron cross and a big gentle giant. Silver and white with black and brown spots, he is so sweet and kind. I saw him born and he was a gift from a friend.

The big love of my life is Tigger. I waited fifty years for him. Mr Kissy-Kissy is a 17 hands Clydesdale with the high step and feathered feet. Moustached and gentle-eyed he is glorious. I rescued him from a hard life in the tourist industry where he was mistreated, the previous owner telling me, 'The way to handle these big buggers is to starve them down!' If I wrote what he looked like then it would move you to tears. He is now ten; we have been together six years living a shared dreaming.

As a child there were periods of no horses; I was then the horse, galloping and neighing into the wind, locked into a suburban yard or the Goodwood orphanage. As a young womyn I died for the love of horses. As a crone womyn the horse is the magic that weaves meaning and life into this Gypsy's dreaming and journey in life. The old man was right. I love no human like I love the horse.

I am called **Red Catherine**. *I am a Romani womyn, Gypsy. I am a playwright, author, poet, builder, storyteller, teacher and healer. I am a womyn who walks with the animals. I live at 'Artemis' a 157-acre womynspirit retreat in South Australia with around a hundred non-humans. My life is dedicated to the Goddess and to the care of the animals of this planet. I still travel by horse and cart and wagon and am known by the big hounds that are my companions. My life is a gift that is full of the magic of living.*

The Woman On Horseback

Claire French

Everybody loves Xenia the Warrior Princess, the archetype of the martial maiden on horseback.

I met her for the first time when I was about twelve: a pen drawing in an old almanac of a regal woman riding a black charger ahead of her war band. Her name was Dolasilla, a sure-handed archer whose arrow never missed her mark. She was the heroine of a local legend in my native Tyrol and she became my heroine. Next she appeared in my French Reader at high school: Joan of Arc riding triumphantly into Orleans.

Many years later, when I arrived in Melbourne, a lonely, penniless migrant, homesick and ready to take the next boat back to Genoa, I met her again. It was when I gazed, transfixed, at the equestrian statue in front of the Victorian Library. 'They have put up a statue of St Joan.' I said to myself. 'This must be a good place.' And it was.

I have never owned a horse. But oh, how I have yearned for one! Riding a horse seemed to me the highpoint of Life, the ultimate of liberation. During my school years in Fascist Italy and in Nazi Germany my experience had been that boys were encouraged to be young heroes, but for girls there was only motherhood, to bear sons and to pander to 'the solace of heroes', as Nietzsche put it.

There was not an ounce of rebel in me. Yet, diligently as I tried to absorb Christian values and political slogans, there was but one basic truth that penetrated my unfolding consciousness with the clarity of inspired revelation: the fact that Hitler and the Pope, priest and party leader were agreed on one universal law: keep women down!

But, I reasoned, a woman was as good as a man—and better, especially on horseback. It was the metaphor for mind over body, of spirit united to natural wisdom, a symbol for what made us perfect.

I decided to stay in Melbourne. And Melbourne was good to me.

But later, as a young housewife and mother, confined to suburbia and unable to reach my potential, I felt trapped again. Books were my only consolation. I read and read, until I found Her again in a hoary Welsh saga. Picture the scene: on a moonlit night Prince Pwyll of Dyfed meets a lady on horseback. It happens on Narberth, the Sacred Hill of his tribe. He had expected a miracle, and she had appeared to him.

'Lady,' said Pwyll, 'where do you come from and where are you going?'

'I go mine own errands,' said she, 'and glad I am to see you.'

'My welcome to you,' said he. And then it seemed to him that the beauty of every girl and woman he had ever seen was nothing compared to the face of this lady.

'Lady, will you tell me anything of your errands?'

'I will gladly. My most important errand was to try and see you.'

'That seems to me the best errand you could have come on. Will you tell me your name?'

'Lord, I will. I am Rhiannon, daughter of Heveydd the Old. I am being given in marriage to a man against my will; I have not wanted any husband and that is because of my love for you… and it is to hear your answer to me that I have come.'

The lady who 'rides her own errands' and who preferred a mere mortal to an other-worldly godling turns out to be the Welsh incarnation of Epona, the Celtic Horse Goddess. She and her foal symbolised Spring, Life and motherhood. She protected horse and rider, draft animals and coachmen and her shrines were found in every stable of the Celtic realms. She was the only Celtic goddess worshipped in the Roman Pantheon, her image forever adorned with roses. The great Spring Carnivals were held in Her honour and the Celto-Roman cavalry squadrons paid her homage. The name Rhiannon comes from Gaulic Rigani, meaning Great Queen, and She was indeed the Great Queen of Heaven, Earth and Underworld. While she reigned, women were held in honour and the Land prospered.

By her marriage to a mortal, Rhiannon divests herself of her divine status and the story goes on to relate how evil powers steal her baby son. She is accused of having devoured him and condemned to serve as a beast of burden, thus sharing in the suffering of horses and donkeys. There is great rejoicing when the boy is found and her penance ended.

She calls him Pryderi, a word that means Care, Worry, Sorrow. And is not every boy a worry to his mother? Pryderi, the Celtic God of Spring and Vegetation, is a hunter, a harp player and a god of healing. His other name is Mabon, Map-ap-Modron, Son of the Great Mother. In the religion of our Celtic ancestors Rhiannon and Pryderi represent the image of the Divine Mother and her Son, and they were often shown as a mare and her foal. With the coming of Christianity, Rhiannon morphed into Saint Madrun, a saint dedicated to the protection of little children. Her shrines showed her as woman on horseback, holding a baby, much as the Christian image of Mary holding the Christ Child on the Flight to Egypt.

Today the tide seems to be turning. Rhiannon/Epona is riding again, choosing her devotees, teaching them how to rule the Land and protect the Earth.

Her sanctuary on the Continent still carries her name: 'Stuttgart' in south-west Germany means 'Mare Garden' and the city's museum holds many ancient icons of the Woman on Horseback, proof of the devotion in which she was once held.

And is it sheer coincidence that Stuttgart was the birthplace of the motorcar, the invention which freed horses from exploitation forever? That Mercedes is the Spanish name for Our Lady of Mercy, who graciously freed slaves and horses alike?

The Great Mother on horseback returns. Even in everyday life. Recently a large equestrian statue of Epona was unearthed near Stuttgart and it will be re-erected at an important node of the Autobahn for the protection of motorists.

I have never owned a horse. Instead, I have found Rhiannon-Epona the Great Queen, and She has blessed me.

Claire French grew up in South Germany and in the Tyrolean Alps. In 1951 she migrated to Australia, working successively as housemaid, grapepicker and translator/secretary before marrying and becoming the mother of a daughter and two sons. For twenty-five years she taught Cultural Studies at the Melbourne Council of Adult Education. She has written several books on Celtic and Alpine goddesses.

Equus Angela Crocombe

I have been enamoured with horses my entire life. They have been in my thoughts, my dreams, my imaginings, for so long I cannot remember a time when I was not acutely aware of the remarkable nature of Equus. I would not be surprised if I was dreaming of horses in the womb, so important are they to my sense of self. As a child, whenever I had cause to make a wish—be it a birthday, shooting star, or the wishbone of a chicken—I always wished for the same thing; a horse.

'But where would you keep it?' my father would ask.

'Under my bed, of course,' I would say.

Eventually, my wish was answered. My parents moved to five acres when I was eleven years old and they bought me a pony. Now my fantasy had a magnificent flesh and bone animal to focus upon, and my love affair really took off.

I spent eight years owning, riding and being with horses every single day. They were always in my conscious thoughts, their hair on my clothes, their distinctive smell in my nostrils, permeating my skin. I went to Pony Club, riding lessons, horse shows, and enjoyed the daily routine of grooming, feeding and riding horses. These were some of the best years of my life.

One day, I was forced to grow up. Horses were no longer an immediate part of my waking life and I felt the lesser for it. But the horses were not to be gotten rid of that easily; they simply took over my dreams. I was not a stranger to horse dreams, but now they took on greater meaning. The vast majority of my dreams have two vibrant images; myself and a horse. We are bound together, through good times and bad, through adventure and disaster, through relationships and solo. I can count on my horses to be there for me, supporting me, spurring me on, carrying me when I can no longer go on.

A psychic has told me I have spent many lives with horses. Another has said I have a horse resting on my shoulder, a spirit guide from another world. My intuition tells me that all this, and much more, is true. Women have spent thousands of years in close proximity with horses, and I believe that I am, like many women, genetically predestined to love them. My close connection with horses is embedded in my DNA. The majority of our ancestors would have kept horses as part of their daily working lives, to help them gather the food, harvest the crops, and as a mode of transport. We have, no doubt, often owed our lives and livelihood to their strength, reliability and obedience. Some women have been so in love with horses they have, like Catherine the Great, risked death attempting to have a horse as close to them as possible.

I dreamt of a horse again last night. This time it was a rangy, white stallion with a long, flowing mane. We rode on and on through paddock and forest together, galloping as fast as we could, my head close to his neck, my body moving in time with his long limbs as they pounded the ground. We had purpose, we were free, exhilarated, completely in tune with one another as we rode proudly into the future together. May our ride never end…

Angela Crocombe is a freelance writer who also works selling foreign rights at Penguin Books. She has had articles published in Melbourne Star Observer, *the Melbourne* Age, Black & White, In Press, *and many other publications. She has written for Disney and is currently working on a series of books based on her childhood experiences with horses.*

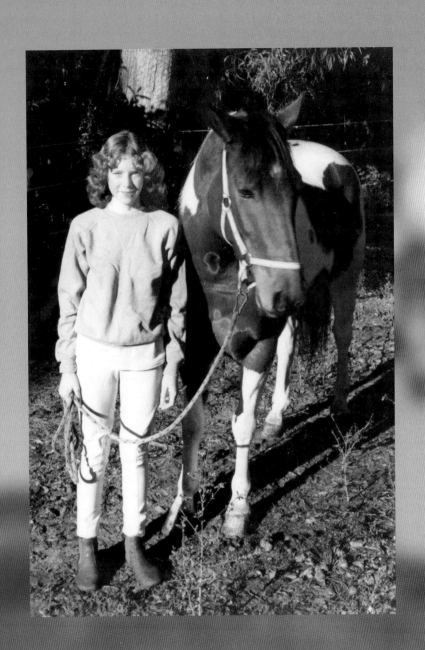

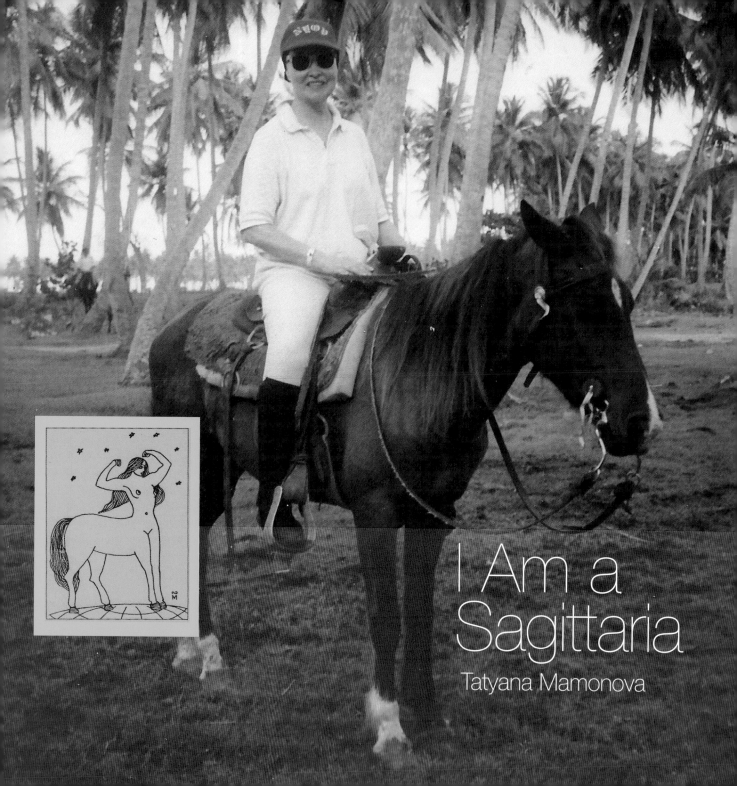

I Am a
Sagittaria

Tatyana Mamonova

Born 10 December, I got my Sagittarius star sign like everyone else who appeared in the world around this date. However, being a female centaur or centauress, I am actually a Sagittaria, according to Latin grammar. The legend says that a centauress is really an Amazon on a horse—practically inseparable.

After my exile from Russia, which happened because I created the first non-governmental organisation in Leningrad, and published a non-official samizdat *Woman and Russia*, I was invited to many countries by feminist organisations. I remember the greeting banners in Canada: 'Welcome, Tatyana'; 'In solidarity with you.' The banners were, in fact, handmade quilts depicting an image of a powerful Sagittaria, a design I had developed with Gena, our samizdat's artist. The Canadian women made a tremendous amount of effort to re-create this sign of Sagittaria in fabric.

This sign has followed me around the Earth. Women from Italy, Greece, Austria, France, US, Finland, UK were attracted to my Sagittaria and reprinted it in their articles describing our *Woman and Russia Almanac*. Only a mythical centaur—half-male, half-horse was known in Russia before a young graphic artist, a nineteen-year-old genius named Nadia Rusheva, had drawn her little centauresses.

Nadia lived a very short life—like Joan of Arc—yet she left thousands of fine pen-and-ink drawings of sassy, playful, teenage centauresses. We just re-created in our samizdat Nadia's idea, revealing a more mature adult centauress—a Sagittaria.

The idea was transferred from the beginning of the 1960s, when Nadia worked on her images, to the end of the 1970s in Russia, then throughout the 1980s with my trips, shows and lectures around the world. In the new millennium we have two real centauresses—our TaTu girls, Lena and Yulia, two Russian musicians, who have been composing together since high school. They fearlessly sing about loving each other everywhere.

My son is their age. I named him Philip, which translates from ancient Greek into 'horse lover'. I have been drawn to horses by some magnetic power all my life—including seahorses. I emphasise seahorses because it is not a female but a male who becomes pregnant and carries the foetus in his belly in this species. Thus, a seahorse frees us from bias. Tired of all that patriarchal glorification of female pregnancy, I admire seahorses for breaking the rule.

At the start of 2004 I went to the Dominican Republic and did something I wanted to do for years—I went horseback riding in Samaná.

I met an unexpected and splendid teacher—a German woman almost seventy years old who now lives in Calais, France. She offered to me her black 'chaps'—the English classic style leather leg covers (also used by motorcyclists). She introduced herself as Charlotte and warned that the road ahead of us might be difficult as she ended up with bleeding calves when she rode this trail the previous year.

I felt uncomfortable taking Charlotte's shiny new chaps, but she was persistent in her generosity. I don't know what I would have done without her because our guides for this one-hour ride weren't useful—two guys constantly showing off with no instruction.

Even though I asked them to find a calm horse for me, I received a Rambo. Rambo refused to listen to any directions. Charlotte was galloping in front of the guides on her horse, Diablo, farther and farther.

My saddle, despite my British chaps, wasn't in English style. It was a cowboy saddle which is much less stable. I thought okay, if it is my destiny, I have to take care of myself. I squeezed Rambo's equestrian belly with my thighs. My uneasy horse went into a gallop!

'Wow! Yeah, Rambo is a good galloper,' said Alfonso, one of the nonchalant guides—in French with a Spanish accent, which I am not trying to imitate—when I was surpassing him.

'Well, I don't have much choice, n'est-ce pas?'

From that moment on, I followed Charlotte. Rambo happily galloped with Diablo through the streets of Las Galeras and onto the beach of Paraiso y Camino del Sol, leaving our guides behind. Charlotte encouraged me with her amiable comments. She inspired me to become a dignified caballera.

Tatyana Mamonova *is an internationally renowned writer. Besides, she continues to lead her NGO and edit her samizdat, both now called* Woman and Earth. *Tatyana has received a number of global awards including the Living Legacy Award (2002), Poet of the Year (1998) and Woman of the Year (1980).*

115

Stormy

Susan Wills

For Catherine (d. 10/4/96)

(letter to Catherine, Easter weekend, 1996)

Catherine,

The phone rang this morning at six a.m. We thought it was Sarah and the baby come. But it was Paul. This day is dismal, grey, it rains for you. I'm playing 'Killing Me Softly' on guitar. How can you be lying there? How can the life in which you built roads in Chile, packed fish in Alaska, sought brave adventures and solace for your heart be quelled so soon? I have tried to find a photo of you but I can't see your eyes, I can't see your beautiful eyes.

(letter to Paul)

Grateful for the sepia photograph of Catherine with Lynette and Stormy. You couldn't call Catherine a 'horsey' girl. Not like Camilla and that set. Catherine is equine in herself. She is more Diana, a goddess of wild things, hunting and the moon.

(letter to my son in utero 26/8/96)

Have I told you about your Auntie Catherine? She is a real live Princess. Of the Cocos Islands. She has raven hair and milky skin and the lithe form of a racehorse. She is a carpenter and she helped me to choose my guitar. Black like Nicholas Cage and Wild at Heart.

(letter to Catherine after Nicholas' birth)

I have heard that departed souls choose new life to send to earth. Three people close to you conceived their first child within a month of your leaving. You sent me my son. You sent a daughter to Georgina and a daughter to Calista. Of these, Iona is most like you. A wild spirited thing with no fear. Will she too be fuelled by the potent power of equine energy? Will the galloping thunder of hooves and the soft nuzzle of hay-scented breath be her at extremes? Will she ride wild into the night and return sweat drenched with heart thundering against steel ribs, hair slicked and flowing, eyes profound? Will she too have the heart of Phar Lap and will the tempest of a storm drive her life?

Susan Wills *lives in Darwin with her partner Andrew and their two sons, Nicholas and Henry. When not chasing her toddler, she teaches English to indigenous students and writes when the moon is right. Her work has appeared in* Cat Tales *and in* True North.

My Horse with a Golden Pole Cheryl Osborne

My mother's family loved horses. My grandparents, Nanma and Papa were great racegoers and horse owners. My mother always claimed to have learned reading by studying the form guide in the Sun. One of my favourite childhood memories is of visiting my grandparents in their large Victorian house by the beach and hearing the sound of whichever race at whatever racecourse being broadcast on the old bakelite wireless. When my mother's elder brother Uncle Ray's horse raced in the Melbourne Cup in about 1960, I was collected from school, changed into a new dress with patent leather shoes and straw party hat and thus experienced my first Melbourne Cup at the age of four. I had a wonderful day with all my cousins whilst my parents, aunts, uncles and grandparents waited for the barrier draws.

Another of my influential childhood horse memories goes back to when I was about eight. Shortly after my sister Fiona was born, Mum and Dad decided I should see Walt Disney's Fantasia one Saturday afternoon. In 1964 it was a big deal to drive to the city with your father to see a matinee. I was so excited but, alas, the queue was too long and we missed getting tickets. As Dad promised we would return next week, this was okay with me. I had the bonus of being taken to the Melbourne Museum in Swanston Street. There, for the first time, I saw the horse that has become an Australian legend. Dad told me Phar Lap's story. My eyes were like saucers when I saw this huge stuffed chestnut horse in a glass case. What a magnificent creature he was to a very small girl!

When it was time for me to have riding lessons I can't tell you how scared I was. Unfortunately on my first lesson the horse decided to canter, rather than trot. It took off with me holding on for all my life, my head narrowly missing a branch of a tree. When my sister learnt to ride in Europe she really got the habit. She looked the part in her riding gear.

One of my favourite memories of Papa was being taken to the Caulfield Cup as an outing from boarding school. We always had a lovely lunch. Then he took me to the stables to see the horses. I thought they were beautiful but at the same time I felt afraid. Give me a small furry cat any day… I thought even then.

So far my story has not been the usual girls' story of her love for horses. I guess my fascination with horses really began when I was in my late thirties. One Christmas I was given a book called Painted Ponies. This became the inspiration for a series of paintings titled 'An Escaped Merry Go Round Menagerie'. I explored and developed my ideas of freedom, love and joy using the different carousel animals, including the horse and seahorse as subjects. The golden pole became not only central to the design, but also symbolised the ties that stop the carousel animals from being completely free.

At about the same time I discovered a papier maché carousel horse in an art supply shop. Images of a younger me riding a carousel horse travelled through my mind. Including the pole, it was approximately 1.5 metres high. It remained in its papier maché form for about twelve months. Amari, my then feline friend and owner, didn't quite know what to think of what was known as 'horse'. I was having an exhibition of my carousel animals and I looked at the still-somewhat-naked, brown-paper horse. Gently I placed her on the kitchen bench. Amari thought this was a great idea, knocking her over several times. After about a week my papier maché friend was transformed from an ugly duckling into a beautiful rainbow-coloured carousel horse. Her pole is painted pure gold as are her long eyelashes and mane. She now graces my lounge room. Whenever I look at her I dream of the times when my golden, girlish locks floated behind me as I rode the carousel horse at Luna Park in St Kilda, safely holding on to the horse's golden pole.

Cheryl Osborne is a visual artist who lives in Melbourne. Her art reflects her love for living creatures. She has exhibited widely both in Australia and overseas. She now shares her life with two cats and a horse with a golden pole.

The Last Melbourne Cup
(the most victorious ever)
Koa Whittingham

The horses galloped only a few feet
Before sliding their jockeys onto the grass
They slowly turned their great heads
To confront the crowd's silent gasp

At once the crowd understood
As they gazed into the horses' wise eyes
Some began to scream apologies
And some began to cry

But all stared in wonder and compassion
As the horses galloped towards the sun
A roar from the crowd echoed through all space
The horses have won!

And ever since then, there have been no races
Except, perhaps, that of a small aboriginal child
Seen racing traffic through the streets of Sydney
On a horse still peaceful and wild

Koa Whittingham *a twenty-three-year-old woman from Brisbane who is currently undertaking a PhD in psychology at the University of Queensland. She has written poetry and stories for as long as she can remember and is currently working on a novel.*

Section Four NightMares

Black Horse

Eve

They say the Dreamtime isn't real. It is. My Horse lives in the Dreamtime and he comes for me whenever I need to escape. He saves my life.

My horse doesn't have a name. He doesn't need one. His body is strong and his mane and tail fly in the wind as he gallops into the Void with me clinging to his back. I saw him almost every day as a child. Nowadays he appears from time to time, like a friend that we love but only meet up with occasionally. But his rememberance is burned into my soul. You might not believe this but I can smell him and feel him and taste him, this Black Dreamtime Horse. It is his eyes that I remember most—black, shiny, warm and full of love for me.

Some say that black is a negative, bad colour. It isn't. Black is the colour of the Void where the Great Spirit lives. That is where he takes me. He came every evening in winter when I was on the school bus afraid to go home. I would rub the mist and damp from the windows and press my nose against the glass to peer outside at the dismal streets with faceless people huddled underneath umbrellas. There he was, standing in the sunshine, waiting for me to clamber on his back and off we would go. We did not come back until I was ready. My horse was patient; very, very patient.

When we returned my body was huddled under the bedclothes, the pillow damp with tears and the smell of a man, my stepfather, spread over my little body and the sheets. That did not matter. I had gone away with my Black Dreamtime Horse into the Void where the Great Spirit lives. The important thing was that I knew that I was loved, very much loved and could go away to another place in another time and be safe. My Horse would never let me down.

Some people have guardian angels. I don't. I have a black Stallion who came from the Void and taught me the power of entering the Darkness and finding the Light and of how to protect my soul, no matter what. My horse taught me how to live without fear. I love my Spirit Horse.

*My name is **Eve**. I was born in Glasgow, Scotland. I watch sunsets, eat mangoes, dance at the drop of a hat, have children and grandchildren, love the smell of log fires, work in the community with mental health groups and love being part of the adventure of life.*

The Goddess Paddock

Lin Van Hek

A body had been found in the Goddess Paddock. People read about it and rang the newspaper to ask why it was called the Goddess Paddock. People were like that, certain things intrigued them. No evidence of any consequence was found. No one knew the identity of the little girl.

The horses knew all about it. They stood on the spot where the child was murdered. There were many of them in this paddock filled with fossils. They all turned to the place in the makeshift fence where the child's dress had been caught in the wire.

They all walked to the fence and hovered around the spot. A yellow thread hung from the wire. They all stood near the old bathtub drinking trough where the murderer washed the blood away leaving a trail in the water. The detectives did not notice the bathtub, and the yellow thread on the fence would eventually rot there.

For a long time, nobody had been to the Goddess Paddock. It was a place where lightning had hit trees and scorched the earth. The locals said it was full of weather. Several decades back, before anyone now alive could remember, people had walked along the track by the river. Then the women had come and with them came the horses. Stables and a barn were built. For years there were the sounds of hooves under a canopy of stars. The

silhouettes of these sleek animals under one large moon. The women were always there, grooming the horses or mucking out the barns, or driving in fresh hay. They rode en masse across country, down to the lakes, resting along the way and letting the horses graze on fresh grasses away from their home paddock. The women lay about under the trees dazed by the midday sun talking together in a mood of serious exultation. The horses snorted and kicked up the grasses as they galloped towards the lakes.

After the great flood, when the river broke its banks and the barns were washed away, the Goddess Paddock seemed a desolate place. People moved from the town by the hundreds. Only a few old timers remained. Then as sometimes happens, after a few years, there was a sudden population explosion. City dwellers moved out to try the good life and the old bridge that had been destroyed in the great flood was rebuilt with massive steel trusses.

One woman now owned the Goddess Paddock. She had ridden with the women as a child and had known all of the horses by name and had slept in the arms of the women in the summer grasses. It was a recurring dream for her, a fortifying virtuous expectant dream that she filtered through her days. An idyllic reflection that became remote as she grew older but none the

less potent and wonderful still.

There were only two people still alive that knew the horses in the Goddess Paddock. Only two people in the town and she was one of them. Only two people who saw the horses and they both had the sight.

After the murder, the woman stepped into the paddock by climbing through the fence. Instantly she felt the menace. The horses crowded in around her. She stroked their eager necks and gleaming flanks. They threw back their heads. The stallions pushed in on her and stomped their feet. She felt an enormous unrest. The police had gone quickly from the place and closed the investigation as soon as they could decently do so. They had not seen the horses. They saw a desolate few acres that led down to the river. That was all.

It was winter and the ground was cold. She easily saw footsteps, soft and pliant as if the earth sank in where the child had stepped. She did not know why she saw this so effortlessly when no one else did.

She saw the child was pinned like a specimen butterfly, unable to move. She had intercepted a suspended moment. She saw them both, the child and her killer as if mummified.

He faced her, translucent in the rain and she knew him for he was the only other one in town with the sight.

A hailstorm had started. Ice fell. She saw it all before her for she had come unknowingly to witness the critical moment. She looked directly into the eyes of the man. He looked back at her. Could he see her? Were they in different times or places? She did not know, she could never be sure for she was not educated about her sight.

She knew that this man's sight was superior to hers, for he not only saw the horses, but he saw the women who rode them. He talked about it in town, the goddesses who wore trousers. He was responsible for the paddock getting its name. Everyone said he was mad and she told no one about the sightings that she herself experienced.

She felt the conversation in the paddock. The child had been on the bus. It had stopped for a meal break. She had no money. He offered to buy her chips. She accepted. They walked. They had two hours before the bus left. He raped her. She did not scream. She had been raped before. He said he would give her all his money. He would marry her. She said she was only twelve and wanted to go back to the bus.

The woman saw his mouth move in a canine bark as he struck the child. Instinctively, she threw herself forward to protect the girl. Time jumped! The man was at the water trough washing his hands. The girl lay still. The horses came in a wild charge, reeling and shuddering and, for the first time, she saw their riders; she knew them all by name. Only the gauze of time was between them. The man ran down the hill; the horses greatly agitated bolted

after him. He began to cross the river at its lowest point. The river that had once been a raging flood was now reduced to a trickle after seven years of drought.

The hail was so harsh on her face that she could not be sure that she had not travelled to an earlier time, perhaps the night during the flood when she was a child and the women decided to move the horses to the other side of the river. As they crossed the old wooden bridge, it cracked and was washed away, taking the women and the horses to their deaths.

She walked back to the fence, she was alone in the paddock. She saw the yellow thread from the girl's dress as she climbed through the fence.

By the time she reached the road, it was dry, as if it had not rained. She still felt the hailstones on her face, she shuddered along her spine and the moon was full and lit the long hard road.

She kept quiet about what she had seen. She still saw the horses but she never saw the women again.

Another body was found downstream; he had been trampled to death, they said. He was washed up against the pylons of the new steel bridge.

The girl's body was claimed by the other man who had raped her, but only one person in town knew that. The woman saw him go into the undertakers and she approached him. She offered to show him the place in the paddock where the child had died.

The man backed away. He had never seen eyes like hers. He claimed his daughter's body and went on his way.

He was unnerved and accelerated very fast out of town. As he turned onto the bridge, at breakneck speed, a dozen women on horseback galloped towards him. The sun was in his eyes. He swerved clumsily to avoid them. His truck hit the bright new steel of the bridge and his neck snapped. He died instantly.

Later she put the Goddess Paddock on the market. It sold quickly to a newcomer, a woman who did not see the horses. She built an ice factory on the corner of the paddock and, intrigued by the name, called her business, Goddess Ice. The place was hit by lightning a few times and workers complained of strange noises on the night shift. Sounds of hooves, stampeding horses.

The woman with the sight continued on with her life trying to ignore her handicap as much as possible. Each night she dreamt the same dream, she saw a child, asleep in the arms of the women in the summer grasses. All around her stood the horses in slivers of sunlight.

Lin Van Hek *loves to sing and ride horses, especially at the same time. As a child, she rode with her grandmother and aunts (see* The Ballad of Siddy Church)*. The horses were kept in the Goddess Paddock and even today Goddess Paddock Road is a secret pilgrimage for many women horse lovers. She has just completed* The Difficult Women's Cookbook *and is presently testing the recipes that were given to her by women all over the world.*

A Holiday Romance

Denise Imwold

For my fiftieth birthday, I decided to take myself on a trip to Ireland and the UK. I felt I deserved a holiday. For the past few years I'd endured enough loss and change to knock the wind from the sails of even the strongest soul, the most recent blow being the death of my ancient little dog Pumpkin.

Normally I enjoyed the freedom and independence of travelling solo, but by the time I arrived in the village of Betws-y-Coed in north Wales, after nearly three weeks on the road, I was tired of my own company. I hated to admit it, but I was lonely.

As I was settling into my lodgings, I pulled back the pink, ruffled curtains and noticed a pony standing stolidly in the far corner of the paddock across the road. A short time later, when I went out to explore the village, the pony had moved to just behind the stone fence, looking up at me expectantly. It was hard to tell whether he was white or grey, because he was so dirty. His mane was yellow, and his most endearing feature was his nose; one side was grey and the other side a fleshy pink, giving him a cheeky and comical appearance. Although he had a pot belly, his bones were protruding, and I guessed that he was old and rather malnourished. As soon as he looked at me I felt an instant connection, a magical meeting of kindred spirits. He nuzzled my shoulder, leaving grassy slobber all over my jacket, and I laughed—I had fallen in love! I decided to name him Tony, after my favourite Welsh actor, Sir Anthony Hopkins.

I asked the owner of the guesthouse who Tony the Pony belonged to. She replied, 'I don't know. Occasionally someone drops some feed off to him, but I feel sorry for the poor old chap—he seems to be starving for companionship.'

On my next trip to the shops, I returned with carrots and apples, as well as a large brush with soft bristles. Tony was again in the corner of the paddock and, when I called his name, he immediately came toward me, his gait somewhere between a trot and an arthritic hobble. He sniffed my pockets and I held out my hand and offered him a carrot, and enjoyed the ticklish feeling of his lips against my hand. I climbed over the fence and began to brush him. The dry caked mud crumbled to dust and was hard to remove, but the rhythmic brushing was relaxing for both of us. It lulled me into a quiet reverie, reminding me of some of the happiest times of my childhood spent at my cousins' farm in western Maryland. They bred racehorses as a hobby, and there was always an assortment of horses and ponies on the property: Sunday, the feisty chestnut; pretty and confident dapple-grey Ginny; and the brood mare Lady Patrick, giantess and brown earth mother, who would let me and my sisters groom her for hours, submitting patiently to our over-enthusiastic attentions.

A routine developed over the next few days. After breakfast I would go for long walks down to Fairy Glen, and sit and meditate by the rushing Conwy River. In the afternoons I would go for scenic drives, or hike in Snowdonia National Park. The autumn landscape was other-worldly and somewhat melancholy—craggy mountains, dark forests and dense mist rising from the valleys—this was Merlin's country. It was cheering to return from my solitary sojourns to find Tony waiting for me, nipping at my pockets for a snack. We'd share an apple, and I'd tell him of my day's adventures.

I wondered about Tony's life. Was he once the beloved pet of a young girl who abandoned him once she discovered fashion and pop stars? Or had he been retrenched from a riding school, awaiting the knackers? It didn't bear thinking about.

On the morning of my departure, Tony was there at the fence as usual. After I gave him his treat, I hugged him tightly, buried my head in his mane and sobbed. God, how I hated goodbyes! As I drove away, I worried what would become of him. Winter was approaching: he had no shelter, and there wouldn't be as many tourists to give him a pat or a kind word. I fervently hoped that another pony pal would come and share his paddock, or that he would find a loving and comfortable home to live out the end of his days.

Several years have passed, and whenever I think of my Celtic odyssey, the first image that comes to mind is that of an angel disguised as a scruffy Welsh mountain pony, who extended the hoof of friendship to a lonely traveller.

Denise Imwold is a writer, editor, and self-confessed book, film and animal addict. Her early influences were Black Beauty and National Velvet. Denise grew up in the United States, and has lived for many years on the Northern Beaches of Sydney. She is currently writing her first novel, which explores the theme of the healing power of animals. At every opportunity, she stops and talks to horses.

Night Journey Marg Peck

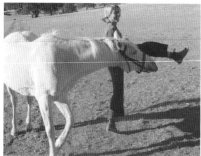

Last night I paused at the edge of darkness,
And I slept with green dew alone,
I have come a long way, to surrender my shadow
To the shadow of a horse.

James Wright

He had been prancing around, spooking at cars and pedestrians. The ground was soft with heavy rain. He had tried to buck and slipped on his side. She was trapped under the horse but still strapped into the saddle. The white of the horse's eye, the trembling of flesh, flaring nostrils. The young girl shouting and screaming, holding onto the horse's reins and hearing that dull thud as her boot connected with his belly.

They were both familiar with fear.

She hated him; she hated this wild impulsive animal that was about to kill her. As she kicked his side, his terror only increased until finally he broke away and galloped down the road.

He dodged cars and slid on the asphalt. She could not hold back her tears. She was overwhelmed with exhaustion and confusion.

The things we know well are fear and terror, the desire to escape.

That is why when you see a horse you are both happy and sad. That horse represents the wildness within yourself you have never dared to become.

She was woken by neighing in the night. It was a full moon. When she came out he wasn't there. She found him pacing up and down the wrong side of the fenceline and snorting, tossing his head. His coat was silver. Steam rose through the dark. He looked much bigger and his tail was up. He lifted each hoof so high he looked as though he was floating.

'Shit,' she breathed, eyes wide. 'How did you get out there?'

There were no hoof prints in the mud, no skid marks. The gates were all locked, the fences untouched. His neck was thick and arched, his head was high. He did not look like the same horse. It was as if the events of the last few days had cast a shadow.

Whenever you see a white horse, know that the spirit is with you.

(Starwoman)

It is still freezing cold outside and a soft rain is falling. He is on the ground again. When I arrived today he was exhausted and stuck, folded on the damp ground. He struggled to his feet, trembling, shaking, unable to bear weight on his right foreleg, and hobbling on his back legs.

How will he be after another five or six hours out there on the damp ground again tonight? If only I had been able to get him into the stable. Walking was agony and it was all he could do to make it to the paddock. His breathing was slow and heavy, his body leant against mine. How can I lose the two things I love most in one week?

Should I be lying in bed crying or out in the cold and drizzle? I feel numb all over, and can't believe that this wailing sound is coming from my body. I can't give in. Get up and get out there. He hasn't gone yet.

I do not know who I am, and therefore do not know what I am doing, where I am, or how to look upon the world or on myself.

I can hardly believe his recovery. We are spending more and more time together; I am sitting quietly by him. He lifts his hoof to swipe away the flies and sniffs tentatively at my arm and hand. I notice the changes in his breathing, feel the soft warm air on my skin.

That deep breathing, a groan from right in his belly as his eyes gently close. I wonder if he knows I am writing about him as he stands there watching me, half-dozing and occasionally sniffing the paper.

His quick recovery reinforces my notion that he may live forever and that my white horse is an endless, timeless, being, a fable—but aren't we all.

***Marg Peck** has had a beautiful white horse named Ace for most of her life. He has taken her on many amazing journeys, and her two little boys are now learning to ride him and to love him as she does. She has been a chiropractor for nearly twenty years, and lives and practises in Castlemaine, Victoria.*

For Drew

Niki van Buuren

On Saturday 18 January 2003, the west and south-western suburbs of Canberra, the capital city of Australia, were devastated by a firestorm, the worst recorded in memory. It was the consequence of lightning strikes igniting Brindabella and Namadgi national parks ten days beforehand. Four lives were lost, over five hundred homes destroyed and hundreds of injuries were recorded. Almost seventy per cent of the territory was burnt and millions of dollars worth of damage was done.

Niki and I were caught in the firestorm when we went to check her horse Drew, and our friend's horse Sunni, who shared a private agistment paddock at Canberra Equestrian Centre in Chapman. Niki suffered severe burns to two-thirds of her body and spent ten months in hospital, celebrating her twenty-first birthday there and finally returning home on 17 November 2003. She has had amputations to her fingers, involving all but one thumb, and has very limited movement in her shoulders and elbows due to ossification build-up as a result of complications from her injuries. We are hopeful that further surgery will help restore some movement, but this will not be considered in the very near future. Niki has begun riding again with the help of Pegasus, Riding for the Disabled, in Canberra recently.

Wendy van Buuren

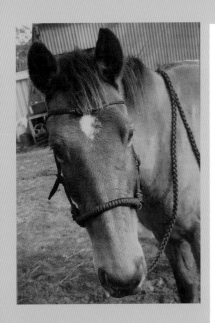

For Drew

At last the sun is setting
and soon the night will fall
the dust is slowly gathering
on the pictures on my wall
My jodhpurs in the drawer
folded neatly, row by row
all the ribbons in the cupboard
from some long forgotten show
There are spiders spinning cobwebs
on my riding boots outside
and I'm left sadly wondering
about how and why you died
Some days I think that I'll get by
some days I do it tough
I did my best to save you
but my best was not enough
I miss the way you'd greet me
when I arrived each afternoon
How your coat would grow all woolly
in the bitter cold of June
I miss your cheeky nature
You were something of a clown
but you'd always try your hardest
Even when I let you down
You always would forgive me
when I didn't get it right
and I pray forgive me now
when I face my toughest fight

I wish that I could see you
and touch you one last time
to create some long last memory
that I know will not be mine
I know the sun is setting
and the night will surely fall
but there's always lamplight shining
on the pictures on my wall
My jodhpurs sitting neatly
that I'll wear again some day
all the ribbons in the cupboard
that I'll never throw away
I cherished every moment
and although it had to end
I never will forget you
you were my greatest friend.

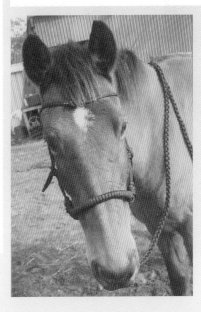

Love is Caleb

Sandra Burr

The first time I saw Caleb I wanted him. He was up on his hind feet, boxing the air. A wispy mid-line of pale honey-coloured hair seamed his tight belly, feathering outwards to a rich red bay that glowed in the Canberra sunlight. He dropped to the ground, his tail splayed over his rump, his pink nostrils squared and blowing, laughter in his eyes. He sputtered like a fizzing firecracker. I stopped dead, stunned by his beauty. The woman holding him spoke quietly. With an air of exaggerated contrition, Caleb lowered his head, took a step forward and, resting his nose on her stomach, closed his eyes.

'He's such a little monster,' the woman sighed. To me he was perfect. I wanted to touch him, be electrified by his energy, run my hand over the velvet softness of his nose, feel his sweet breath on my skin.

'If you ever want to sell him...' I heard myself suggesting. Then, as I drove away, the voice of reason kicked in, listing all the sensible reasons why I should forget him. What about Rikki? Wasn't one horse enough? Then there was Achilles (retired). I couldn't afford another horse. I didn't need another horse. Besides Caleb was too small, too young and he was an Arab—I had only ever owned quarter horses. Luckily Caleb wasn't for sale—but he hovered spectre-like in my subconscious.

Six months later his owner rang and my wish came true. Caleb was mine and from that day on my life overflowed with love for this cheeky, spirited, optimistic, affectionate little Polish Arab. He settled into the herd, taking his cues from his elders and driving them to distraction with his unrelenting invitations to mock fights and races. At two years old he was too young to ride, so I determined to show him as much of the world as I could. We went on walks together, played games, went swimming, he met the farrier, the dentist and went on float trips. I ponied him from Rikki, whom Caleb idolised. Life was his own private playground and he lapped it up. Nothing fazed him and when it was time for his first ride, he stunned us all by casually stopping to scratch his ear with his hind foot, oblivious to the unaccustomed weight on his back.

Caleb has a wicked sense of humour. I once looked up from mixing his feed to see my mobile phone disappearing down his throat and I only just managed to crank his jaws apart in time to save it. Another time, I was leading him from Rikki when he grabbed a rein and dragged us halfway across a playing field before I could persuade him to give it up. On the rare occasion that I told him off, he would rest his shovel-shaped chin on my stomach and sadly close his eyes. He was all spark and cheek one minute and soft and smoochy the next. I loved him without reservation—but then everybody loved Caleb.

Then his herd split. Trish took her horse Tenzin and Achilles to their new property in the mountains. She asked if she could buy Caleb. Absolutely not—never—he was mine. Shortly after, Rikki joined them in retirement. Caleb stayed and within days his world began to crumble. Little bumps and bruises escalated into debilitating injuries and I could no longer ride him. I bought Myst. She barely tolerated Caleb. I moved them both to new agistment, hoping he would make new friends. He didn't. Instead he stood pawing at the fence in frustration, ripping his heels and breaking my heart. Something was badly awry. I tried everything—even an animal communicator, but nothing worked. The only one I didn't listen to was Caleb.

During his first year at the new agistment, Caleb had a severe reaction to the spring clover. The pink skin on his white nose and legs burnt and blistered into weeping sores. I couldn't put him through that again, so Trish agreed to have him for a spell.

'It will only be for a few weeks,' I told him. 'Then I'll come and get you.' He pushed his head under my arm and sighed. My eyes filled with tears.

The boys were waiting for us—one chestnut, one bay and one palomino. Caleb lifted his tail high over his rump and flew to them. He paused to exchange sniffs and then invited them to run. And they did, streaming flat out down the gully in a frenzy of farting bucks, led by one speeding, very happy Arab. Finally I understood what he'd been trying to tell me. I could love Caleb without making him a prisoner of my heart. So I set him free.

Sandra Burr was first smitten by horses in primary school, a passion that has endured to this day. She is a Canberra-based freelance writer who has published many articles about horses and is currently venturing into the fields of fiction and poetry. Sandra shares her life with her horses, her dog, her family and some great friends.

My Friend,
My Confidante,
My Horse, Schantelle Edgecumbe

My first pony came when I was seven. I have had numerous horses ever since. Although I have loved each one deeply there was one mare that will always have a special place in my heart. Her name was Sasha.

Sasha was an aged 14.2 hands-high bay mare of unknown lineage who was given to me for my fourteenth birthday. Her head was too large, and her forelegs were too short. Her conformation certainly left something to be desired. But I loved her.

Sasha had the kindest and sweetest disposition that I have ever known. When growing up I was teased an awful lot at school. I didn't have any friends and I didn't know of anybody to talk to except Sasha.

No matter what happened, Sasha was there for me. There was always a shoulder (or a mane) to cry on when I came home from a hard day at school. Sasha not only gave me a lot of confidence in the saddle, but a lot of confidence in life as well. She didn't care if I was ugly, or fat, or unpopular. The only thing that mattered to her was that I took proper care of her. That I brushed her after a long trail ride. That I gave her enough food and fresh water. That I loved her.

When I turned fifteen the schoolyard taunting had became too much and had eroded my self-esteem. I became deeply depressed and thought that there was only one way to end my pain. I felt like I was standing in a room full of people, screaming for help, and yet nobody was listening. Nobody, that is, except for my beloved horse. I cannot recall the number of times that I sat in the small shed on our property, a sharp knife suspended over my trembling wrist. Every time the blade touched my skin I would hear Sasha's shrill neigh over my own sobs. Her call brought me back from the dark place I had created inside myself and reminded me of just what I had to live for.

Her. What would happen to her if I gave up?

This scenario always ended with my arms tightly clinging to my beautiful mare's neck, my salty tears soaking into her thick, black mane. Sasha and I had many wonderful times together until, sadly, she was put to sleep in November 2001, when old age became too much for her. I will never forget my sweet Sasha and how she showed me just how wonderful life can be. Rest in peace, dear friend. You will never be forgotten.

My name is **Schantelle Edgecumbe**,
I am nineteen and live in Adelaide,
South Australia. I am currently studying
to be a professional counsellor. I have
owned horses since I was seven.

The Beginning

Polly Klein

When I was a child I used to ride horses. I wasn't a great rider, but I loved doing it. The sound of hooves clomping against rustling leaves was one of the most peaceful sounds I could think of. The smell of leather in a tack room permeated my body leaving me feeling as soft and supple as the leather itself. As important as those things were to me, being around the barn and riding was also the only time I felt free. Free from my life which was, at the time, very miserable in an abusive home.

At age thirteen, I finagled the use of a horse to ride whenever I wanted. I would pack up my riding gear, get on a local bus, and head for the barn. It was incredible. I rode Chunky everyday and it was pure bliss. A month or so into this, I decided to enter a horse show. I was really nervous. I had shown before in school shows, but this was a real show. I knew I would be competing against people who had much more training than I did. That was one difference. Another, more important difference was that most children in the show had at least one parent with them who was just as into the whole show thing as they were and who helped them with everything. I was by myself.

The day of the show arrived and before my first jumping course I fell off the horse during a practice jump. I wasn't hurt, just scared. With no one there to coach me, my fear took hold of me and I didn't get back on the horse. Instead, I pulled out of the show and never tried to jump again. Before I could regain my confidence, the trouble in my home life escalated and I was grounded except to go to school. As hard as it may be to believe, the grounding lasted virtually uninterrupted for the next six years. Riding was ripped out of my life in one fell swoop. During those years I would often comfort myself with the idea that, if I made it out of my parents' home alive, I would buy myself my own horse. I day-dreamed that my horse would be 16 hands tall, a bay with a white blaze. This dream got me through a lot of horrible nights and was certainly a large part of how I maintained any sense of normalcy.

Actually, when I did leave home, I didn't have the money, time or even the interest in buying a horse. It wasn't until my early thirties that I got near a horse again for any prolonged period of time. Due to a car accident, I returned to riding at a therapeutic horseback-riding center. I did a lot of my physical therapy on a horse. I remember when I first walked into a stall to groom a sweet old mare for riding. The smell of hay and horse swirled around me but I found myself terrified that I was going to be hurt. The fears I had developed through the years of torment at home had paired up with the fall at the horse show and I was paralysed.

I pushed myself past this feeling and found my love of horses and riding returned almost immediately. Just as quickly, my fear disappeared. I regained most of my physical strength while I rode horses. When the opportunity presented itself a year and a half later, I was finally able to buy my own horse, Arrow.

Arrow was a find. He was just six years old; healthy, nice, and relatively bombproof. I could do whatever I wanted with him and he just went with it. He was a bay with a white blaze. And though he was a little smaller than my fantasy horse, at 15.1 hands, he was perfect. Sometimes I would show up at the barn where I kept Arrow, just to look at him and remind myself that I did it. This was my horse!

It came as quite a shock to me when I fell off my handsome horse for the first time. Horses are prey animals. What this amounts to is in the wild, they eat grass while other animals eat them. So to defend themselves, their first instinct is to flee whenever they find anything out of the ordinary. Their genetics say, 'Run like hell first, ask questions later.' This is what happened with Arrow.

I was out on a trail ride with Arrow and another woman who also had a horse at my barn. I really enjoyed riding with Debbie and her horse Walter and found it easy to melt away the stress of the day whenever we went out on the trail. On this particular day, we were riding on a mountain trail and I was leading the ride with Arrow. We were walking down a trail we had been on numerous times before. I was chatting away with Debbie when, all of the sudden, Arrow spooked at a log. He jumped straight up in the air but came down off to the side of the trail. I went straight up with him but came straight down off his back. Time moved very slowly as I fell. I can clearly remember thinking, 'Oh, this is going to hurt.' Then with a thump, I hit the forest floor.

Upon hitting the ground, I felt thirteen. While I saw the big fir trees, the dirt of the trail and Debbie, I felt exactly as I did in the wake of the horse show. I thought to myself, 'This is the beginning of everything going wrong. I am going to have to give up Arrow now.'

I could hear Debbie asking if I was all right. Was I all right? I hadn't even thought to check to see if I really had hurt myself. I was trapped in this event that I perceived as marking the end of my world. I tried to get up. Hmm… everything seemed to be working. Nothing was really hurting. I hadn't really done anything but bounce off the horse and it seemed I had landed on a very soft patch of ground.

'Yes, I'm okay,' I called back as I finished standing up. But I wasn't really okay because my next thought was that all I had to do is give Arrow to Debbie and call it a day.

But just then I realised something was different. When I turned to look at Debbie, she wasn't sitting there with her hands out ready to take Arrow away from me. Other than wanting to make sure I was okay, it looked like she thought I would attend to Arrow myself and then get back on to finish the ride. Didn't she know? This wasn't how the story went. I was there. I knew.

'There. There?' I heard a voice say. 'Well you might have been there before, but you're currently here on Squawk Mountain. This is your horse. Even if someone gets him off this mountain for you, guess what? He'll be waiting back at the barn. Not only is he not going anywhere, but he's your responsibility. If you don't get on him, how will you get off this mountain? Fly? You're not hurt. Arrow is perfectly safe to ride. It's okay. Get back on him.'

'Who is that?' I thought to myself. 'Whose voice is telling me these things?' Didn't they know I was scared and helpless and at the mercy of whatever and whoever was around me. But this voice sounded familiar. It was not critical; on the contrary, it was convinced of my capability. This was the voice I was hoping for when I fell at the horse show. The voice I hoped would have said, 'Bad luck, but you're okay so try it again.' A voice attached to a parent who would have helped me climb back on the horse and who would have been there to cheer when I cleared the jump the next time. Then I realised that voice was mine. It was my thirty-four-year-old self telling my thirteen-year-old self just what I needed to hear. This wasn't the beginning of the end. It was the beginning of the beginning.

I looked over at Arrow, who was nonchalantly standing off to the side of the trail. He was none the worse for the wear following his tangle with his mistaken predator, the fallen log. He wasn't even breathing hard. He was just standing there, patiently waiting. Waiting for me to climb back on. Waiting for us to begin. And so, we did.

Polly Klein, *owner of Tonglen Healing Arts for Animals, is an animal communicator and healer. She is a Reiki Master and Certified CranioSacral Therapist for large and small animals. Polly lives and works in Issaquah, Washington with her horse, three dogs, two cats, parrot, pond of goldfish, and husband.*

Champions

Brenda Coulter

This child I loved
quick-silver beauty,
moon-blue eyes
questioned, searched,
laughed and cried.
Farms covered wooden floors,
pop-stick paddocks
held valuable mares
while foals
played chasey
around plastic trees
and bolted away
from the red and black train

Under the gum trees
hobby horses
won ribboned rosettes
for dressage
and show jumping,
clearing jumps
more a test for rider
than horse.
Two friends
made up this trio
of champions.
Dasher, Cloudy
and Aintree Boy
stabled by her bed
munched hay,
while the moon-blue eyes
saw again
her dreams
of victory.

Brenda Coulter *won a scholarship to study piano and singing at the Elder Conservatorium. She also gained teachers' and performers' diplomas in speech, drama and classical ballet. She has had poems published in seven* Friendly Street Anthologies *and in 2002 gained her masters degree in Creative Writing. She has an abiding interest in the use of music techniques in the remediation of specific learning difficulties especially with visually impaired children.*

The Horse Guard

Lyn McConchie

I was riding home one Sunday. It had been a long day out in the country, and both my small mare and I were tired. I was sixteen, and Leasan was three. An onlooker would have seen a skinny girl with long black hair riding a chestnut mare; a real brumby of a horse, with a roman nose, big blocky hooves and lightly feathered fetlocks.

I'd paid fifteen pounds for my horse and I adored her. She was incredibly gentle, affectionate and smart. I didn't care that to anyone who knew horses she was clumsy-looking, slow of pace, and with an ugly head. She was mine, I was hers, and that was all either of us cared about.

The paddock where I kept Leasan was isolated and it was dusk, shading towards dark. Not that I was afraid. I'd lived in this town for years and never known any danger outside my own home. The paddock gate was nestled at the end of a short alleyway between other properties, and a small copse of trees hid it from view.

We were almost at the gate when Leasan shied. Instinctively I gripped with my knees and balanced against the heaving swing of her body. I'd ridden bareback most of my life and this day it had been so hot I hadn't bothered again although I'd recently purchased a rather second-hand saddle.

I made soothing sounds but Leasan shied again and this time I looked where her ears were pointing—at a deeper shadow in the trees. A figure slouched towards me and a voice hissed demands and threats. It was 1962, and I didn't even know what some of the words meant.

Hands reached up to grab at my waist, trying to pull me from Leasan's back. I clung like a monkey, kicking out, yelling protests. I knew we were where no one would hear me. I could hope for no help, and Leasan was a young mare. I knew from her movements that she too was afraid.

I gripped her mane fiercely, feeling fear-sweat start out across my whole body. The hands were slowly dragging me loose and I screamed then, in rage and terror, fighting to cling to Leasan. In another minute we'd be separated and I guessed what would happen then.

It never did. Leasan spun, striking out as she half-reared. I felt one of her feet strike home and heard the yell of surprised pain. She dropped to all four hooves and her head shot out like a striking snake. Teeth must have gripped, there was a howl, as he was tossed to one side almost under stamping hooves.

She spun like a dervish, kicking out at the dark figure, teeth snapping at him savagely. He broke and ran then while, sweat-soaked, I clung to a lathered back and crooned my horse into calm again. I never knew who he was, but I changed paddocks the next day, picking a larger, more open field with no alleyway to the gate and no trees to hide it.

I never knew what prompted my small gentle mare that night either. Perhaps it was my smell of fear. I must have reeked of that. Perhaps it was that she was a mare and her protective instincts were aroused. All I knew is that she saved me, fighting for me as hard as, twelve years later, I fought for her when she inadvertantly drank poison. I lost that battle, but in a way she never died, not so long as I remember that night and a small chestnut mare who fought with all her heart for me—and won.

Lyn McConchie started writing in 1990 and has sold seventeen books and seen some two hundred of her shorter items published. Her most recent works were a reprint of her humorous non-fiction book Farming Daze, *and the publication of the sequel,* Daze On The Land *by Queensland Press, Avalook Publications. Lyn is an animal lover with a farmlet, two Ocicats and a personal library of around seven thousand volumes.*

Fur Therapy

Lorelei Dowling

It's late January, the day before Australia Day and, as I leave an exhausting rehearsal for Friday's concert, the crisp but fine day slowly begins to live up to its true definition of what minus eight is like... a fine snow begins to fall. By the time I reach the farm there's a snowstorm brewing. Susanne runs in, late, 'See it's your fault—it was fine this morning. Pity you had to work!' she says with a grin as she gets on her horse, Velvet. My white part-Arab, Scarlet, is really not into snow. She snorts her disapproval as I saddle her up.

We ride into the eerie white landscape of hills and woods which surround both sides of the farm and I reflect on how romantic the countryside looks when it is covered in snow. It's not exactly congenial to ride in though... Both horses are slipping around. Velvet starts bucking in anticipation of galloping but the snow is getting heavier so we hold both of them back to a trot. As we approach the farm we spot a man ascending the hill in the snow. He walks alone (unusual without a dog) and heads for the thick woods. He pauses from the trek to take a breath and turns... I think he sees us but when I wave he doesn't respond.

'That's really strange,' I say to Susanne. 'Two days ago I was galloping along the edge of the forest and suddenly Scarlet became agitated. I pulled her up only to find that a man standing in the woods was watching us. I yelled out, 'Hallo,' but he didn't reply. I should have told the Springnagels because he then started walking towards us...'

'Yeah, you've told me this story before... Hey, did Frau Springnagel tell you that the sisters found a body just on the other side of the woods?' interrupted Susanne.

I know this sounds like a beginning of a detective story... but it's not meant to be! This is my life as it is now and as romantic as it sounds—and mysterious—it wasn't always like this. My name is Lorelei and I am forty years old. I hadn't ridden a horse until late 2002 and now I ride nearly every day. My whole world revolves around horses.

Three weeks before my thirty-ninth birthday my whole world fell apart. I felt like I'd lost everything. I had badly overworked for years. The result: burn out. I had turned my back on my private life and suddenly found myself alone. Alone in Vienna that is, speaking hardly any German and realising with a jolt that all I had done in life was build a career. I felt I had sold my soul to my work and forgotten to live and enjoy life on the way. I was deeply depressed and went to see a psychologist.

I realised that I had few friends and no family in Vienna, and worse, I was very lonely. I really wanted the companionship of a dog but as I toured so much it was an impossibility. I felt that at this stage of my life I wanted to experience new things and face fears I'd never faced before. I wanted to learn something totally new and unrelated to my life. I decided to face one of my biggest fears: learning to ride a horse. To exhaust myself physically was a way I knew I could get out of the depression I was in. To my surprise I found that in Vienna it was quite cheap to learn to ride. The stables in the Prater were geared towards adults learning more so than children because the horses were huge!

I applied all the skills I knew from being a musician to learning to ride. After four months I really wanted my own horse to practise on. To improve my German I read all the ads for animals in the papers. One day I found a notice for leasing a Shagya-Arab. In my very bad German I rang the owner and then trekked the hour-and-a-half out of Vienna to the small village. At that stage I didn't have a car and I spent over six months hitchhiking out to see Scarlet every day.

The best part of leasing Scarlet is that she is looked after when I go on tour. Also now I won't tour unless stables can be found near where I am working. In Gent, I was taught Horse Whispering with an Irish Tinker and Appaloosa. In Graz, I improved my jumping and had the chance to ride a Halflinger. In Barcelona, I will learn Spanish riding. In Australia I have lessons in Centennial Park and have horse trekked in the Snowy Mountain Range.

When I return to Vienna, I can't wait to drive straight from the airport to the farm. One of the most amazing outcomes of horses in my life is that I have lost over twenty kilograms. And I am fit. Something I had never been. I feel alive and very happy.

When I walk on stage to play these days, my mind is often back on the farm, sitting on my beautiful Scarlet. As I launch into a solo, I am away riding along the mountain ridge, riding into a balmy night, deer silhouettes running beside us as we ride into a pink sunset.

I have never played as well. Fur therapy is certainly better than psychotherapy.

Sydney-born **Lorelei Dowling** *has lived in Vienna, Austria, since 1995. She is the Solo Bassoonist/Contrabassoonist with Klangforum Wien, Austria's full-time Contemporary Music Ensemble. From 1989 to 1992 she was a member of the Sydney Symphony Orchestra. She bi-annually returns to Sydney.*

The RSPCA Horse

Coral Hull

The rspca horse

Just stands in the paddocks starving,

In the wind & rain, his little back rug rag taggle,

There are a lot of lonely horses out in valleys with mountain backdrops,

With one report of cruelty a day, of neglected horses

Without the grooming equipment to keep the coats clean & healthy,

Without the herd for company, without the independence

To leave the property, without the work needed to survive,

Without the purpose of what it means to be a horse,

Many people, particularly the young, would like to own a horse or pony,

But how much time, hard work & money, is involved in looking after them properly,

A suitable paddock, or supplementary feed if the grass in their paddock is low,

Shelter from weather, or a horse that just stands in the fog, tail spoilt,

Knotty, thick & still, hanging like bracken,

Vaccinated then left to rot in the sodden hectare, ribs like broken fencing,

Killing the will from the inside, that the inspector overlooks,

When the horse is discovered, standing there, knee deep

In mud, thin, undernourished, forgotten,

A toss of the mane, a stamp & a snort, to compartmentalisation,

To kilometres of other segregated horses, never to be nudged or run with,

The solitary rspca horse at the end of its tether, at the end of the line,

Soon be to be sold off as pet food, a bad investment, timely, big, bigger than

The paddocks, as big as a heart or the country, these displaced horses,

Financial difficulties, too big for money, remember horses,

Herd bred & herd born they should not be kept on their own,

& keeping horses tethered in stables does not work,

Remember them in a herd, for the last time, on the ramps, at the knackeries.

Wild horse to ridden horse to rocking horse,

& those slippery merry-go-round horses, the reins of real leather & real

Strands of hair, now face to face with your own trumped up version of nature,

The wilderness knocked out with a chisel,

They are as wooden as the carnival music sliding up & down the poles,

As empty as the big white swans with the seats inside, & those mirrors

Rotating in the middle, where the ticket collector stands

Smoking, as money grabbing & hollow as the rides,

You are left floundering, on the way home, without the strength to carry you

Through your crisis, before your anxiety begins, & again you must grab for the reins,

Of 6,000 year ago horses that rushed the plains in herds, before the undergrowth,

Streams & forests, before the night set in on horses,

The industrial age of the horse, the technological age of the horse,

Horses are receding, as a physical animal they are effectively invisible,

Their grace & muscular power, their independence & will to life,

The joy of wind in the gallop, the landscape they move through, their story,

We are losing everything of horses.

Coral Hull *is the author of over thirty-five books of poetry, fiction, artwork and digital photography which are available through her own publishing label Artesian Productions. She is an animal rights advocate and a vegan and has spent much of her life working voluntarily on behalf of animals and the environment. Coral is the Editor and Publisher of* Thylazine, *a free biannual literary and arts ezine focusing on Australian artists, writers and photographers working in the areas of landscape, animals and in other areas of special interest, with a strong emphasis on indigenous Australian culture.*
www.thylazine.org

Destiny...just meant to be!

Kate Danby

My heart beats quicker as we approach the Livestock Marketplace.

It's Friday. The day the horses are auctioned.

Each Friday is Black Friday to me because it heralds heartache and sadness as I watch semi-trailer after semi-trailer full of horses being driven away. With soulful eyes, confused and bewildered by their circumstances, they stand in frightened silence.

On this particular Friday we were drawn to the market, with the intention of speaking to people who were selling their horses, in an effort to find out why. We wanted to let them know that there were other ways to sell their horses... ways that would give the horse a better chance.

We walked along the alleyway, heads down, trying not to catch the eye of any of the horses. There was a woman with a grey pony, a child's pony that

hadn't made the grade. I looked left into a pen and saw a gorgeous big thoroughbred with whip marks all over his rear and his racing plates still on his feet. I went further with my heart in my hand and saw a superbly-cared-for quarter horse with children climbing all over her. Why was she here?

Further down the alley we stood next to an old timer, a horseman of days gone by. I was trying to catch what he was saying to a companion when my eyes shifted sideways and I caught a glimpse of chestnut and white. I felt eyes burning a hole in my back and, as I turned toward his stall, those liquid brown eyes engulfed me.

He was a big, ungainly thoroughbred. A crooked white blaze ran down his nose and uneven white socks ran up his legs. He was no oil painting but my heart beat faster, harder, as he held my gaze. I looked to the old horseman who followed my eyes and he said, 'You wouldn't want to get stood on by those feet.' I looked down at the chestnut's feet and I found myself smiling... sure enough, they were big, real big. They matched his uncommonly big ears.

While telling myself to walk away, I slid through the bars of the stall and started to run my hands up his legs and along his back and under his belly and over his head and down his nose. All the time repeating in my head... I have five horses, I can't afford another horse, I won't buy another horse, I have no money, I don't have the time to care for another horse, my husband will kill me... but I just have enough time to get to the bank before the bidding starts... but no, I can't take home another horse! Then I made a compromise with

myself... if he is to be bought by a person looking for a pet, I'll let him go, but if I see him being sold to a meat buyer, I'll have to bid for his life. I turned to leave his stall. I was unprepared to bid and needed to get to a bank but, as I left him, I heard him sigh. I turned back... people all around me... he was looking at me and I was hearing him. He hated it there, he wanted out... and he wanted out now. He was confused, unsure, frightened.

I ran to the car, sped to the bank, returned with money that was destined for the telephone bill.

The bidding began. The quarter horse mare was safe... thank god... others though were falling to the meat buyers. My heart was leaking sadness as we reached my chestnut's stall. The bidding began; two pet food buyers and a buyer for horseflesh to export overseas. No way would I let that happen here... we started bidding and didn't stop until he was safely sold to us.

I knew nothing of this horse's history except that he was five and bred to race but, thankfully, I now knew his future would be secure. He was coming home to family and friends.

At home, my vet told me that he was sound and he was healthy, but the

determination was that he was 'terminally slow'. For a race horse that meant his life was not worth the money it took to feed him. A life used and abused and then discarded.

But to me, his life was precious, a gift.

I named him Picasso, because his blaze is off centre. At first he showed all the usual signs of having been hurt once too often and had lost trust in humans. He would swing his head away in anticipation of a blow if you happened to raise your arm near him. It made me ache with pity for him.

But even after all he'd been through and all he'd seen, he found it in him to forgive us humans for our faults and for the treatment he had been delivered. He let go of his fears. He relaxed and accepted my care, my friendship and my love. In return I get to spend my life in his company.

I couldn't be more grateful.

*As a young girl **Kate Danby** dreamt of bringing her riding school pony home to look after him and love him. Now, many years later, on a property in the Dandenong Ranges, Kate lives the dream with her eight equine friends who 'just happened' to find their way into her home and into her heart. Her life is her horses and her horses are her life!*

Diary

Helen McLennan

Tuesday

Rode Gorgeous George along the Perimeter track and out to Long Trail today. The bush is spectacular in this early spring. Brown and common boronia scent the air and everywhere spider grevillea and geraldton wax flowers sprinkle pinkly and redly and whitely over the branches. The banksias have thrown giant, wizened pods to the sandy floor and new banksia flowers sit up on the cankered branches like orange candles on a Christmas tree.

At the end of Long Trail, I dismount and sit on a rock, looking out over Coal and Candle Creek. I admire the cool blue of the inlets and watch the wind catch the grasses by the hair, dragging them down to the mangroves. Every now and then a light zephyr wafts a gust of warm air up to me. I smell eucalyptus oil, boronia and wild orchids. Heavenly. It's free of man-made noises but the birds call, occasionally a whip-bird or the ding of a bellbird. Goannas are rustley in the undergrowth, the wind soughs through the sparse leaves of the scribbly-gums and Gorgeous George snuffles around trying to find blade of grass on the scrubby track.

When I get home, I can't put George back in his paddock. A pair of spur-winged plovers have their three ground-coloured chicks in there and are fiercely defending them. I try to get in, but they have an organised method of attack. One comes from the back of me. The other aims straight for my face. The spurs are very sharp. I'm not keen to take them on. George and I retire in consternation. Woman with horse overboard. George looks at me as if asking 'now what?' I tell him I can't believe I've been driven off by two birds.

Wednesday

Maria and Rose are with me. They've come to Sydney from the north coast for the funeral of a beloved and venerable aunt. Maria's inherited her auntie's emerald engagement ring. It's a clan gift. It means more to her than her own which she chucked in the trash years ago. She doesn't need a partner in her life anymore; now she has Rose. Rose was conceived on a wave-lashed rock a thousand miles away from any city. She's wild like the sea. She might be a Silkie because she swims like an otter and sometimes it's as if she lives in different skins. She rides my filly Tantrum out with me. Tantrum and Rose seem to have known each other forever. I'm jealous. I've wooed that bloody-minded little mare for two years and she's stayed aloof the whole time. Still, there's something about watching the two of them communing with each other, so tuned in. Rose hardly moves and Tantrum steps around and up and over fallen logs and rocks like an angel. Which she isn't. When we get back on the road, she doesn't even flinch when the garbo's truck rumbles past. It stops, grabs a green wheelie bin as if it is going to strangle it, heaves it high into the air and shakes the life out of it into its stinking maw. Tantrum stops, stares, then shakes her head as if to say 'humans!' I wonder, what exactly do they know about each other, these two young females. Rose sits unmoved, a Mona Lisa smile on her secret, fairy face.

Thursday

Maura rings, hysterical. Contemptible Colin wants a divorce so he can start afresh. He's re-mortgaged their family home. Now all Maura is entitled to is a half-share on a big debt. She has no money for a good lawyer. Colin denies ownership of the four houses she knows he bought last year. Maybe he's sold them. He says he will pay the boys' school fees. Maura must pay for Emma. He didn't want a third child. Especially not a daughter. So he doesn't see why he should support her. Colin is worth roughly twenty million dollars even with the foreign exchange rate. Nice.

Friday

Visit Jane at her Welsh Pony Stud. Hannah, a neatish, black mare is in labour. We plait up her tail and bandage it to keep it clean and to stop the placenta wrapping and tangling in it. Horse placentas dangle for quite a while.

The poor pony is a maiden and doesn't know what's happening. She keeps kicking at her belly and stares round to see if there's a wild animal attached to her sides. We can see the strength of the contractions as they ripple down her flanks. She lies down. She gets up. She stretches her neck and comes over to us for a cuddle. 'Poor thing!' says Jane sympathetically.

'Huh!' I say. 'You got her like this, putting her in with Sioux. Bet she never asked to meet up with a stallion. Or signed a consent form!' 'Ah well,' says Jane. 'Brood mare or dog-meat—take your pick. She's got to pay her way like the rest of us.'

Hobson's choice I think. Or caught between a rock and a hard place. I watch the grunting mare and see the unborn foal's little nose and forefeet, still neatly parcelled in the sac, push out of the vulva, then disappear again. We tie a soft rope around the hooves next time they make an appearance and help the mare by gently taking the strain when she contracts. Within minutes the foal bursts out in a rush, the sac breaking, placental blood and fluid all over everything. A bony, black filly.

The mare is up on her chest in minutes and makes deep rumbly noises in her throat, whiffling her nose to get a scent of her baby. We pull junior round to mum and she starts to snuffle and blow and lick. In one hour, the little filly is up on trembly legs, rootling for the milk bag, swollen between the mare's back legs. Hannah has lost interest in us, totally focused on the foal and looks well pleased, despite the ghastly, blood-streaked curtain dangling out of her vagina. We tie it up in a plastic breadbag so she won't step on it and tear the placental bed out too quickly.

As we leave them happily whickering to each other, I think about that seven-month pregnant Afghanistan woman held on board the Tampa last year, lost in the Arafura Sea. I bet she could see Christmas Island from the tanker. I bet, like Hannah, she had no idea what was going on.

Saturday

Have Maura's kids over so she can try to talk some decency into Colin. Good Luck.

The boys take turns riding Gorgeous George round the yard. Emma doesn't want to ride. 'He's too big,' she explains, 'and he smells and the flies go round him.'

The boys double-up to save time. George gets tired of doing circuits. He does a big, grunting poo, then puts his head down to eat grass. The boys yell and kick but Gorgeous George knows they can't do anything about it. He ignores them. They slide down his neck and roll, laughing, onto the grass. Emma complains about the flies and the smell of the manure. The boys tell poo jokes.

I take them to the beach and we get full of sand and eat too many icecreams. Emma is sick on the way home. 'I want Mummy,' she wails but Maura's still not back when we get to my house. When she does come Emma is asleep on the couch and the boys are drugged by televison. Maura is so pale she's see-through.

'Her name is Star. She's twenty-eight. I asked him how long he thought it'd be before she wanted kids too. What if they're all girls? Will he wait another fifteen years before he abandons her?' She contemplates this idea. 'He'll be old by then. Old and alone I hope.'

When they've all gone, I feed up the horses. They're not in the least grateful, standing aloof like monarchs by their empty bins while I wait on them, hand and hoof. I love it out here at this certain time in the early evening. The sun drops its glare and drips softly like honey down the trunks of the stringy barks, making them look almost edible. The paddocks look like one of those calm, sepia prints, the contented horses gently swishing tails and crunching chaff, striped by the long shadows. It's peaceful, even with the plovers fiercely defending their three dun-coloured chicks. The parents shriek and warn, drawing me away from the babies who pretend to be part of the ground. Plovers are a pain in the arse, but they're good parents and at least the dad stays around to help.

I think about where Maura is. Swept away on a sea of motherhood. No compass. No way back. No foam-maned horse to mount and gallop to the safety of firm ground. She's adrift on the Sargasso, a black and impenetrable sea, weed-choked and haunted.

Helen McLennan lives in Sydney and breeds Morgan horses. A former rodeo pick-up rider, she now trains and competes in dressage as well as raising her family. Instead of sleeping, she writes short stories and is currently working on a novel about the Sydney horse world.

Life's short
cut to the chase
malignant growth
surgery
one month
chemotherapy
three months
radiotherapy
an other month
doctor-free-zone
one month
let's ride

Young Dudley of the even trot
ink-green forest
white blue stretched to the limit sky
iridescent silver sable grass
swishing proud gauchos
cantering
care less
across the coastal plain

He hits the beach
ninety miles
sedate
cautious of these sea horses
snorting foam
Ach—never mind
endless sand ahead
let's ride
'You said you'd wait.'
Grinning helplessly
'Hell…
my life force just got the better of me.'

Thanatos—
Be Damned

Francesca Bass

Francesca Bass was born in suburban Australia in 1943 and travelled in the back of a ute with her sister, two kelpies and the fridge, with her tired mother and cane cook father. He died in a car crash when she was fifteen, leaving a pregnant widow. This same mother was also killed by a car when Francesca was thirty-five. Francesca is married and is a psychologist in private practice. She is passionate about her sisters and horses.

Horsewoman

Pat Hodgell

Imagine a middle-aged woman in a laundromat, listlessly reading notices on a public bulletin board as she sips stale coffee.

'99 Chevy: only 99,999 miles; bongo lessons; residential cleaning...'

The stairwell at home is spattered with brown, following yet another of her mother's explosive bouts of diarrhea. Fouled underwear thumps in the washer.

Cemetery plot for sale: nice view...

It seems like a year since, over coffee at a Denny's restaurant, she arranged for her father's cremation. During exploratory surgery, they had discovered widespread colon cancer. Two weeks later he was dead, never having left the ICU. The consummate artist, he sketched angels on 3'x5' cards until drugs stilled his hand.

That was March in Florida. This is Wisconsin in April, only a month later.

Her parents divorced when she was two years old, leaving her to be raised by a grandmother in the same house that she has shared with her mother since the latter's retirement. Her only sibling died before she was born. As a child, returning from school, she used to open the drawer to say hello to the tiny packet containing his ashes. My brother in a box.

Bookcases, cheap...

She has grown up to be an author with a distinct dark streak and several fantasy novels to her credit. She has a contract to write another book in the series, but how can she when her mother keeps wandering into her study to ask, 'Who is alive, and who is dead?'

Good questions, really.

Bridal gown for sale, never worn...

She has never been married, never even been in love unless one counts various cats, most now also boxed ashes on a shelf. She certainly never wanted a child. Nonetheless, now she has one—a professor emeritus once the chair of a university art department, now eighty years old with wild white hair and a bewildered expression, wanting this, wanting that, never satisfied, never leaving her alone. Goddamn Alzheimer's anyway...

Riding lessons...

A pause. She remembers as a child bicycling down Vinland Road, stopping at the white fence to scan the paddocks beyond for horses. What a passion she had had for them then. What a hunger. Oh, if only she had known someone at the stable, someone who might have invited her in...

Could this be the same place? She squints, near-sighted, at the address. It is.

Returning home, she finds the house full of smoke. Her mother has tried to defrost a frozen dinner on the gas range: 'But I was hungry.'

By noon the next day, the woman's legs bend like rubber, her buttocks are black and blue from posting in an English saddle, and she has discovered that one does not fall off a horse the same way one fell, all those years ago, in a judo class. If nothing else, it's a lot farther to the ground, and there are no mats.

But the world has changed.

Six months of lessons follow. One hour of peace a week in the sweet shadows of stall and arena, living out a childhood dream. But it isn't enough.

She decides to buy a horse. Moreover, she wants one she can help train, as research for the stalled novel, as an escape.

A saddlebred mare has recently come into the stable. Used exclusively for breeding, she is six years and has barely been touched by human hands, much less ridden. Perfect.

Winter passes. Every day, the woman and the trainer work with the mare, lunging, long-lining, driving, and

occasionally riding her. Slowly she learns, but in the stall she bites and kicks like the wild thing she still is.

'She hates me,' says the woman sadly, rubbing a bruised leg.

'No,' says the trainer. 'She's afraid.'

'She hasn't been cuddled enough,' adds his assistant.

The woman tries to remember: Did anyone ever cuddle me?

Her mother starts to wander away, and to hitch rides back with strangers.

Her daughter puts her into a group home. She hates it. The phone rings constantly. 'Take me home or I'll eat broken glass.' Instead, she climbs out a window and starts to walk home in her nightgown. The police catch her within a block. Another time, she sets a fire, hoping to escape during the confusion.

This is horrible, thinks the daughter. At least I waited until Dad was dead before I buried him. What kind of a person am I?

The phone rings again. She leaves for the stable, closing the door on its desperate appeal.

A year passes. The woman turns fifty. She continues to visit her mother every week, but she also changes to an unlisted number and goes to the stable nearly every day. Sometimes she takes her mother.

Her mother is there the day that the mare comes back without a rider and the trainer sprints to the rescue. He arrives just as the woman emerges from the tall grass and swings back into the saddle. She doesn't tell him until later that she was not only thrown but dragged. In fact, over the past year she has been thrown repeatedly by her skittish mount, dragged face down over gravel, and hurtled backward down a deep drainage ditch. To her surprise, none of this has greatly upset her (except the ditch) nor has she been much hurt. Perhaps she isn't the timid, weak person that she always thought she was.

Meanwhile, there is such peace, riding through an autumn wood or across an open field under the great dome of the sky:

She gives me fields of white lace

Brushing her shoulders

Brushing my shoes

Leather creaks

Ears twitch

Grass braids in the wind

White butterflies dance around us

Like snow in August

And sometimes, in the stall, the mare quiets to her touch. They stand together, her arms around the sleek neck, the velvet nose on her shoulder, cuddling.

This is my horse, she thinks with wonder. I'm a horsewoman.

The mare sighs; then, deliberately, she steps on the woman's foot.

They decide to breed the mare to the trainer's stallion. The mare is an old hand at this. The stallion is not. On his first time, he nearly falls off on top of the woman, who is holding the mare's head. The second time, he gets it right.

Eleven months later, the woman kneels in the deep straw of the stall, one arm around the new-born foal, who is nibbling at her ear, the other around the mare, who is licking the foal's back. They had never thought that she would let them near her baby. In three years, how far she and the woman have come together.

Mothers and daughters. Mares and foals. Women and horses.

Out of so much grief and guilt and fear, somehow, has come this small, perfect creature.

Then the mare bares her teeth. Enough.

The horsewoman retreats, absently rubs her bruised arm. Sometimes life bites, she thinks, but it goes on.

P.C. Hodgell is a professional fantasy writer with three published novels and a number of short stories. She knits, does stained glass, teaches Wisconsin Gothic at University of Winsconsin Oshkosh, and chases four cats around the house.

Section Five WorkHorses

Dress-up Donkeys

Donna Jackson

After my sister and I left home and my father died, The Family expected my mother to sell the house and move into a small flat and be no trouble.

Instead my mother sold the family home and went for a drive and saw a house with two paddocks. She bought it without looking in the house. She had decided to collect, train and breed donkeys. Her plan was the donkeys could pull someone, in a bunny suit, in a small cart at Easter. At Christmas, Santa could appear in the same cart but with different decorations. She would drive the cart. She found out later that there were also many requests for donkeys at Christmas to walk down the aisle in churches with Mary and Joseph.

It was difficult, she said. 'Everyone's dad, who has an inflated ego (because he's got to play Joseph), thinks he can handle a donkey in a church. The donkey is carrying his daughter who is playing Mary (usually a non-rider) and she is wrapped in a sheet, riding side-saddle. There is smoke and music and people waving palms. They all jump up and brand donkeys as stubborn and badly behaved if they so much as sneeze in this situation... I tell them you can have the donkey in the church with your wobbly Mary and pushy Joseph but you will need me to lead the donkey and handle it going down the aisle. So we have Mary, Joseph and me, the mystery Arab, entering Bethlehem. I also appear as an Arab with Santa and the Easter bunny and no one has asked me why, as yet. I have a rabbit suit in the pipeline but I draw the line at dressing as a bearded elf.

'Back in the 1920s and 1930s no one would dare laugh at donkeys. Donkeys were famous for helping sick men during Gallipolli. That's the Big War. Donkeys carried sick blokes, while bullets flew overhead, left, right and centre. Did they get a medal? Did they get a statue? Nothing! We hear all about the horses, on and on about the horses in World War One. Let that be a lesson to you if you ever decide to jump in a burning building and save someone.

Just think of the donkeys and call the Fire Brigade. They get paid to be helpful.'

My mother became the President of the State Donkey Society after a very short period of time. The women in our family often know how things should be done and we like to help other people organise themselves.

She was unfairly demoted from this position after only eighteen months due to what was referred to by Beryl Anderson, (replacing President, small Jack with bad feet and a sway back called Pharlap who my mother calls Dogmeat), as The Incident at the Donkey Gymkhana.

The Donkey Gymkhana involves a series of events, including obstacles for the donkeys to manoeuvre in and out of with their little carts. In another event, donkeys parade in a circle without carts and are judged on temperament and beauty and behaviour. Ribbons are presented.

As part of her Presidency, Mum introduced The Donkey Fashion Parade at the conclusion of the Gymkhana. It very quickly became the most popular event the Donkey Society had ever had. Mum drove all around the state with her friend Kate, who is a retired dressmaker and they helped people design costumes in the build-up to the Gymkhana.

This was a good outlet for her. (My sister and I have refused to wear costumes developed by her since we hit High School.) She sewed a cat suit, which she encouraged me to wear daily for several months until I developed heat rash. The rash became infected. The skin specialist told Mum she was not to dress me in the woollen cat suit until the rash was totally gone. I have not been back in the cat suit because, even years afterwards, the heat rash has never quite cleared up.

Prior to the Big Donkey Gymkhana a break-through in animal costume design came to Mum in a vision. It came while she was doing the dishes, wearing pink rubber gloves. She attached rubber gloves to either end of a broom handle and put a shirt on the broom handle. Mum then secured the gloves and broom across the donkey's back. The two forelegs of the donkey had pants slipped over them.

This new design enables donkeys to appear as a quite convincing replica of a person from the front as you see the forelegs in costume and the outstretched arms with two rubber hands. The head of the donkey can have a hat or wig added to hide the large ears. After this breakthrough in donkey costuming there was some excitement as people prepared their donkeys to come to the parade not as things but as people such as Humphrey Bogart and Cher.

Part of Mum's push for presidency had been her skills in publicity and her election platform had been largely based on her claimed ability to re-profile donkeys in a positive light in the media. She had a track record due to the success of one of her very photogenic donkeys. Pollyanna had appeared with celebrities such as Santa and the Easter Bunny in the mainstream media several times. She sent out media releases across the country and attracted a considerable press contingent to the Donkey Gymkhana.

My mother who had been so helpful in terms of other donkeys' outfits had kept her own entry in the event top secret. This was the subject of much speculation among the other entrants. She wouldn't even show my sister and I what she was up to in the spare horsestall at her house. The stall had a new padlock on the door when I went to have a peek. We had to wait with the other entrants at the side of the oval to get a look at her entry.

The other hopefuls included a small boy of seven or eight years called Charlie who had dressed his donkey as an elephant. This involved a grey, pool-cleaning pipe attached to the donkey's nose and a complete grey body suit his mother had stitched for the donkey, made out of pairs of cut-up, grey, ladies' pantyhose. It turned out the kid's father sells in hosiery. This outfit could win. There was a donkey that had been spray-painted bright green. (It was supposed to be a grasshopper but it just looked like a big green donkey with green cardboard wings on its saddle. Pathetic! No competition for Mum there.)

The other entrants included Elvis the donkey, and a donkey dressed as a hot dog. (Lots of red balloons with helium tied in a line along the back of the donkey and two very long cushions as rolls either side of the donkey's back. The donkeys were very well behaved and seemed to be enjoying the attention and adulation. The Cher donkey's owners had put their donkey (whose real name is Bob), on a diet as he had got loose in the top paddock and whacked on a lot of weight just prior to the competition and had difficulty getting into his G-string. Cher/Bob was looking a bit desperate and hungry in his green-sequinned thong.

Just before the parade started, Mum appeared out of her large horse-float wearing a dressing gown and leading Jasper, who had a silver bucket over his head with eyeholes. He had broom-handle arms and rubber gloves, all of which were sprayed silver, as was his suit made out of cardboard. She nodded at the other competitors passed the reins to my sister and disappeared back into the float.

Mum reappeared with Dinky, who had a broom handle across her back with hands and a straw hat with straw poking out of it and a checked shirt and old pants full of straw.

Finally Mum appeared with Pollyanna in a very fluffy orange bath mat around her neck and whiskers— Pollyanna had been spray-painted all over orange.

My mother whipped off her dressing gown and, underneath, she had a red-and-white-checked short dress. She whacked on a wig she had handcrafted out of straw.

It was easily recognisable: Mum was Dorothy, and the three donkeys were Lion, Scarecrow and Tinman from the Wizard of Oz. They were a team. One huge entry and they were a dead-set cert to win.

There were three independent judges who had been brought in for the Donkey Gymkhana. They usually judge horse gymkhanas. The rumour was the lady with the long ponytail was seen to smirk occasionally at the donkeys during the judging last year. As a result, members of the Donkey Association Executive took it upon themselves to surreptitiously watch her this year for any sign of mocking-type behaviour.

The donkeys and owners paraded in a circle around the judges. All the donkeys seemed very proud and presented well except Cher/Bob who appeared distracted and edgy, looking for food.

'First prize in the Donkey Gymkhana!

Dorothy and the Tinman, Scarecrow and Lion!

Second prize the Hot Dog Donkey!

Third prize Cher!'

Things only started to go wrong during the presentation ceremony. The donkeys and owners lined up to get their ribbons with first place in the centre and second and third either side. The press moved forward and all the donkeys stood very still as flashes went off and the television crew took a close-up, prodding around the donkeys' heads for a shot for the end of the news after the weather.

Unfortunately Cher/Bob chose this moment to lean over and snatch some straw out of the Scarecrow's straw-stuffed hat. The little boy with the elephant donkey was then dragged into the winner's circle by his donkey who also wanted some straw. Mum tried unsuccessfully to push off the Hot Dog Donkey who made a lurch for her straw wig.

By the time my sister and I jumped the fence and headed to the presentation arena, the area was in chaos. The film crews were dashing in and out of donkeys, and shouting and filming and flashing and waving their arms about, which is why the alarmed Grasshopper donkey began pig-rooting, kicking other donkeys and hopping about.

Unfortunately I was involved in the sequence, which featured in the main bulletin on the news that evening. I was filmed holding half my mother's straw wig with wild costumed donkeys all around me. Little Charlie who had been holding the Elephant donkey came to hide behind me. The film grab then shows Cher/Bob the donkey lurch towards the remainder of the wig as the boy peeps out. The little boy is then bitten viciously and graphically on the face.

Little Charlie was taken away in an ambulance.

Mum made an outfit for Charlie for when he came out of hospital from the skin grafts. It was a donkey costume.

The media has been banned from any future Donkey Gymkhanas.

Donna Jackson: I was born a short legged, strong little girl who walked like a wharfie. I was born optimistic. I don't know why. At sixteen I met my birth mother. This is one of the stories she told me as I remember it.

Bareback Rider

Amanda Owen

The knocking came loudly into my dreams, accompanied by the gruff, irritated voice of Mike Zorrelli shouting my name from the other side of the caravan door. Snuggling more deeply into my blankets, I covered my head, trying to hide from the inevitable for as long as possible. His knocking grew more urgent as his voice became unbearably persistent. I had to acknowledge my existence in the bed.

'Yes,' I hissed.

'Time to wakey wakey,' he shouted, triumphant at his sadistic awakening.

It was quarter to six in the morning and cold and wet outside—a typical English winter-turning-to-spring morning. I tried to reconcile myself with the fact that in ten minutes, I would be outside mucking out the horses and feeding the animals. Then I would be bedding down the ring.

Sandy, Hazel and I were bareback riders, performing with a traditional travelling circus around Britain. Every day we fed and looked after the animals. All the animals—the horses, the llamas, the performing dogs, pigs, and my favourite, Jack, the donkey. Our routine was this—we fed them at six in the morning, we fed them at lunchtime and we fed them at eleven at night. We mucked them out, groomed them and exercised them. Every day. We helped put the tent up, we put the seating out, we performed in the show. We sold toffee, popcorn and tickets. We trained with them in the morning and at night after the show. After the last punter had gone home or to the warm cosy pub, we were being put through our paces by Mike, ringmaster, owner of the circus, horse trainer.

I love it when people look at me dreamily when I say I was a bareback rider. The audience sees you in your skimpy costume dancing about like a fairy on the horse. On the other side of the canvas is mud and slush to pick through in your ever-so-dainty black slippers with diamante sparkles and sub-zero temperatures to negotiate in fishnet tights. I was not born into it. I thought it would be romantic too. That is why I changed career.

I was originally an acrobat. One day at a master class for acrobats, a tousle-haired man turned up to watch us training. After the session, Mike came up to me and asked if I could ride horses. I had ridden a horse once, when I was seven. It had trodden on my sister's foot when we had got back to the stable.

I had avoided horses ever since. He said that I would be perfect as a bareback rider and that he would like to hire me. I told him I was an acrobat, not a bareback rider.

'I control the horse and you do acrobatics on it. I don't want anyone who thinks they are going to ride the horse. Only one boss here.'

Certainly there was no possibility of anybody other than Mike being the boss. He ran the show. Completely and utterly. There was no arguing with Mike. So I became a bareback rider, and I fell in love with my horse, Shiraz. Except that Sandy thought she had the big horse's heart as well. We settled on sharing him, each of us whispering sweet nothings into his velvety ear, when we thought the other wasn't around. He listened patiently to us both.

The bareback act came in the first part of the show, after the clowns' 'exploding car' act and just before the interval. It ended the first half on a high. Sandy, Hazel and I leapt on and off Shiraz as he cantered around the ring, we collected scarlet and green hankies from the ring's sawdust floor, knelt and then stood on the broad back of this steady steed. Later, we came on with the 'little and big' act—a stallion, Joela, accompanied by Kipper, the bad-mooded Shetland with an inferiority complex. At the end of the show, we were in the 'exotic' act, leading the llamas, Beau and Bandit, and the horses around the ring in a parade. Beau did not like me. I had to guide him onto his pedestal and sometimes, when we were in the ring and I could not escape, he looked me in the eye with a steely gaze, drew his head back and spat at me with all his

might. Once I repaid the favour. This wasn't the only sparky relationship going on.

As the touring show was about to come to the end of its yearly season, I became aware that Hazel had an intimate relationship with not just Shiraz. Sandy sneered, 'She's in Mike's trailer every night. She's allowed off the early morning mucking out and feeding. She doesn't have to do any more grooming. She's on the easy jobs.' Turns out she was on jobs like derusting and oiling the swords of the 'ladder of swords' for the fakir act.

Sandy and I were furious at the extra workload but not as furious as Mike's ex. One night she came back to the circus. Sandy saw her prowling around. The next day Shiraz, Joela and Kipper were not in their stables. Apparently, she had paid for the horses originally and she was claiming them back. Months later we heard she had taken them to her mother's who had a small farm in Cornwall.

Mike's early morning call came as usual, 'Time to wakey wakey.' I replied, waited for him to retreat, got up, dressed, looked in at the empty stable and left on foot. I was a bareback rider with no back to ride on.

Amanda Owen was born in London and moved to Melbourne in 1996. She now has the good fortune to enjoy both cities, working as a performer, musician and teacher. She practices yoga, soprano saxophone, handstands, equanimity and solving cryptic crosswords with varying levels of success.

Cat Friday

Rebecca Gorman

My hurtling body hit the crossbar of the iron gate with the kind of thwacking thud that a sandbag might make if you dropped it onto cement. Cat Friday was a bitch of a horse, but beautiful. Sixteen hands plus, black and Jaguar sleek; a real V8 mare. My driving skills were decidedly four-cylinder.

I had told Pip, the stud master, that I wasn't up to galloping her in a large paddock. At nineteen, having bluffed my way into this stable-hand job, I could barely manage her regular track work drill. We'd trot to the bottom of the track that meandered through a small forest of gum trees. This was a little circular affair and we'd go round it a couple of times, warming up the horses before they galloped up the steep hill track. Once at the top, Cat Friday would simply pull up and the sack of potatoes (me) that had been clinging to her back would sit up and take up the reins as if it knew what it was doing. It was a terrifying daily routine, but I'd come to this job with a chip on my shoulder that needed shifting.

I was a farm girl, who, despite years of burning around paddocks on ponies, could not really ride. Dad had tried, of course. All five of us had been taught the basics on my brother's pony Penny. Penny taught us to grip in the pig-root, duck on the approach to trees and to fall off when she suddenly reversed direction. Then, when everyone else was at boarding school, Penny's foal, Katoot (no idea!) came of age, was broken in and became mine. He was a beautiful ride. You could open gates on him and he'd go from a walk straight into a canter. He made me think I was a rider. That was until Henry came home from school with a need for speed. We have a spectacular photo of Henry atop Katoot, who is rearing high in the air, front legs pawing the sky. Henry's right arm is held aloft like a Musketeer, like Zorro, like a little shit who wrecked my obedient horse. They were the holidays that Katoot learned to gallop. He never changed gear, and I hardly rode him again.

Dad's growing cancer stopped him from riding, and kept him in Sydney for hospital stints in the days before chemotherapy when they just cut the growth out bit by bit. There were no trips to Pony Club where I might have perfected the barrel-race and justified a smart wardrobe of jodhpurs, tailored jacket and felt-covered riding hat. Perhaps my pony-love was as shallow as all that. But attached to a horse you're bigger, you've got power and independence, rather than being the snot rag at the end of the family.

As my father died his slow death and the drugs made his tummy protrude in a Father Christmas kind of way, I imagined black stallions puffing softly at my verandah door, beckoning me for a night flight. But even without the escapism, I can justify through my own breeding, my love of horses. For instance, horses from our farm were sent to fight in World War One. There's an apocryphal story about one of them escaping from the shipping yards in Melbourne, and making his way home. And Grandpa Ted had a racehorse, Riverina Lad, that won a Wagga Wagga Picnic Cup. Another one of my photos shows the two of them, proudly cheek to cheek, as if they are both gentlemen of some standing. Henry framed it for me one Christmas. And Dad had a string of horse stories that embedded the bug. He was a man who took enormous care in the small tasks of life, like bathing his littlest and waiting patiently as I learned to sit on the toilet. 'Take it easy little Bec, don't strain, just let it come,' and we'd chat until it did. The story I begged for most was the one in which he and his brothers would strip off, toss the saddles to the ground, and ride their horses through the dam after a hot summer's day of stock work.

So here I was now on a stud in southern Western Australia, attempting to live out my dream, but knowing I wasn't up to the task. Perhaps Pip knew I was there under false pretences. Perhaps every girl lies about her experience in order to get her first horse job. Perhaps he thought I'd rise to the occasion and make that first triumphant inroad into conquering the fear of a charged thoroughbred. But I had no illusions. We trotted down the road and into the paddock. As we turned in, I again said to Pip that I didn't think I could hold her. 'Yes, you can,' he said. It was all very well for him—he could ride. He knew then what I know now: that to handle a Cat Friday you needed your confidence on display. You needed to lock in your arms and swing back on your heels so that she'd feel so beautifully directed that she'd just wait for the instructions to come from head office.

But Cat Friday knew the boss was out to lunch so she may as well go home. She cantered eagerly down the paddock and then, once we'd turned for home, galloped straight at the exit. For those long terrifying seconds as we pounded towards the gate, I wondered whether I might manage to stay on as she took the hairpin turn onto the gravel road that led back to the stables. But I may have needed more than a racing saddle to achieve that, maybe a fighter pilot's ejector seat with a three point harness. Instead, I flew through the air and hit the cross bar of that wide, silver, iron gate, and slid down it like the Road Runner Coyote. I waited for the wave of pain. When it came I was mildly pleased, given that no pain would have meant no feeling.

Cat Friday ran home and I never rode her again. But I recovered and perservered, and eventually got my amateur jockey's licence. I rode trackwork wherever my radio jobs took me: to Albury, to Brisbane, to Randwick in Sydney and, bizarrely, to Chile. And then I finally came home to Wagga and rode at the picnic races. My Uncle Kerry had disapproved of race riding, telling me the night before that jockeying was no place for a woman. But he was first into the mounting yard when I made third place. And I've got that photo too. I'm in the colours of the horse's owner and trainer John Cocking, Uncle Kerry's arm is clamped around my shoulders and we're both beaming.

Rebecca Gorman *grew up the youngest of five on a farm at Yerong Creek in southern New South Wales. She is a journalist with ABC Radio National's* Life Matters *program, as their workplace specialist, but her idea of a good time involves riding along a deserted beach whilst singing an Irish ditty.*

A One Horse Tale

Sharman Horwood

I have loved horses all my life, but I'm a city girl. Opportunities to go riding have been rare. So uncommon, in fact, I never really learned to ride. On the few chances I had to ride, just getting on a horse and having it move beneath me was exciting enough. But one horseback riding incident at Lake Louise, near Banff in Canada, stands out in my mind.

The horse's name was Kate. I felt completely comfortable with her. She wasn't quite white, more a light grey colour with darker charcoal splotches under her belly. She wasn't young, and she didn't look like she had much energy. In fact, with her head tucked down near the paddock fence, she looked half-asleep. The leader of the trail ride, Andy, looked at her, looked at me, and told me she was the horse for me. He was grinning.

It was a clear fall day, the snow visible on the mountains, Lake Louise choppy with a cold breeze. And there were few tourists about. It was a beautiful day to go riding. We led off at a very slow pace, which suited me. I shifted around on the saddle, and patted Kate's neck. She whuffled back. Or seemed to. I didn't care if I was imagining it or not. I was on a horse. I leaned over and rubbed my hand over Kate's neck once more. She turned her head, leaning into it as best she could while still walking. Poor girl. She must have a dozen different riders in a week, and not many showed their appreciation by the looks of it.

I settled into the saddle and prepared to enjoy the ride, slow and uneventful. Just me and the horse and the peaceful Rocky Mountains. A jay chattered at us from a tree as we rode beneath it. Peace and quiet, nature at its best.

'There was a grizzly sighting near here yesterday,' Andy announced. I was startled. 'How near? Like around the lake?' He smiled. 'No. No, it was higher up, next to the pasture where we keep the horses overnight.' At Lake Louise, there was only room for the stables. Land to use for anything other than tourists was limited. 'Anyway,' he continued, 'no bear will come down this far with people around.' That wasn't exactly true. Bear maulings happened every year, usually near campgrounds, though, not at Lake Louise.

Andy was smiling again, a superior satisfied smile now that he'd made me uncomfortable, and himself seem more like a man. I reached over and patted Kate's neck. 'No bear will come near us, girl,' I told her. She whuffled again. 'Hey, she talks!' I announced.

If anything, his grin spread. 'Only to those who talk to her,' he joked. He kicked his heels into his horse's sides. It took off at a brisk trot. Kate promptly followed, her hooves prancing on the rough trail. I bopped up and down, feet jerked out of the stirrups. Pulling on the reins, I somehow grabbed the saddlehorn to keep from falling off.

Kate stopped dead. She didn't walk again until I had control of my seat. Andy looked back over his shoulder, laughing outright. 'A little green, are you?' But I was a paying customer so he took pity on me. He rode on at a more cautious pace.

Frankly, I wasn't ashamed of being a little green. I didn't need to gallop around the beautiful lake to enjoy the ride. It didn't need to be a brisk gallop to be an adventure for me. I was quite happy plodding slowly along. I was on a horse, a nice horse. I leaned over Kate's neck to tell her what a good girl she was. She rolled her shoulder, enjoying the attention. We'd reached a long, fairly level stretch of the trail. The lake glittered in the sunlight, the breeze across the water brisk and cold.

'Giddyup!' Andy's horse broke into a quick canter. Kate immediately lurched ahead to follow. I grabbed at the

saddlehorn again, my knees clinging tightly before I slid off. Kate stopped again. She refused to run. Andy looked over his shoulder and reined in. 'That's odd. She usually likes to gallop along here. She even pushes ahead of the slower horses.' He'd intended a race he knew I couldn't win; he was feeling a little cheated out of his fun. 'Pull over and go ahead of us.' But every time we tried, Kate refused to lead. By now I had the distinct impression she was taking care of her rider. In fact, when we turned for home at the far end of the lake, she refused to trot back. She stayed in the rear, sedately looking after her rider all the way to the stables. I came back the next day. She deserved every carrot and pat I brought her.

Sharman Horwood is a science fiction/fantasy writer who teaches English as a Second Language in Seoul, South Korea. Her first published short story is in Catfantastic IV, *and she has written a textbook published in Korea for ESL, titled* North American Discussions of Today. *In between writing two novels, one of which is a sequel to an Andre Norton novel, she has also collaborated on an alternate history novel,* Queen Of Iron Years, *with New Zealand writer, Lyn McConchie.*

Joyce Pilkington and Kurumba Cassidy
Mary K. Hughes

Joyce Pilkington and her Arabian horse Cassidy, are from St Arnaud in Victoria. As a team they have been on the Victorian endurance riding scene for many years. Now that Joyce is in her seventies and Cassidy, at twenty-three years old, has outlived many of his equine mates, they are still planning the long distance rides they will attempt in the year ahead.

Joyce remembers most of the facts about Karumba Cassidy. Where there are gaps, her husband, Bob, chimes in from the background.

'When I first saw him, in 1986, Cassidy was a six-year-old pure Arabian gelding. Another female endurance rider brought him to my attention. She said that he did not have enough spice for her... that he was too quiet and, while bred for endurance, was more likely to become a Pony Club horse. This suited me as I particularly needed not to have to fight an excited horse at the beginning of rides. Cassidy was a leggy and relatively quiet type.'

After Joyce rode him once or twice she made up her mind, paid the deposit and organised for him to be floated home—he was hers.

Now, at the beginning of 2004 and heading for his twenty-fourth year on earth, Cassie, Joyce's long term endurance horse, is a real Australian legend. Just like Joyce herself. At the start of the year Cassie had completed 15,800 competitive kilometres. Bob reckons that the two would have done at least an extra thousand kilometres per year in training on top of the competition.

'...Cassidy used to shy when I got him and he has bucked a few times, but oh yeah, I love him... I'd be a bit silly if I didn't, wouldn't I?' says Joyce. But when asked to compare her relationship with Cassie with her forty-nine year marriage with Bob she just cannot, '... I dunno... not easy to compare them,' she chuckles with a hint of embarrassment.

But what about how it all started? How did Joyce get into horses in such a life-long fashion?

'... I was three years old when I had my first horse... we kids all used to ride her... I had to learn so that I could ride to school, which was about six or seven miles from home. I had white hair at the time and it is white now...' Bob chided her, 'It's grey.'

'... I have had seventeen horses all told and Cassidy is one of the two outstanding ones. The other is dead now, Hall's Viraq, who was also a great endurance horse.

'Cassie watches out for me when I am around and even if he cannot see me he can sense when I am coming back, he calls out... especially for his tucker. What has made Cassie such an outstanding horse? Well, it has to be his feet. They're all white but they are tough. No problems shoeing him and the farriers love him.'

Joyce and Cassidy train in the country around St Arnaud, central Victoria, where Joyce and Bob have lived since 1978. Joyce's profession was nursing and riding was, and still is, her passion. In fact, endurance riding and the lifestyle which comes with it has been the focus of their lives for twenty-plus years.

Cassidy has five times completed the Tom Quilty Gold Cup One Hundred Miler, Australia's premier and coveted annual endurance riding event. Together with Joyce, as a pair, they also completed one of the toughest rides—the four-hundred-kilometre Shahzada marathon, in the challenging sandstone ranges around the Hawkesbury River region in New South Wales.

Over the years Cassidy has won many national awards and so has Joyce—lightweight distance horse and light weight distance rider.

But it has not all been easy or without complications. Despite Cassidy's stunning record of 110 successful rides without a vet out, Joyce was herself 'vetted out' after the Victorian State Championships in 1998. After the ride, another one hundred miler, she collapsed, and was taken to hospital in an ambulance. She subsequently had a pacemaker inserted. 'I want to see you come in next time on your horse, not in an ambulance...' she recalls the cardiologist saying again and again when she returns for regular check-ups of the heart device.

Joyce is proud of Cassidy. Bob is proud of Joyce. Fellow endurance riders are proud of this pair and their absolute capacity to keep going, even in conditions that others may shun. 'I have never come off him. I have always ridden in a stock saddle and he is always reliable... not until I got to know him, all those years ago, did I like him. Cassidy has grown on me, even though he is not really an affectionate horse...'

Whatever the bond, it is an extraordinary one. Both Joyce and Cassidy are breaking records, as much now for their mature years, as for the successful distances they have achieved together. Once it was only Cassidy but now they're both grey.

And they are, by any measure, rather special characters.

Mary Hughes *has been actively involved with horses since early childhood. Her passion for endurance riding and for promoting this family and age friendly sport keeps her extra-curricular hours very full. Apart from participating regularly herself, Mary is the Membership Registrar for the Victorian Endurance Riders Association and an occasional freelance contributor of horse articles for various publications.* ♘

How Many Times Do You Have To Fall?   Susan Hawthorne

I think I rode a horse before I could walk. I say this because horses were a daily part of my young life. My mother was known for her horsewomanship and reputedly rode thirty miles a day. This surprises me more now than it did then. That's a long way to ride on a daily basis. It puts her in the same league as bushrangers like Captain Starlight.

The horse. The dark horse. The white horses of the sea. Light horses. The pony. Black beauties. Silver brumbies. Mares of the night. Rustled horses. Work horses.

The smell of a saddle, the feel of leather, the way your nose fills with the combined smell of horse and leather as you pull as hard as you can on the surcingle. Indeed, the whole language of horseriding is its own kind of world.

My father too rode extremely well. I watched him often enough as he sat astride a vexatious horse. When war came in 1939, he at first joined the Light Horse Brigade. But he soon realised that the era of horses was on its way out and he threw in his lot with the Air Force instead.

As I grew up with the scent of horses, sheep, cattle, poultry, pigs and dogs in my nostrils each of them kindles in me a kind of nostalgia, for now so many of our lives are lived without this daily interspecies interaction. But for my dog, I would be entirely bereft of animal companionship. It has its consequences, of course. That anguished sense of loss when an animal you've treasured dies, is not replicated in any other experience.

The horse. The hobby horse. The circus horse. The merry-go-round horse. The flying horse. The race horse.

One day when I was about nine, I travelled with my father and brother to pick up Lord Bambi, a racehorse my parents had bought. We sat up in the front of the truck, high above the world. The gates, which had been constructed around the open tray of the truck, seemed to sing as we rattled our way along the dry dusty roads.

The horse was truly majestic. His coat shone burnished black. In a certain light you could see the deep reds in the coat. On the way home we sang It's a Long Way to Tipperary and The Road to Gundagai, triumphant in our acquisition of this beautiful horse.

A loud banging interrupted our song. Hooves clattered against the roof of the truck. And then silence.

My father pulled the truck over to the side of the road and, as he clambered out, insisted we stay right where we were. I peered through the narrow window of the back of the truck to see Lord Bambi lying beside the road. His coat still glinting in the late afternoon sunlight. His eyes wild with fear.

My father returned to the truck. He pulled out the rifle from behind the driver's seat. My brother and I sat quietly, assiduously looking forward. We heard the shot ring out and my father climbed back into the truck. Even the truck seemed weighed down with sadness. The trip home crawled and I was hoping that we would never arrive. Perhaps we could inhabit some nether world where we'd never need to tell my mother and my sister that the horse they were so looking forward to fondling, to grooming, to whispering to, to riding was never going to arrive.

Somehow we survived this tragedy, and we went on to get delivery of the chestnut Jet, another racehorse whom we backed at the Ardlethan Picnic Races, but who always came last. We imagined how our lives would have been different if Lord Bambi had been racing.

The horse. The rearing horse. The bucking horse. The rocking horse.
The pig-rooting horse. The galloping horse. The dead horse. The bareback
rider and horse.

I galloped into adolescence on horses who allowed me to imagine another world. A world without saddle or bridle. Between the gallops were the falls, and with each fall I counted my way towards the objective my mother had set. She said, 'You can't say you can ride a horse if you haven't fallen off at least 276 times.' I was on my way to becoming the horsewoman my mother had been.

Susan Hawthorne *grew up on a farm near Ardlethan*
in New South Wales. She has lived in Melbourne for
the last thirty years and works as a publisher,
academic and writer and in her spare time indulges
in her passion for aerials. She is the author of
Wild Politics *and* The Falling Woman.

The Vet Check

Linda Dicmanis

'**Come on, Henry.** There's only five minutes left!' I waved the timecard at my strapper. I didn't want to be eliminated from the competition because I'd missed the deadline for the final vet check. 'Stop panicking,' he replied, grey eyes glinting from his sun-browned face. 'Just trot Hobbs out once more so I can make sure he's okay.' I yanked on the lead rope. Hobbs pulled his head out of his feed bin and flattened his ears. He shuffled into a limping trot. I couldn't believe it. After almost fifty hours in the saddle, clambering up goat trails, falling into wombat holes, sliding into rivers, here we were, with the final obstacle standing between us and the title of Endurance Horse. And Hobbs was lame. I felt as though I'd been kicked in the guts.

Hobbs strained at the lead rope, angling for the only blade of grass he hadn't vacuumed into his mouth in the last five days. Passing a vet check wasn't a matter of do or die to him, but getting to that bit of green certainly was. Henry swore and rushed to Hobbs' side, running gnarled hands over his back, then down his legs. Bile rose in my throat. 'I think I'm going to be sick.' Henry pushed back his Akubra and his gaze fell to Hobb's soup-plate hooves. He bent over, picked one up, and swore again. 'Get me a knife!'

I grabbed a pocket-knife and handed it to him. Henry jabbed it into a lump of clay wedged beneath Hobbs' hoof pads and pried it loose. 'Trot him again!' I pulled on the lead rope, hands shaking. Hobbs trotted after me, his steps even. He was all right. 'Go!' shouted Henry.

I took off with Hobbs to the vet arena as if the hounds of hell nipped at our heels. My fingernails dug into my hands. The slightest unevenness or laggardly trot and he would fail the vet check. And Hobbs never trotted when he could stroll. Henry arrived as the vet did the routine checks. He slid something into my hand. I looked down and almost swooned with relief. A pocket-sized spray can. Our secret weapon against a horse that infinitely preferred eating to moving.

The vet turned to me. 'Hand it over.' Relief turned to despair. 'But I need it,' I cried. 'He won't move without it.' 'Yes he will,' replied the vet, confiscating the can. Easily said for someone with no stake in the outcome. Especially someone who didn't know just how important that spray can was. Hobbs hated the hissing noise spray cans made. Nothing could make his eyes ring white with fear faster, or produce a high-stepping trot an olympic dressage rider would kill for.

I stared at the three flame-orange witches' hats. This was it. The final test of fitness of the four hundred kilometre Shahzada, the toughest endurance ride in the world.

The peanut gallery laughed, waiting with macabre glee for Hobbs to fail. To them he was a cart horse with flat feet, legs like tree trunks, and rump the size of a barn. He was a 'wannabe', an outcast, not fit to share the trails with sleek, wiry Arabs with high-falutin' pedigrees. They never saw what I saw: a glorious white horse with a mane and tail that glittered in the sunlight. Nor did they share the trails through hail and sleet or see the moon rainbow from his back in the middle of the night. All they wanted to see was Hobbs fail the final trot-out. And the vet had taken away my spray can.

I lined Hobbs up and stared at the first cone, like a one hundred-metre sprinter focussing on that narrow corridor between two painted lines. Come on Hobbs, you can do it. I drew a deep breath. Seconds ticked by. Then inspiration dawned. I turned to Hobbs, clenched my front teeth together, and hissed. Hobbs threw up his head as though a tiger snake had bitten him, and ran. Hauling on the lead rope, he surged past the peanut gallery. I ran beside him, trying to keep him on the track. It had to be the longest trot out in history. One cone and turn. Second cone. Keep trotting Hobbs. Don't bob. Don't stop. There's the final cone. Turn. I ran back towards the vet and he lifted his thumb up! I stopped dead. We had done it, Hobbs and I. We had shown them. Hobbs had won. He had earned the title, Endurance Horse.

I threw my arms around him and burst into tears. Hobbs just stood there, curved ears twitching, a bored expression on his face. He pulled the lead rope from my hand and strode off in search of the next tussock of grass.

Linda Dicmanis *was born in Adelaide, South Australia, directly opposite Victoria Park Racecourse, so had no choice other than to be horse-mad from birth. She has written a fantasy novel about a unicorn, that won the Blue Fringe Arts Festival Literature Award in 2003. Linda competes on her two horses, Hobbs and BJ, in eventing, dressage, show-jumping, and endurance. She is currently learning the art of sidesaddle. In her spare time she paints and draws horses. She lives in the Blue Mountains, west of Sydney.*

Lorna's Story

Lorna Oldaker and Maralann Damiano

We had horses all our life. When Dad was alive, we had a buggy. It was a big buggy that had two seats, one facing forwards and one facing back. It had a hood over the top of it and there were steps on each side which came up in between the two seats. We sat in the front seat, with our backs to the horse. Her name was Fanny.

We would go over to the cemetery and we would put some apples between the two seats to eat on the way. We used to go from Cambrian Hill to Addington on Christmas Day, about thirty kilometres, and back again at night time. I don't know how long it took because I was only a kid then.

Fanny fell into the creek one day. They got her out but she was in the water far too long and died.

After Dad died in 1922, when I was nine, it was up to Mum and us older girls to take care of things. We got a Prince William cart, a two-wheeler; the seat was in front, and there was a board across the back. We used to sit on this with our backs to Mum. It was a good cart, a lovely cart.

Mum would get Nell, the new bay horse ready, and put her in the cart. We'd then go the five miles to Ballarat. When we were older we could do it too; my sister Jess used to ride the horse but I didn't ride the horse 'cos I hated them.

We used to go out in the cart to collect wood which people gave us. We also scythed hay for feed and put it in bags and threw them over the horse's back and took them back to the cowshed.

Mum used to drive into Ballarat of a Friday with her eggs and her butter to sell. Sometimes she would leave Nell at Norton's the grocers, and go in by tram. When we had to catch the tram, Mum would drive us in and, when we came to a certain hill, if Nell saw that tram there, she would go like hell.

Mum also took us to church in the cart, although sometimes we'd walk. At show time, Mum would take us to the showgrounds which, at that time, were on the lake.

In those days, that's how we got around. Usually Mum would get the horse up from the stables in the paddock and yoke her up.

One day my brother Norm went down to get Nell. She must have been asleep because, when he touched her on the rump, she kicked and broke his jaw. She was usually a quiet horse, but he must have surprised her.

I used to go down to the Sobey's to look after the children. One time Mum came to take me home. She left the horse and cart at the gate with the brake buckles on the wheels. All of a sudden there was a noise and Mum said, 'That sounds like my cart going. Someone must have came along and frightened Nell.' She went all the way from Sobey's to our place with the wheels locked. The Sobey's followed in their cart. But Mum was not going to be bossed around by a horse. She made her go all the way back to the Sobey's and then go all the way home again.

We sold the Cambrian Hill farm when I was about twenty-one and came to Ballarat. I couldn't tell you what happened to Nell. We left the cart at Dowlings but it disappeared. We never got any money for it.

Lorna Oldaker lived on farms most of her life. She grew up on a small farm. When married she moved to a poultry farm and later to a mixed farm with wheat, oats, sheep and milking cows. She was always very involved in the community. Although now limited with her movement, she keeps busy with craft, Scrabble, jigsaws, her children and their families.

*Her middle child, **Maralann Damiano**, has a background in community work and has been office manager at Spinifex Press for the last seven years. She lives with her partner Sharyn and has two daughters and five grandchildren.*

Can You Feel It?

Alayne Renee Blickle

'Can you feel it?' Inger called to me from across the show grounds' warm-up arena. I looked over at the smiling face of my coach. A sea of riders separated us, riders who were also warming up their horses in preparation for their turn in the show arena. 'You're in the groove now, Alayne. You. And Pepper.' She grinned and gave me a double thumbs up. 'You guys are getting it!' I smiled back gratefully and reached down to pat my little bay mare.

It was an hour before midnight on a drizzly June night and in a few minutes it was to be my turn in the big indoor arena to ride and 'do my stuff'. Pepper and I would be performing reining pattern nine in the Non-pro Reining Classic. This was the big night for the show and I was riding with all the big shots from my region, my friends as well as role models. In fact, I was to go one horse after the highest scoring run of the night, a tough act to follow for one little Pepper, who only learned to rein and slide about six months ago, as well as for her rider. After years and years of working at this I was finally looking forward to my first full season of competing.

Across the show grounds, in the dark rain, my trainer walked with Pepper and me to the show arena. As we arrived, the wind picked up and started to blow. Pepper and I stood at the entry gate, gazing into the big indoor arena, bright lights dazzling our eyes. My heart pounded as the crowd cheered for the rider before me as she ended her ride. I looked around. Could I really be the next one to go in that big arena all by myself? Am I ready for this? Is my horse ready? For eight years I had been working towards this moment—riding, riding, riding.

Finding the right horse is something like trying to find the right dance partner. Years of lessons, studying the rules of reining, working out, training hard. But I had a new coach this year and things were different now. Things were fun and somehow it didn't seem such a struggle to do well. Standing at the entrance gate I had on my new black chaps, designed just for me, and my new hat, the kind that won't come off when you're riding at mach five, which I planned to be doing in just a few minutes. Pepper's saddlepad matched my fancy emerald-green silk shirt. I reached up to my neck and felt the amethyst necklace; another reminder of the support I had, this from my cousin living five states away. Pepper and I had been practising, practising hard all winter. Working with Inger, learning and learning. Pepper and I both wanted to do this thing called reining and do it well. Silently I rehearsed my pattern in my mind, how Pepper and I would ride each portion, stride for stride. Am I ready for this? Is Pepper the right partner? Is she ready? I worked to focus my concentration as I felt my heart pounding.

It was my turn now. All eyes turned towards us as Inger, Matt and my good friend Sheri wished us luck. From a far-off place, I heard the announcer call out my name, '... next in the arena, Alayne Blickle riding Chili Pepper Chex.' My dance partner and I stepped one step into the arena and the gatekeeper closed the gate behind us. I cued Pepper to take the left lead. Immediately and obediently she responded, loping straight down the arena to the far end, building speed as I asked her, stride for stride. Inger was right. I could feel it; Pepper and I were ready. And it felt great.

Alayne Renee Blickle, a life-long equestrian, is passionate about horses—as well as the environment. She and her husband live outside of Seattle, Washington (USA) where they raise AQHA horses on their ten-acre farm and compete in reining events. Alayne is the creator and director of Horses for Clean Water, a program that teaches environmentally-sensitive, horsekeeping education. Alayne speaks and does presentations across the country and is a contributing writer for national as well as regional horse publications. Visit HCW the website at www.horsesforcleanwater.com

Joey   Anne Deal

She was a beautiful, part-Arab bay mare, seven years old, full of spirit and barely 13.3 hands-high when I purchased her from a friend who had successfully ridden her in endurance rides. Her name was Marooba Juie Bey but I preferred to call her Joey. When I first rode her, I was quite wary because she seemed temperamental, highly spirited and, at times, difficult to handle, especially if a group of riders was present.

It took me twelve months of gentle, reassuring handling to win her trust and for me to feel confident enough to take her in our first endurance ride together.

Endurance rides are from fifty kilometres upwards where the horse's fitness is as important as the completion time. Before this, we trained intensely for six months in the bush near our small farm. A close bond developed as we learnt to understand each other's personality. When we went on a ride together she liked to take her time for the first five kilometres or so and sometimes she stumbled so much I thought she was either lame or tired. When we headed for home her pace quickened and I had to learn very quickly to stay in the saddle and move to the rhythm of her extended trot. It was then like floating on air. It wasn't until years later that I realised her stumbling was merely an affectation and that she was very sure-footed.

She was always a bit unpredictable and insecure, sometimes shying at the tree we had passed one hundred times before or pig-rooting without warning, I suspect, if she was feeling good. If riding in a group she would prance on the spot until allowed to be in front. Later on she learnt to respect me more as leader and these behaviours became less frequent.

After a number of weeks of training, sometimes for thirty or forty kilometres at a time, Joey became very good at working out my training plan and adapted her pace accordingly, without me giving her any obvious cues. They must have been very obvious to her however, because she would stop when I began to think it was time for me to walk or run beside her. She would break into a trot or canter on flatter country, slow to a walk up hills or rough ground and stop when she felt we both needed a toilet break.

The first endurance ride was a steep learning curve for both of us. I was inexperienced and she was nervous and very excited. She had bonded too well with her floating companion and couldn't bear to be separated, so all night before the ride she ran up and down on her tether neighing loudly. In the morning she was a lather of sweat and I was sure that she would have no energy. I took the fifty kilometres slowly. She surprised me by finishing easily with a very good recovery heart rate.

We went on to do a number of endurance rides, each one becoming a bit longer and more challenging. I became a stronger leader, and floated her alone so she relied on me solely for company. Gradually her insecurity disappeared. She became quietly gentle but was still capable of energetic exuberance to get her through the long rides.

She became so quiet she made a reliable mount for my daughter who was just starting off in Pony Club. At the same time she had the fire and passion to complete an endurance ride.

Joey amazed me several times by her calmness in handling a difficult situation. Once was on a country road on a high, narrow wooden bridge over a river. Joey always hated bridges and often shied at the sides. This time we had just started to walk across when I heard a car travelling very fast, down the hill on the other side. The driver wouldn't see me until he or she was on the bridge because trees and a curve excluded the view. I had no time to get off. I stiffened and hung on tightly. Normally she would react to my fear but, this time, she took it all in her stride and didn't panic. The driver screeched to a halt only

centimetres away and apologised profusely. Joey walked calmly past as if nothing had happened.

Another time, in winter, on an endurance ride in mountainous country, we came to some steep, snow-covered tracks, downhill. Unperturbed Joey skied down on all fours, for several kilometres, with me holding on anxiously. We arrived at the bottom safely, without incident.

She was warm and affectionate and would always greet me with a soft breath on my neck. Sometimes she would leave her nose close to mine for a minute or so, completely relaxed, and I could feel the comforting rhythm of her breathing. I treasured these moments together. She whinnied several times, expecting a titbit. If I had nothing she would walk slowly away, turning her back on me.

It was a difficult time in December 2003 as I was forced to accept that Joey, my close friend and companion for twenty-one years, was near death. Her condition, symptomatic of a brain tumour, was slowly draining her strength and the necessary decision had been made to put her down. With an overwhelming sadness, I held her head gently in my arms and recalled these events and experiences we had shared together.

Anne Deal *has always had a love of horses. She is a teacher and lives in a secluded valley near Castlemaine in central Victoria which she shares with her husband, two dogs, several 'borrowed horses' and numerous families of possums.*

The Black Horse

Jenny Barnes

Of all the horses I worked with, during the few years I worked in a small country racing stable, a horse called On Offer stood out. He was a big strong thoroughbred, near black in colour, similar to the Black Beauty of the old television series and he had a patch of white on a hind heel, just like the champion Kingston Town. When I first started working at the stable, I was told that he may try to stand over me as he had only been gelded a few months earlier, as a late three year old.

I never had any problems handling him but he wouldn't suffer fools and would think of ways of showing up his handlers if he felt they didn't show him enough respect. If you hesitated leading him out of the box, you'd soon have him rushing past then spinning and rearing in front of you (as I did once when ducking a pigeon) but otherwise he was very calm to handle. Goose, as he was known around the

stables (derived I was told from acting 'like a goose' when he was a young colt), would never kick and would only try to bite when his girth was being tightened, usually accompanied by his nearside front hoof aimed for your foot.

He once went to Randwick for a race and, in the middle of winter, it was expected the track would be soft (the way he preferred it), to give him a chance in the race. When we arrived it was hot and sunny with a dry track. He looked to have no hope but tried his heart out, eventually finishing fourth behind a brother to Kingston Town in class record time! The jockey came back and said 'not good enough' but for us it was a fantastic effort for a country horse who preferred the wet conditions and never came close to running a class record on the tracks he usually raced.

Late in his career I was presented with the strapper's prize for the best turned-

out horse for a country cup. He would stand perfectly while being groomed and would be turned-out for each race, with his tail plaited, checkerboard on his rump, hoofs black and coat shiny. He ran well that day but, unfortunately, early in the race, another horse broke down in front of him and he was struck on the knee and the ensuing injury saw the black horse spelled for over six months to recover.

He knees had always been a problem and, with his preference for the wet conditions, preparations were usually centred around the winter racing. This resulted in the horse emerging from his box each day very stiff in the minus-six degree temperatures. After walking (ridden or led), he freed up and would head out for trackwork. To prepare for starting to ride trackwork at some point in the future, the trainer decided that I should ride, instead of lead, On Offer

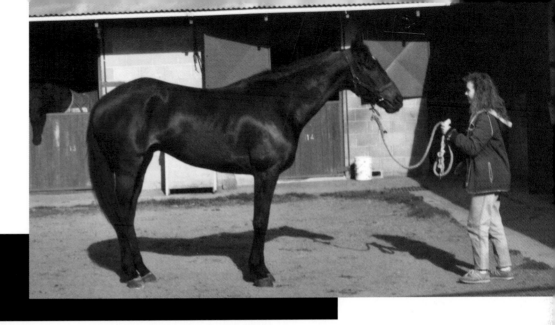

and a few others in the morning, before the regular riders arrived. The first time I was legged on, he took off with head in the air at the trot, until I stopped trying to fight and put hands down near the wither and sat still. After that I never had problems but another track rider insisted on a more severe bit after they continued to fight, the result being that when ridden by that person he always went around with his head too high. I refused to ever put that bridle on him; it wasn't the horse, it was the rider, but being young there was little I could say.

The black horse had a lot of personality traits that made him stand out from the others. Once, when taken outside to the nearby round yard to stretch his legs, was on the toe due to the adjacent Pony Club grounds holding a competition. He seemed to settle and wandered to the far end of the yard before turning and charging straight at me, standing outside as

stud stallions sometimes do in yards with fences far higher than this one. As soon as I stepped back, he turned away and seemed to stand there 'laughing', as if he'd played a horsey practical joke.

Another time, he and another horse were being brought in from a paddock to be floated to the stables. I arrived before the float so headed out and caught him, first putting him in a yard, before collecting the other horse. While I was catching that second horse, the float turned up, and so I was stuck holding the other horse while Goose decided to put one over on the other handlers. This was a horse that knew how to float and would walk on with anyone; well, anyone he didn't dislike. The handler this day happened to be the track rider who insisted on the harsh bit to ride in. He refused to get onto the float; just planted the front feet on the ramp and stopped. Eventually with the help of a passerby, and a rope

around his rump, he finally decided he had enough and walked on. Next, they attempted to load the other horse while I watched, and soon the float started moving and squeaking with the other younger, inexperienced horse refusing to go near the ramp. Wondering what was going on, I opened the float door to find Goose looking at me with that same 'laughing' practical joke look; at the same time he stopped moving, and the float stopped squeaking, and they were finally able to load the second horse.

He got his revenge on another handler he didn't seem to like. The stable had a new strapper and they took it upon themselves to do additional grooming of the horses due to race the upcoming weekend. They took to the tails with scissors, doing an awful job. I arrived on the Saturday morning and just knew there was something wrong with the black horse. I pulled the rugs off to find that his beautiful thick tail had been cut so badly (as he'd had the tail clamped down as they snipped) it resembled that of a broodmare rather than the show-horse look that had been attempted. The next time said strappers gave the horses extra grooming, they were working on a back hoof, positioned under his tail. Knowing full well where they were, he lifted his tail and proceeded to relieve himself and they were in the perfect spot to be covered from the shoulder down. Needless to say, after that, the strapper left any extra grooming of the black horse to me.

Now this brings up another memory: he would never 'go' in front of me. This made swabbing a problem, as the strapper has to witness the collection and sign the sealed bottles as a witness. I'd have to turn and look outside before he'd even think of complying with the swabbing steward and, once, he came and stuck his face right in front of me to block what I could see! He never did this in any situation with the men associated with the racing stable. Perhaps he was trying to be 'macho' as, unlike other horses, he'd also refuse to react if he had a small wound that needed the purple antiseptic spray. Most horses pull the leg away but the black horse would stand there, and I could see it must have been stinging with the way the foot would quiver, but he'd never pull the leg away. He was too macho for that.

On Offer finished racing after stepping in a hole and suffering another knee injury. He wasn't the soundest horse and, apart from the stiff knees in the mornings, he also usually raced in bar shoes due to suspected navicular problems and, after that final race, he just took a couple of odd steps when being led out to the truck. On arriving at the stables he seemed fine but the next day the injury was obvious. Again I knew something was wrong when I got there for the afternoon—he just didn't look right, standing in his box. I was later told he had been badly lame that morning and was diagnosed as probably needing an operation to return to racing. Due to his age, he was instead sent for a spell and, at some stage a few months later, was given to the then-girlfriend of the property owners' son (unbeknown to me until many months later). Years later I found out that she was well known in the showing scene, so can only assume he became a show horse but I could never find out any further details beyond that.

Jenny Barnes grew up in Canberra, in the Australian Capital Territory. She is a photographer specialising in horse racing, equestrian and pets, with photos being published in several national magazines, her website and an internationally published book. Jenny also researches the careers of famous racehorses presenting champion profiles on her website. Jenny lives in Adelaide.

Bay Rose: the Last of the Great Walers

Janne Ellen

I've always hated war. War never made any sense to me even when I was very young and knew little about patriarchies and warrior cultures like ours. I believe my anti-war belief came about because of my love of horses and one horse in particular.

I came from a family where my mother's uncles holed up in a cave with lots of ammunition and were going to shoot anyone that tried to conscript them off to World War One.

On the other hand, my Dad's older brothers were also country boys but enlisted in the Light Horse Brigade. Uncle Stan came back 'loopy'. When I would ask what was wrong with him, I would be hushed-up, with mutterings of how he had had to shoot his horse 'over there'.

Bay Rose was our horse's name and I was very small when we got her, so I don't remember where she came from. I don't have a photo of her because drovers didn't walk around with cameras. She was a big horse and very strong. As befitting her name she was bay with a black mane and tail. All our horses had their colour preceding their names which I guess was a bit peculiar but seemed normal to me.

My father said Bay Rose was one of the last 'Walers'. Every good and bad habit that she exhibited was attributed to her breeding. There was plenty of both. She won all the prizes and money at the local shows and gymkhanas for those working-horse events. No one could beat her. Mum made a full-size horse rug out of her ribbons. People would clap when Dad rode her into the ring. 'That's a Waler,' they would say.

On the road, at feeding times I would measure the chaff and oats into kerosene buckets to be tipped into the horses' nosebags and strapped on to feed. The bags were a hessian number with a halter-type fitting. They came up close to the horse's face so they could eat without spilling the precious feed. Grey Peggy, the old docile draft-horse that pulled the wagon; Black Betty, my little pony (a touch of Timor in that one, my dad said); Bay Mathinna, named after that poem dad loved about a horseman from the Dandenongs; and Bay Rose. 'Don't give any oats to that bloody Waler; she'll walk sideways for two miles,' he'd say. Only my father ever rode her as she did dance sideways for the first two miles.

I was a small and puny kid, but I did have the occasional small ride on her when she was worn out after a day's work. My father kept watch while I tried to hold her. 'Can't wear the buggers out, those Walers.' I felt so proud on that beautiful strong dancing horse.

'That's how come there are none left,' he explained, 'they took them all to that bloody war in the desert because they were the best. None came back.'

Dad told me Walers were a crossbred horse from a light half-draft, a racehorse and a touch of Arab stallion. I wasn't sure if that was just another white Australian rural myth, like most of the stories. Being a drover, Dad's knowledge of the bush was a bit more realistic than most farmers. It took me another forty years before I realised that what passed for information about the Australian bush from white men was mostly wrong. That's what myths are for, to distort reality.

Bay Rose was the hardest horse to catch I have ever known. No training her to come with a call and a bucket of feed. She would watch you coming, halter hidden behind your back.

As soon as you got close she would toss her lovely head, shake her mane, roll her eyes to white, and take off. Arms spread out we would try and herd her into a corner. After much running and mucking about, she would give up and stand and put her head down for me for the halter. I swear that horse laughed at me. Of course, it was because she was a bloody Waler.

Uncle Stan was in the Battle of Beersheba with his Waler that he had taken with him. At Beersheba the 800 Light Brigade horses hadn't drunk water for forty-eight hours. In desert heat, with soldiers fully equipped. Under heavy fire, they ran the charge for five kilometres to secure Beersheba for the British. No wonder poor Uncle Stan was loopy. He still wore his battered slouch hat with the emu plume and wouldn't talk about war. They hadn't told the poor bastards that they couldn't bring their horses back. Mostly they took them out and shot them.

Everywhere we lived, we built a stockyard out of poles with tree limbs for rails. Mostly they were lashed together with twine but sometimes we would find some old nails and carefully straighten them out with a hammer on the chopping block. (It was World War Two!) We had some old tin and made a bit of a shelter for at least one horse to get under in the perishing winters. Bay Rose, being boss of the horses, usually was in the shelter. Unfortunately the feed bin was always attached to the back so that it was nailed through the tin onto the rail. Every feed time, dragging a kerosene tin of feed, I would have to duck under her to get to the bin. She was always very excited and frisky at feed time and invariably would take great delight in pushing me against the back wall. The bloody Waler.

She never bit; she never kicked, even at shoeing time. She rarely ever spooked. Nerves of steel that Waler. My baby sister, at two years old, crawled under her hind legs and was hitting her on the under belly. My mother screamed and screamed, as she had a brother kicked to death by a horse. Dad just called to my sister and she crawled out. Bay Rose didn't move an inch, just turned her head and, with her beautiful brown eyes, looked at the toddler. A good temperament, the Walers.

We moved to Wollongong when I was a teenager so that all us girls could get work. Bay Rose came with us. The only horse to do so.

My father took very ill, our family became fractured and I never found out what happened to her. Last I knew she was on a smallholding of a friend we had made there. I hope she ended her days there.

Research tells me they were considered the best horse in the world. Reared in the New South Wales bush (hence the name Walers), one bloke called Byrne, in 1848, said of them... 'the race of horse at present in use in Australia is not to be surpassed in the world of symmetry and endurance.' They sent five thousand a year to the British to fight the colonial wars. In 1986 the Waler became a registered breed. Their old origins were Arab stallions from India, thoroughbreds from England, mares from Chilli and Peru and light draft horse. A multicultural horse.

My dad would have been pleased to know Bay Rose was not the last of the great Walers.

Janne Ellen was born in 1938, grew up in western New South Wales and moved to Wollongong in her early teens. She became an industrial worker and one of the first women trade union leaders. She became an active feminist from 1960, a founding member of Women's Liberation and has worked extensively in the area of women and violence. Her last job was the co-ordinator of Wollongong Women's Centre. A founding member of Herland Cooperative (Women's Land), where she fell in love with horses again, she now lives in Wauchope and occasionally teaches Women Studies at Adult Education.

Johnny Appleseed and Life on the Road

Zohl dé Ishtar

Laying back into the bale of fresh hay, I studied the huge black hump that swayed casually before me. I reached out and rubbed it with my free foot. My other foot held the rein, hanging loosely across my large toe. I lay back, sighed and watched the clouds playing in the resplendent blue sky. The morning had begun.

It was a morning like many other mornings before it, and many which would follow. No matter what the weather would send me or how much the road changed, there would always be this dependable, luscious black prominence dancing before me. I shut my eyes and dreamt. The chinking of the dangling harness, mingled with the clip, clop of hooves meeting road as Johnny Appleseed plodded along, slowly, gently, and in control. He knew where he was going: straight ahead, along the road. To another town, and another adventure.

Johnny Appleseed was my constant, and best, companion. I had rescued him from a knackery; he had rescued me by opening up the extraordinary possibilities of life lived on the road. We were in this together, but we were not alone. We took with us a menagerie of puppets, who spent their days looking out the back window of Ishtar, our elaborately decorated, horse-drawn circus wagon, waving at cars as their drivers slowed to contemplate the spectacle which meandered languidly before them.

Cars often stopped, and people piled out of them lining the road, cameras and children at the ready to capture, open-mouthed, this unexpected moment of colour and splendor. Sometimes Johnny Appleseed would stop to greet them, seeking an apple or carrot. Or I might jump down to catch snippets of local, national and international gossip which would decipher the lay of the land or become fodder for our upcoming performance. As we drove into the towns, children would stream across school playgrounds yelling, 'The Gypsies! The Gypsies are here!' Shops would empty people into the streets, and they would line the footpaths pointing to the horse, the wagon, the puppets. The circus had arrived in town!

It was Johnny Appleseed who drew the greatest attention. He was so big, so black and so beautiful that he, by himself, personified 'adventure' and 'carnival' in everyone's imagination—mine included. Clearly, it was he who held our troupe together. Without him neither myself, nor the wagon, nor the puppets (who kept on insisting that they had lives of their own) would have been there, manoeuvering our way along the road. It was his gentle patience which made it all possible, so easy.

We'd pull up at the local park, and people would gather. I'd jump down from the driving seat, and the puppets would come alive. They told stories of where we had come from and why, and they invited the children to come and play with them at noon the next day, under the big ghost gum, five miles back down the road. Then we'd turn the wagon around and go back to the tree by the creek that I had picked out earlier and set up camp.

I would unharness Johnny Appleseed and he would relax and graze idly for the afternoon. Before long the locals would arrive. Dressage ladies and girls on high-stepping ponies, boys doing tricks on BMXs, even leather-clad bikies revving their steeds and strutting their stuff. Local farmers would stop by to offer a bale of hay, some fresh vegetables, a set of horse-shoes, or access to a shower. After cooking my lunch, I'd collect firewood for the evening, mend a puppet or a prop, soap the harness, or shoe Johnny's huge Clydesdale feet. The visitors would begin to dwindle as dusk fell, and I'd sit alone stirring the fire and listening to the night begin to stir. It was a good life!

The next morning, when the kids arrived, bringing their friends and their folks, the puppets were waiting for them. They were a motley crew—circus performers and old bushwackers—sitting around the fire, hanging off the wagon, always getting up to mischief, playing pranks on each other. They talked of life on the road, voiced highly dubious opinions on the state of the world, and encouraged the children to be creatively courageous. Johnny Appleseed was an attraction in himself, and he sometimes gave rides to the local children. Involving both wandering nomads and settlers as participants in an extraordinary world, the performance ignited a spark of colourful, expansive possibilities that poured promises into the small expanse under the old gum tree.

A local journalist would arrive, insisting on an interview with a group photograph which the locals could show their kids when they grew up, and the story would spread on to the next town of how Ishtar Pedlar's Touring Children's Circus was heading their way. After another night spent by the creek, Johnny and I would harness up and push on. We weren't going anywhere in particular, just to the next adventure, somewhere along the road.

Zohl dé Ishtar built her gypsy wagon ('Ishtar') at the age of twenty-one and set out in search of a dream—life on the road as a circus performer/puppeteer. Creating a horse-drawn circus, she travelled around the back country of south-eastern Australia in the early 1970s. This was the beginning of a life spent 'on the road'. An adventurer, she (tongue-in-cheek) claims to have inherited the urge from her great, great-grandmother who, known as the 'Black Hawk of Cork', lived in a wagon in Ireland.

Section Six InterBeing

Creatures

Ann Game

All of us have in us
Some of the horse
Vladimir Mayakovsky,
On Being Kind to Horses

The Buddhist monk Thich Nhat Hanh speaks of inter-being, a principle of universal interconnectedness. He says '"to be" is to inter-be. You cannot just be by yourself alone. You have to inter-be with every other thing.'

Horsepeople, then, are people who experience the human form's capacity for horseness, an enlivening spirit connecting humans and horses. They know that horse and human are not separate entities but, rather, live with and through each other, inhabit each other. In this sense the human is comprised of the non-human, we are mixed beings, creatures.

I was in England, about to present a paper on catastrophe, when I heard that my horse had become paralysed. The grooms had found her at breakfast time, on the ground; a healthy young horse, she was unable to move her back legs. For months, KP could barely walk, collapsing and falling, distressed. There was no injury

and exhaustive tests found no cause. Two years later, she can move beautifully, her paces are impressive. But the trace of the paralysis is still there, as a bodily memory. This teaches us about horse-human interdependence. My teacher and I have come to realise that KP's retraining shows, in exaggerated form, what occurs with any horse in training.

During the hospitalisation that followed her collapse, KP was alone in a stable, and very unhappy. I was still away at this time, but KP would say 'take me home' whenever she was visited by Karen, our teacher-trainer. And then when she did go home, she dragged Stuart, another trainer, all the way down to her paddock.

Being with those she knows and trusts not only makes KP happy, it has been the basis of her healing process. She is in some ways more dependent upon people than are other horses in the yard, but she is just as sociable with horses too: her vulnerability makes her generally more social. Because of her disability, we humans have had to learn to listen to her particularly carefully. It has been even more imperative than usual that our horseness be called up in this healing process. KP's dependency has drawn

attention to the mutuality in horse-human relations.

KP has had to re-learn to move. This has been a process of trial and error. Three months after the collapse, I tried lungeing her, assuming that she couldn't yet carry a person on her back. For a few strides, even a circle, she would move with co-ordination, but then, heart-breakingly, she would begin to fall apart. Then, at the suggestion of an acupuncturist, I started sitting on her, walking, to develop her muscles. I was very cautious about possible damage to her legs, and every time they gave way, my body would collapse in identification—a response that retrospectively I consider inappropriate for its lack of support. But KP seemed eager about our rides and so we persisted. When we tentatively tried trotting, at what seemed to be KP's request, improvement was unmistakable. Each time we trotted, co-ordination was better, perhaps only for a few strides, but enough to give hope. KP and I had been doing this alone until Karen one day saw us trotting and insisted that we return to the arena for lessons.

The more we rode, the better KP moved, though we were careful to keep at her pace, taking her cue. But when I asked KP to go up to canter for the first time, she fell apart, no longer knowing how to do it. Karen had to push me to continue, 'Ride as if she were cantering properly.' I was to canter. Although I found this difficult when something else was going on under me—my body wanted to take up this disorder in sympathy—Karen's hunch worked. By maintaining my seat and a relaxed canter as best I could, KP was able to sort herself out, surprisingly quickly. But I had to hold and support her, give her confidence. To help her to remember canter, my body had to take up this movement. The between horse and human movement of canter had to be generated for KP to get in the flow, into the rhythm.

In the light of the experience of KP's regaining movement, I would say that my initial cautious response was not one of true sympathy but of identification. Identification is inappropriate in these circumstances: when I identify with you, your situation becomes mine, and I am then unable to provide the necessary support.

True sympathy involves a fearless capacity for otherness and difference. I had to canter, in sympathy, for KP to

canter. Whenever I followed my immediate impulse and imagined that human interference was not helping matters, it pointed to the obverse, to an attachment to humanness. We are necessarily in a relation; the issue is finding a way to live this creatively. What is called for is a forgetting of human self in a between human and horse way of being. KP taught me this.

Ann Game *lives in Bondi, Sydney. She teaches at the University of New South Wales and is the author and co-author of a number of books, including* The Mystery Of Everyday Life *(with Andrew Metcalfe).*

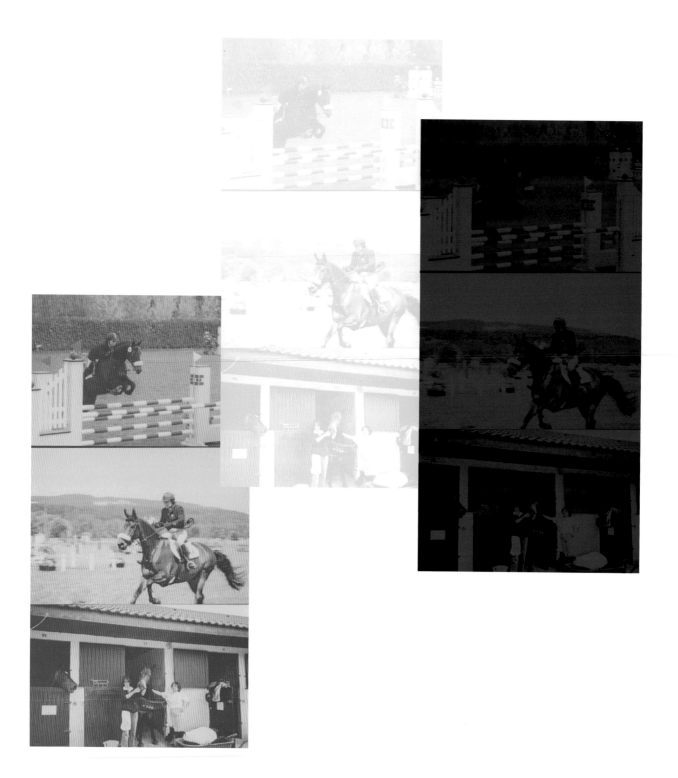

Dreaming of Pegasus, or Quin's Story

Lynda Birke

Hello—my name's Quin. She says I'm the only man in her life, which is true. I've known her about six years. We have a pretty good relationship, if I may say so. It's based on lots of trust—meaning that she has to trust that I'm the one in charge. That sounds sexist but, trust me, it works with her. She does her feminist thing, trying hard to pretend that (sometimes) she controls things, but it really isn't so.

After my food, my next favourite thing is parties, because they give me plenty of opportunity to show off. At parties, I have a different name—The Publisher. Pam, who looks after me, reckons I've published two books: 'A hundred and one ways to annoy your groom' and 'Two hundred ways to trash your lorry' (I'm quite good at that—I get too excited and have made several dents in our travelling house).

I know I sound cocky (I am!), but I'm pretty talented. Apart from rearranging window frames and cornbins in the lorry, I'm also good at spotting hidden dragons. You have to be careful of dragons. They hide behind dressage letters in the arena, behind jump wings, underneath poles, and—especially—underneath the rug thrown over the door. Dragons must be avoided at all costs. I practice my sideways movements to show the dragon what's what, but she always objects. Spoilsport.

My best friend is Polly (short for Polyphonic) who's a bit smaller than me and usually jumps speed classes. She's also good at spotting dragons and being a know-it-all. We have a new friend now, Cassie. Like us, she came from Ireland. She doesn't do dragons so much, but then she doesn't do walking either, much to humans' irritation.

The parties we go to are jumping shows, which I love—jumping is like flying. Sometimes we go on a ferry to Europe. I know these shows are important so I can really show off. These international ones are for Veterans—not me, though—it's her who's getting on in years and qualifies as a Veteran Rider. A few times she wins prizes for the 'leading lady'. What a joke! As though the clear rounds have much to do with her!

And I'm Lynda. I know who's boss in my relationship with Quin. It isn't me. Quin's a bay thoroughbred, 16.2 hands-high, and utterly opinionated. Actually, all three are pretty opinionated, which is what makes them good at their job—jumping. And he is the only man in my life. With his ego, there wouldn't be room. The two girls are 16 hands, but are not the only women in my life: my partner realised long ago she must accept the way our lives revolve around animals. Holidays, day-to-day routines, everything depends upon ensuring our horsey family is looked after.

I've been around horses most of my life. People kept telling my mum I'd soon grow out of galloping around the hills (and get into boyfriends). She's still waiting, on both counts. Even before my first riding lesson, I monopolised the kindergarten rocking horse. Later, it was, and still is, a long love affair. Once you've kissed those soft muzzles, felt the gentle power of a horse's back, or gazed into those liquid brown eyes, there's no going back.

I trained as a scientist, in animal behaviour (no jokes about Quin, please). So, I learned how only humans (or perhaps primates) could do things like deceive or make jokes. Those stories are still told. Scientists believing that have not met my animal friends. Deceit? Meet my dogs deceiving each other to get the best chair. Joke? They didn't meet Laddie, the horse who got fed up with bathtime. I know grey horses always think it hilarious to wait until they've been washed, then seek the biggest pile of poo in which to roll. But one day, he simply grabbed the hosepipe in his teeth, turning it directly onto his human...

To me, Laddie—and several other horses I've known—was a practical joker. And what else is Quin's perpetual search for dragons to spook at? He sees dressage markers every day; and as for things lurking under jump wings... it's funny how they never seem to be there when we approach a jump. Dragon Spotting is Quin's jokey schoolboy routine.

As for claims that horses are less intelligent than us—complete rot. Living with horses convinces me they're pretty clever. We think we're teaching them things—jumping, half-pass, galloping faster—but really we just have to learn some of their language. Dressage or jumping you do together, unlocking something in both of you. I don't teach horses—they teach me.

I sometimes encounter the argument that riding is exploitation, because it involves domination. I worry about that: but then I think, how can a little person like me dominate a large horse? It's impossible (anyway, whoever argued that never met Quin). For me, riding's a choreography, a partnership each of us knows in our bones. I once read an article describing jumping, racing and dressage as fulfilling the dream of Pegasus—being one with the horse and feeling like flying. That's why so many of us love riding. Exploitation, maybe—but the horses seem to enjoy these tasks, too. You simply can't make a horse jump if it doesn't want to.

Flying, dancing—I think of these metaphors in my relationship to horses. What we do, we do together. I barely have to think how to approach fences with Quin or Polly, because we've been together so long. Often, they know before I do, what I'm going to do (not that that's always desirable!).

The pas-de-deux of jumping or dressage movements depends on trust, and learning to communicate in deep, non-verbal ways. Of course, some humans treat horses abysmally but, on the whole, it's pretty hard to build relationships with horses if you do that. Good relationships rest on love. I lost myself in those beautiful brown eyes decades ago, and I'm in love forever with these wonderful creatures. And I think they love me, too.

Of course we do... but please don't tell her too often, or she'll get all sentimental. We're glad she's written how intelligent we are: perhaps she's beginning to understand a bit about us. Humans aren't too bright—but they do (usually) remember to put packets of mints in their pockets, which we appreciate. And at least she knows WHO has to have the last word.

Lynda Birke is a feminist biologist, who has written several books. She has a passion for animals and took early retirement from Warwick University, at least partly to spend more time with horses. In the last couple of years, she has been on the British Veteran Riders' show jumping team (with Quin, of course). She lives in Shropshire with her partner, her partner's son, and various non-human friends.

Horsefeathers

Beth Burrows

Dear Editors,

It has come to our attention that Beth Burrows is alleged to have some affinity for horses. Nonsense!

Burrows was born, promisingly enough, in the Year of the Horse. However, she was thrown from the first horse she was put upon. Further, she never yearned for a pony. Not once. And she never made drawings of horses. Not one. And she was thrown from the second horse she was put upon. Under peer pressure at age ten, she rented a horse. The horse stepped on her foot. When the foot healed, she rented another horse and rode without incident. In the mid-1980s, she was thrown from still another horse. She broke three ribs and didn't laugh for a month. Subsequently, Burrows has made no attempt at a relationship with horses.

We share these salient details with you in the hope that questionable 'horsepersons' like Burrows will find no sympathy between the pages of your undoubtedly brilliant and horse-sensitive book.

Sincerely,

an equine friend

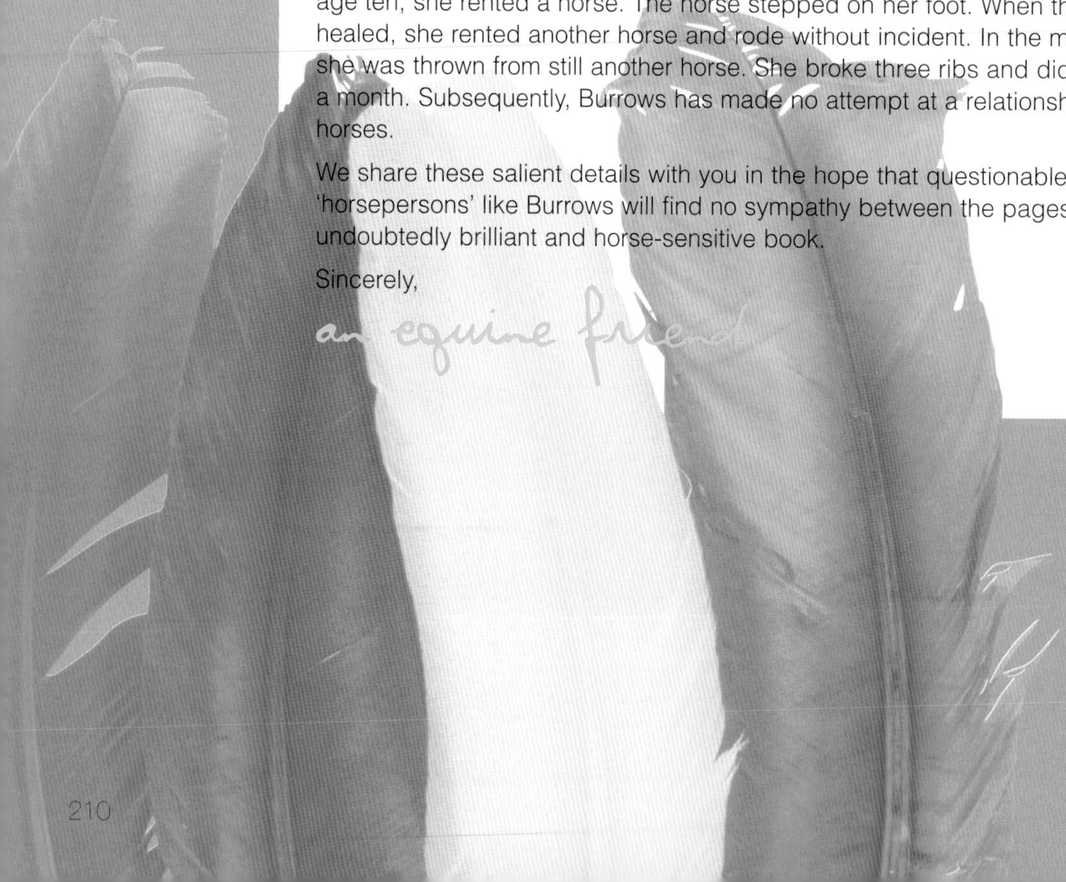

While not a horseperson, **Beth Burrows** does a passable job as president and director of the Edmonds Institute, a small public interest group in the United States. She advocates for biodiversity, social justice, and peace. She is not a bad person, just a person without a horse.

Talent
Elizabeth Campbell

'she's got loads
but she needs to jump
from technique
not scope—being up
is about
relating
to the ground—good—
make her round—keep
that ten foot stride—ask
for more
contact—if you need
ride her shoulder-fore—circle—
flex
her—can you see her inside eye?—don't
let her dictate the pace
or race them—let her
knock em—it hurts—she'll jump higher—
she'll learn
to judge her take-off—now—
the treble—
good—good—good
—tell her
she's good—she is—
this is all new—
now the wall—how
did that feel?—okay—
she's a mess—that's enough
for today—she's getting
the idea
and—don't worry—if she hits it
it will fall.'

Elizabeth Campbell was born in
Melbourne in 1980. After years of
begging her non-horsey parents, she
got her first pony, Honeycomb, at
thirteen. She now owns a beautiful
thoroughbred mare, Dutch Valentine.
Elizabeth is working on her first
collection of poems, a number of
which are about horses.

The Smell of Love

Gwin Harris Steph

Have you ever smelled a horse? Have you ever held a horse's head in your hand and gently pulled it close to your chest, inhaling deeply, from the very bottom of your lungs, while you kissed the forehead, and said I love you?

Have you ever lifted a horse's mane and buried your face in the neck, in one of the softest places on earth, the place where nuzzles are? Have you buried your face even deeper, losing yourself in the intoxicating essence of green grass, freshly mown meadows and sweet horsey sweat?

I will always have my horse's smell with me. It is in my heart, and, forever until the end of time, embedded in my memory. The smell will always elicit comfort, the wholeness of the animal and my relationship with her, the simple parts as well as the complex.

My horse's name was Star. She graced and shared my life until she was thirty-one years old. Star was an unwavering constant for me. There was a concrete stability in the forces between the woman and her horse. It was made up by both a mutual need and a mutual want, each changing its expression as the years unfolded, as time marched on, and youth begat older age for each of us.

I first saw Star when she was eight and I was twenty-seven.

She was in a paddock with dead and dying mares, stallions, geldings and foals. The ground shockingly littered with corpses. The horses, like Star, who were still alive, were starving to death. I brought her home to green grass and, sentimentally said now, my heart smiles to say, home to the tenderest of loving care.

She thrived and became healthy. We were both young, adventurous and independent. She would graze for days in the open pasture, coming for water, pets, and to let me know she was okay. She was capable of withstanding horrific summer heat and drought, and brutal winter cold.

I loved it when she would take her nose and nuzzle my neck, sniffing and telling me secrets in my ear while chewing on my hair. She, the gentlest of gentle spirits, made me laugh, on the inside and the outside. She had a nature and a heart that knew no borders when it came to me, and the joys, trials, and tribulations of my life.

There is a saying, author unknown, 'Serenity is not freedom from the storm, but peace within the storm,' and peace within the storm is something that I could count on when I was with my Star. I would stand at the barn, watch her eat, talk to her, and feel contentment. I treasured her.

Several months before she died, old age caught up with Star and she changed from a competent animal, one who had had foal after foal, alone and without trouble, to one less so. She became slightly disoriented on occasion and was not always sure where she was. It did not seem to distress her.

One day, I found her miraculously unhurt, physically stuck in brush, as if aliens had deposited her in a thicket.

It took five chainsaw cuts to free her and she flinched not once at the loud noise. The veterinarian said she was calm because she knew I would find her and save her. From then on, she remained in a large pen, carefully babyproofed by her uncles.

Sometimes she would become hindered by the most innocuous of barriers. A tree, perhaps. I would say she was roadblocked and then help her find her way out of the jam she perceived herself in, much as she had done for me, many times, in her own special way.

She would follow me back to her food and water and be happy.

Sometimes I think I see her. This must be her way of letting me know she is with me. And I listen for her—the sound of her hooves coming down from far up on the hill. Even in death, it remains a comfort sound.

Gwin Harris Steph lives on a ranch in Texas. She was born in New York City, daughter of an American woman and a French man. She appreciates the simple things in life such as that which nature and good hearts provide.

Change

Heather Cameron

She gave birth sometime in the night; there was no one there to record the exact time, other than herself and the ghost-moon which hung low, just to the right of the fence separating the small patch of land she called home, and the gully running the length of the school grounds which fanned out beyond the rise. The pain in her belly had begun at dusk, but she had silently shivered through that beginning time, and moved slowly to the shelter of the trees, beyond the eyes that may have recognised the signs. It was not that she didn't trust the man and the woman—it was more that she sensed this was a time to be centred within herself, to be free of the human world that swirled around her in confusing patterns. The night time was still, the warmth of summer lingering in the sweet air, and in the darkest spaces beneath the trees she gave birth to her first born; shivering becoming the heaving, ageless rhythm of labour, at once known and yet unfamiliar to her. She nuzzled the wet muskiness of her newborn foal; he snorted his surprise at her soft touch, standing on legs that barely held and finding the richness of her milk as she whinnied her breath across his flanks.

The hens in the enclosure next to her field clucked their happiness to her before the sun had broken the surface of the ocean to the east of her shelter. As the sky filled with the red streaks of dawn, the world she knew took the shape and form of day, and it seemed to the tired mother-mare that the noise filling the field sang welcome upon welcome to the newborn. Much later the woman wandered through the wooden gate that led from the buildings to the orchard, and out to the field. The shock of finding the mare standing with her sleek, wobbly foal rendered the woman frozen; her silence was familiar and the mare calmly waited for the woman to grow accustomed to the thought of a secret night-filled birth. 'Oh, you clever, clever girl,' murmured the woman as she moved to run her hands along the mare's neck, her eyes following the progress of the shaky too-long-legged foal. She did not like the woman coming close and gently tossing her head, she shepherded her offspring away, moving back to the shelter of the trees, calling warning to the woman. She relaxed when she saw

understanding on the woman's face, and then simply watched as the woman sat on the ground in the long summer-dry grass and cried; her tears as silent and as incomprehensible to the mare as they usually were.

When the man stood and watched her run freely through the long grass, her foal beside her, kicking his legs out behind him in the sheer excitement of stretching and finding the wind rippling across the skin, she heard him laugh and saw the wetness in his eyes. He often sat on the low bench by the old water trough at the top of field, just watching and sometimes calling out to her when there was an apple or some sweetness in his hand especially for her. His voice was soft as water, and she would lean her long nose into his shoulder, nuzzling him as he whispered to her. The woman came less often to the field; she would sit in the orchard when the days cooled into evenings, but often she would lie staring into the spaces beyond the field, looking far beyond where the mare and her foal lingered. She rarely bought apples to the field with her, but sometimes would walk the length of the fence line at dusk,

breaking into a run and kicking her heels out as though racing some unseen foe. The mare watched as the man and the woman skirted around each other, wide gaping spaces between their movements, their voices—the increasing silence between them resonating dully in the passing summer-hazed days.

And then came an autumn day when the woman stood in the field and cried as she ran her hand along the warm, sleek back of the foal. 'Goodbye little one,' she whispered, 'Grow strong, and run fast.' Raising her hand to the nose of the mare, she cried in long, stabs of sound which made the mare twitch and shiver. She did not see the woman again. The man continued to come to the field, often empty-handed and always with a slow, dragging gait that made him seem older; he didn't laugh any more when she tossed her head and chased the wind across the wintry iciness of the field. Instead he watched the foal who had grown into a strong, sleek yearling. Sometimes he would bring others with him, and they would stand and talk about the length of stride the yearling had, and how fit he looked. It was at these times that

the mare would shiver as she caught the scent of strangers and change and, moving to stand between her offspring and the men, she would toss her head in challenge, and together they would race to the fartherest edges of the field, as though racing some unseen foe.

Heather Cameron *lives on the Surf Coast of Victoria with her partner, and two sons. Among many memories of horses in her life is one special day when her maternal grandfather, who bred and trained horses in Southland, New Zealand, sat her on the back of a young horse named Trusty Scot. A beautiful horse, he went on to win the New Zealand Trotting Cup, and a special place in the family folklore.*

The Tail of a Terrible Horse

Jilll Mather

'He was a rotten horse really!'

In the 1940s, following the war, my father decided that he would buy me a horse. I was seven years of age.

'A horse!' My mother, city bred, was alarmed. 'She'll be killed. Mark my words!'

My father's good idea came dangerously close to a divorce when he tethered the horse to a post that supported her crop of luscious green beans.

He stood 14.3 hands-high: a bright bay with a black mane and tail. Gelded at four years of age, he retained the high crest of the stallion. A strong horse with only the faintest remnants of a distant thoroughbred ancestor. This was the legacy of finely boned legs and neat, well-placed hooves.

Somewhere in the deep dark recesses of his brain, he hid a craftiness that was to surface as a force to be reckoned with in the fourteen years I owned him.

Each day, each ride, was challenge. Catching him was the first test he put me through.

Now picture this… a long paddock with a steeply rising hill culminating in a small flat area framed by magnificent macrocarpa trees with low sweeping branches.

After an initial approach, with my rope halter in hand, he would stand transfixed until I almost reached him. With lightning speed and a gleam in the eye, he would gallop past me and stop. Just out of reach. For almost an hour this game would continue until at last he would stand trembling on the flat patch. Shivering like a delicate leaf

on a tree, he would grunt as I placed a hand on him.

Thereafter another game would ensure that the saddling-up process was as prolonged as possible. Sighing heavily, he would lapse into a jellified mass of tortured flesh sagging sadly as the saddle was placed on his back. Huge intakes of breath ensured the saddle would slip when the girth was tightened; no matter how many times.

The bridling took place without incident. He was complacent by this time. Asleep, even with his bottom lip extended so that a cup of pink flesh hung from his head. Eyes half-closed. Head drooping almost to his knees. A sorry sight brightened only by the sight of food.

His name was 'Artful Lad'. Oh, how true it was! He was nicknamed 'Fatty' because he was, according to all, 'a good doer'. Little wonder really for, as soon as feed became less abundant nearing winter, he would leap the fence and visit a nearby vegetable garden where he wrought havoc. He ate his way through the carrot patch, the cabbages, silver beet and anything else that caught his fancy. Thoroughly satiated, he would return home to wait at the gate, too swollen with ill-gotten gains to jump back in again.

The phone ran hot.

He had a sense of humour matched only by cunning. The ride to Pony Club on Saturdays was interesting. He had been known to collapse into a large pool of muddy water with me on board. Not for long; suddenly I would find myself wallowing in filthy water and then, to cap it off, he would shake any excess off, spraying me liberally in the

process, looking reproachfully at me as if I caused the incident.

Ring events were entered with mad enthusiasm—if the mood took him, or the opposite. He was unreliable in that way. Plunging recklessly towards jumps he would leap over, gazelle-like, swooping around the ring like a champion. Being of a light build, I would hold on while he took control.

Perhaps he would decide that it was all too much trouble and slouch along, a sad and miserable sight. No amount of prodding, or encouragement would alter the mood. Not until we turned for home. Suddenly the sorry sack would turn into a bounding lively animal, full of the joy of life. A bin of chaff and oats waited for him at home. Life was wonderful wasn't it?

The day came when after fourteen years I was moving on, and had purchased another horse. A small girl and her father came to try him out. I'll swear he knew because he put on such a turn of bucking and plunging, never before seen, and they left. Finally he was sold to a good home and I trust he gave them years of fun and games, because despite all the years of uncertainty, I really loved him. But he was a rotten horse.

Jill Mather is a former feature writer for international/national publications, received a recent award for Best Documentary on 'The Plight of the Desert Horses' and also an award for the Best Film Script. A lifetime of writing, all subjects. Published a novel, numerous commissioned works. Qualified teacher, television presenter, broadcaster. Had thirteen stories broadcast on the National Network.

The Horse Whisperers

Doreen Dunsford (as told to her daughter) Cathie Dunsford

'Got the five quid, Joy?' I whispered.

'Yes. Keep it quiet or Dad'll wake up,' Joy whispered back. Dad was a printer in Devonport and often stayed up late getting his work finished. He was proud of his job.

We got up at five a.m. and the rain was pounding the window panes of our run-down house in Bayswater, Auckland. I pulled on my new jodhpurs Mum had made. Like many of our friends in the 1940s, we couldn't afford new clothes, or a saddle, or for that matter a new horse. But my older sister Joy and I had been saving our pocket money for over a year and had five quid in a rusty biscuit tin. We'd seen an ad in the local rag: 'Handsome horse for sale. Five pounds. A real beauty. Come and see for yourself.' So that's where we were going. Our place was surrounded by empty paddocks, and we figured a horse would love to be there. And we wanted that horse more than anything. Ever.

We both jumped onto the back of Joy's stubborn Sabu, hoping he'd be in the right mood for a trip. If he wasn't, he'd just sit down! Luckily, he was chirpy that day and we rode the ten miles or so north. When we saw Bronzie, it was love at first sight. A real whopper of a horse! As bronze as a statue, as wild as the blackberries we picked in summer. The horse owner had a booming voice and made sure he had our five quid in his pocket before he'd let us get near Bronzie. He seemed glad when we told him we'd never had enough money for saddles and always rode bare-back. We found out why later. I climbed the fence and jumped onto her back and that was the first time she bucked me off. Joy counted another nineteen falls into thick, ochre clay and grey mud squished deep by the heavy rain, before we got

home to the paddock. There was mud from tip to toe, caked thick over my new jodhpurs mum had made. I had to sneak to the sea, wash them and hang them dry on the tea tree so that she'd never find out. But as soon as she glanced through the window and saw a wild horse crashing about in the paddock, she suspected what we'd been up to. Gradually, she got used to Bronzie whinnying us to sleep and awake. We couldn't afford to have her shod so I had to ride her in the paddock and along grass verges, but never on the hard stuff.

Nobody but me could ride Bronzie. She still bucked me off every time I got on, but after a year, the bucking became less frequent and I could whisper in her ear. Years later, I taught her to jump over fences then took her to the gymkana. Much to the chagrin of all the nicely dressed, saddled rich kids, Bronzie beat the lot of them! Every time! We won every single race every year for years. I beamed with pride. My Bronzie. Eventually, we got a second-hand saddle for her.

One day, we all went to the gymkhana and a well-known horse trainer came up to us. He asked where we'd got Bronzie. I told him. He laughed, a big hearty guffaw from his belly. 'That bloody fella. He'd sell his bloody mother! Your Bronzie, lass, was a rogue horse well past its best when that fella sold it to you. Would've been pet food if it wasn't for you lassies. Ha ha! A right rip-off. Fancy him getting five quid for that bugger. Nobody could ever ride her and she certainly wouldn't take to a saddle. You're a right little horse-whisperer, you.' He laughed and laughed and Joy and I looked at each other in amazement. No wonder she'd nip you every time you went near her for years, until she got used to us. Still, we'd saved her from the meatworks.

Doreen Dunsford is a patchwork and tapestry artist who loves horses and lives on Milford Beach. **Cathie Dunsford** is the author/editor of twenty books in print and translation. Her latest is AoToa: Earth Warriors. She is director of an agency which has brought 174 authors into print: www.dunsfordpublishing.com

Star Louise Duval

Beloved friend for fourteen years. Died 22 October 2000, approx. twenty-eight years of age.

Impatient nose nudged gently as you waited for the piece of apple. Whiskers brushed over my hand as you grasped the treat, teeth carefully avoiding small fingers. Blissfully you crunched, juice dribbling from your lips. Contented you then stood quietly as I brushed the dust from your coat, stamping occasionally at the ever-present flies. Ears flicked back and forth as you listened to the low whisper of childhood secrets. Hopes and dreams shared, tears shed into your long black mane. Deep brown eyes gazed knowingly into mine; warm air ruffled my hair as you offered comfort.

Years passed.

You were happiest when left in peace to endlessly graze or to doze quietly in the shade. But the magic bond grew as another little girl learnt to love you too. My daughter's first word was 'Star' as she called you up to get your daily offering of carrots. You stood quietly when she toddled up and begged to be lifted up to sit on your broad back. The love of horses had been passed on.

But too soon, you had gone. We cried together, for we had lost a friend. Even now, years later, she'll remember you and say how sad it is that her little brothers never got to know you. I cry for lost childhood and unfulfilled dreams, but most of all I cry for a gentle wise old soul. I hope the pastures in heaven are always green and there are no flies to disturb your dozing.

Louise Duval lives with her husband and their three children in Perth, Western Australia, along with their two dogs, two cats and a Shetland pony. Her love of all animals, but especially horses, led her to pursue a career as a veterinary surgeon. Even with her busy life, horses still play a special part. Her daughter has also been bitten by the horsey bug and has recently started attending Pony Club.

I Remember, I Don't Remember

Margaret Carmichael Leonard

I remember riding my first horse.
I was two and had a small roll of blanket tied to the front of my father's saddle—but I don't remember how I got there. I remember we were droving sheep, and suddenly one broke free, and the horse instinctively trotted to return it to the fold. I can remember how excruciatingly uncomfortable it was, as I was anchored only by my father's encircling arm. I remember I was highly indignant. I screamed at him to let me down, sobbing, 'you have shaken my libber out.' I can't remember saying that, but I remember my brother saying it many times to prove his superiority to be able to pronounce the letter 'V'.

When I was four, I remember owning my first horse, a little black mare named Topsy, a hand-me-down kids' pony. I can't remember having any real disasters on her, as long as you don't count jumping a sleeping cow but, after all, by then I was an experienced horsewoman! I do remember Topsy would put her head down to the ground so I could put on her bridle. She stood against a log for me to clamber on her back. I can't remember how big she was, but I remember my father's attitude that small ponies encouraged poor riders as it was too easy to fall off: I assume she was a good-sized pony. I remembered this when we bought our daughter her first pony: her Cassie is 13.5 hands-high.

I don't remember Topsy being passed on to the next kid in the chain, but I do remember she died when I was seven. My father said Topsy had her tea, then lay down and died; I remember feeling satisfied with that. I learnt much later that death is never that easy.

Until I turned eleven I remember a herd of neighbours' horses being brought for me to ride and civilise, for their young owners. Eventually, my mother who was afraid of horses, must have called 'enough'. My next horse was a 'real horse', a very perky chestnut that I could realise my dreams on in the show ring. She was called Dolly, a stupid name I remember thinking. I can remember when Dolly died; she would have been near to thirty years old.

I distinctly remember when my husband cashed in an insurance policy to buy me my next horse. I was thirty-six, with a three-year-old daughter, and recovering from breast cancer, and going through a not-so-positive stage in my recovery. The horse was a magnificent Arab-Quarter cross Paint Horse, and something you would kill for, if he did not kill you first. He was in need of a lot of attention as he had recently been gelded, and still remembered his former status, and naturally, at that time, had a complete hatred of

men. Because of this I was the one who had to do most of the handling of him until my husband was able to win him over. I do remember startling many people as we careered partly out of control until I built up the strength to hold him: well, I liked to pretend I was in control, but I remember my daughter considering this was debatable. His name was Sirocco, which suited him, as we were one with the winds in spirit and speed, as we raced through the years.

My beautiful soul mate—the memories are still painful from having him put down twenty years later when he suffered from a cerebral haemorrhage but I was able to say my loving farewell to him before he was painlessly put to sleep. I could not bear to be present, but my husband held and comforted him, and I remember being reassured that he died peacefully. Since then my husband's handsome black Thoroughbred-Stockhorse cross has been put to rest with dignity, and we often remember the pleasure we had in all our adventures together. Our daughter's little black mare Cassie spends the rest of her days in a paddock next to us so we can share her last memories.

I stand with Cassie's head in a bucket of horse muesli, which ensures her health in her old age. She contentedly munches as she pushes close to me. As we share a warm compatible silence, I remember all the other times we have communicated through feed and touch. She deliberately but gently noses my hand out of the bucket, but obviously moves her velvety muzzle closer to my body so we are sharing the satisfaction of the meal. I run my hand down her furry neck, and ruffle the cottonwool softness of her forelock, and smile to myself at the long feminine curl of her eyelashes over her huge milky black eyes.

As she licks the last grains from the bottom of the bucket and sighs with satisfaction, I whisper to her, 'Goodnight my sweet black princess, sleep softly, but do not allow Pegasus to wing you away into the night. Please wait until morning when I can cradle your head in my arms, and comfort and reassure you as we remember the many times I have done this previously.' She languidly escorts me to the fence. I feed her a carrot for dessert and farewell. We both turn away reassured there will be another day.

Margaret Carmichael Leonard
thinks she may have been born on a horse's back on a farm near Wangaratta, Victoria. She worked as a teacher in Victoria, New South Wales, New Zealand and Bangkok, the latter where she and her husband spent two horseless years. They now live in Bacchus Marsh with two geriatric horses and a cat. When not waiting paw-and-hoof on the freeloading livestock, she is writing a book on her time in Bangkok.

Lesson One: Thinking Outside the Square

Anna Bianchi

Dolly was nothing so refined as her name, Alcheringa China Doll; nothing so delicate as a china doll, and never a fragile, rosy-cheeked young miss. Dolly was a large horse with squat legs that was awkwardly and ignominiously called a pony. She had the one redeeming feature of a 'gentle eye', and this was sufficient enough for us to consider her suitable for our children's first pony.

As a young mother trying her hand at horse handling for the first time, Dolly was my introduction to the world of horses, and my first challenge. She was a bit of an old maid; at times grumpy, but always self-satisfied and self-sufficient. Dolly knew best, despite, in our eyes, a lack of training. We soon found that a kick of the rider's heels only meant 'go forwards' or 'increase your speed' when it suited her. The first canter, and the first rush of willingness that I ever felt, was when her foal had escaped down the country road where we lived and, leaping onto her back, we galloped hastily in pursuit. For a moment there, the wind blew quite briskly past my face, and there was the thrill of moving across country at speed. But once the foal had been retrieved, it was the same old dull, leaden walk all the way back home.

Despite being bought for our young children as 'safe' and 'bombproof', she was, we thought, desperately in need of some discipline as well as a respect for us. The children were still too young, so it meant me having to do this. I was willing. I was well read.

Lesson one, I decided, was to be on the lunge—where, standing firmly and safely on the ground, I was to drive her on a circle around me by using yelled commands and the crack of the long lungeing whip and, by the lowering of my voice and whip, she was to slow and halt. These commands, of course, were to become increasingly subtle visual cues, and were to result in our increased safety and pleasure. It was easy to visualise the resulting amenable, soft, angelic, white horse with the gentle eye: the China Doll of her name.

As lesson one commenced, I was confident and hopeful. Dolly stood willingly and patiently as I put the halter on her large horsey head and attached the lunge rein under her jowl. I draped the long rein in safe loops in one hand and then raised the lunge whip in the other. As advised by horse-riding books, I made a triangle with sides of rein, whip and horse. I stepped back, pointing the whip at Dolly's rump.

'Walk on!' I gave the command with a deliberately motivating tempo and a waggle of the whip. Dolly stood still. Why move? She looked inquiringly at me.

I called to my watching friend to assist; to help explain to Dolly what I, the driving person in the middle of the imagined circle, meant. My friend took a hold of the halter on the outside of the supposed circle. And as I again ordered, 'Walk on!' my friend walked off. It also looked, for a moment, as if Dolly might also finally understand.

Goaded on by my voice, the cracking of the whip and the leading pressure on the halter, her weight momentarily shifted forwards... then her hesitant step forward stopped. She turned away and put her head down to snatch a mouthful of grass. There was no malice in her eye. There were no violent movements or aggressive gestures like ears laid back, turning of the rump and raising of a leg, the baring of teeth, or swishing of the tail in resistance. Just passive resistance.

She will do as I command, I thought. Just got to increase the volume of the voice and show more determination in the body language. Crack! Crack! The whip licked at her hocks and flicked her tail. More determinedly she turned away out of the circle, pulling the lunge rein and jerking me off balance. My feet were turned in the direction that she wanted to go. The friend leading on the outside was bowled off her line by Dolly's hefty shoulder, but she managed to step sideways to avoid Dolly's feet that, in the drama of the moment, seemed more suitable for a 17 hands-high horse than a 13.2 hands pony.

Pulled off our line and our intentions badly out of shape, my friend and I became more determined and we yelled instructions to each other—the horse in the middle between us still quietly unyielding. I moved further back and again the friend on the outside pulled hard on the halter. But in trying to tug the horse forwards, she found only an unmovable weight.

'Trot on!' I lashed with tongue and whip. Jog, jog, jog, the friend emphasised the imperative nature of our command in the running steps that she took, or at least attempted to take. Dolly remained still, but now turned in to face me, a little surprised at this wildly gesticulating person in the middle of the imagined circle.

I moved further behind her, stressing that I wanted her to move away from me, forwards onto the circle. Suddenly— neither my friend nor I could really appreciate how—the circle began to materialise and take shape. One body stood in the centre, only rotating enough to keep a watchful eye on the two bodies orbiting around it with circular precision and at a brisk trot... my friend and me.

There we were, in all seriousness, thinking that we were teaching the horse, but the more I moved behind Dolly and the longer she stood still, the faster and further I went, and around and around I went. My friend mirrored my every move, until we were going around and around together, faster and faster, more and more unwittingly. While the two of us were bellowing out our instructions and demonstrating wildly what we wanted, Dolly was actually the one in the controlling seat. She was the one calmly doing the driving, and we were doing all the hard work, loudly and inelegantly, first one way on the circle and then the other.

At least, that is, until it suddenly dawned on my friend and I how easily we'd been put in our place by the horse, and how funny the reversal of roles had become. We roared with laughter, splitting our sides in the hilarity, while Dolly appeared oblivious to this peculiar turn of events, at most, relieved at being out of the focus of our attention.

The children came home from school later that afternoon, eager to go for a ride. By then, my friend and I had laughed loudly and long, and marvelled at the ingenuity and wisdom of the horse, and from then on, left much to her own devices, Dolly turned out to be the best nursemaid and teacher one could ever wish for. She quietly and patiently stood still as they brushed her all over, plaited her mane and tail with ribbons, and stuck rooster feathers and all sorts of adornments in her forelock and tail. They were able to swing from fence posts on to her back, and safely crawl between her legs. She progressively walked, trotted and cantered as their ability to ride increased. She withstood the humiliation of fancy dress with indifference, and willingly jumped obstacles as each child rider chose.

She turned out to be an amazing assessor of human nature. She listened to each child, or didn't, as she deemed appropriate. She stepped delicately and deliberately one foot after another for the most timid child, but with the flick of the heels and duck of the head she would on the odd occasion dump a loud, rambunctious child on the ground.

She 'loved' her kids, as only a horse could. We parents, who had previously thought that we knew best, just stood back in wonder and delight. Lesson one complete.

Anna Bianchi *lives in Adelaide, South Australia, and is a mother of three who has just bought the 'first pony' for the next generation, her grandchildren. Anna's great passion has been forming relationships with all the different horses that she has known (besides all the other people in her life, of course!), and believes that they can teach us so much about ourselves. Her ambition is to finish her book on the three-day event as an Olympic sport, which will save the world!*

Barn Fire

Sally Armbrecht

This a love poem to Tesoro, my Arabian pony, who was killed in a barn fire in 1989 along with twenty-nine other horses.

I would have slit your throat,
my two hands clenching the knife
as I stood beside you whispering tender words,
wanting you to listen, listen to my voice
to distract you from the flash,
the blade stroke up.

I would have slit your throat,
felt the fire of your blood course down my forearms,
would have faced your cue ball eyes
as your ton of beautiful flesh crashed down into the sawdust.
Would have caught your falling head
and eased it down, cradled it above your blood turning black,
your eyes going blank.

I would have slit your throat
to have spared you that first scent
of burning acrid wire and dank hay,
the nervous snorts of two   ten   thirty   horses
turning frantic as flames flowed like water into the first stall,
then the stamps and scrapes of hooves pawing doors
that strained and rattled against their metal latches.

If I had known when I slid the latch home
that I locked you into a pyre, locked you out of this earth,
I would have slit your throat.
I would not have failed you.

Sally Armbrecht spent her childhood riding horses in West Virginia, USA. She is currently travelling. Her passions are reading and writing, the natural world, and human rights issues.

You Ask Me About My Horse, You Ask Me About Myself Alessina Brooks

My horse and I are inseparable. When I ride him, we ride together and as I wrap myself around his body, my two legs become four and his head and neck are as sensuous in look and smell as any lover's could be. Together we go forward with a power that is as exciting as it is undefinable.

And my horse dreams? When I can't sleep, he comes to me and I brush and brush his coat until it gleams and my eyelids grow heavy from the effort. Sometimes we ride together in the stillness of the night to places we have visited in the daylight. Yes, he is magic at any time, but especially when he visits me in my slumbers and takes me to places far away with effortless strides.

His name is King. I met him first as a school horse when he was only four years old—after he had walked away from his drought-ridden paddock, thin and neglected. I rode him as a young, highly impatient, swift, surefooted creature—we used to fly together over parched fields in the summer.

And within a very short time, I somehow knew he was to be with me and I wasted no words in telling his owner. Life turns unexpectedly. I was taken away from him for a while and during this time King went sour, in fact,

'downright dangerous'—to be sold as horse meat. He was offered to me with great caution and a $250 price tag.

I hesitated but knew in my heart there was no argument. So he came as was destined, to fill a part of my very being. There is truth, I'm sure in the saying that 'animals find you'. King has taught me many things but, above all, to step outside of my own space and share my world with another—without inhibition and with only the purest of thoughts and movement. King is now twenty-three. I respect his age and ride him most times bareback with ease and a bit he hardly feels. He is always the gentleman, waits patiently at gates, waits patiently should I fall, waits patiently in turn for his food.

One day, I will be left with only memories—but for now, my horse dreams can be topped up whenever I visit him—waiting, waiting, waiting for his carrots, sugar cubes and a loving pat.

Alessina Brooks *is joint owner of The Images Publishing Group and Peleus Press, publishing world-class books on architecture, design and lifestyle. Qualified as a Behavioural Scientist, she is passionate about developing business systems that facilitate harmonious and productive work flow environments as well as studying the way in which humans interact with their animal friends.*

The Orphan Foal

Helen McIntyre

Having a big mouth has always gotten me into trouble, so it is nice that on at least one occasion it all ended up okay. At the time I had three grey donkeys and one day, watching them while chatting with a friend, I said, 'If ever anything happens to one of my donkeys and I decide to keep having three and not cut down to two, I think maybe my next one will be a brown one.' So, of course, about two months later I received a frantic phone call, Fat Kate, who had already killed two foals and was not supposed to get pregnant again had dropped a foal and was attacking it. The owner was desperate to find a home where it could be hand-reared and the word had gone around that I was looking for a brown donkey. Yeah right, who left out the 'one day', 'if ever I only have two' and the 'maybe'. So Pollyanna came into my life, she at twenty-four hours of age and me at fifty-four years of age.

First move, off to the vet to have her checked out to see if Fat Kate had damaged her, to have her tubed full of milk and given any other treatment the vet thought necessary. First, weight, fourteen kilograms. My kelpie dog weighed eighteen! Then, before treatment, the vet asked, 'What's her name?' I think names are important, so I frantically searched my memory banks for a 'positive' name to give

her all the help I could. Of course, Pollyanna! A survivor if ever there was one. She was always glad, even positive enough to be glad crutches were a better present than a doll as she didn't need them. So Pollyanna it was. Why, oh why, didn't I have time to think further. Pollyanna was also an interfering busybody who always knew better than anyone else and thought she had the right to direct everyone along the lines she chose. Polyanna has worked very hard to live up to her name, especially the bossy side of it. If only I'd thought, 'Topsy, she just grew.'

So home with Pollyanna, Divetalact milk powder and instructions on all the things to watch for and worry about. I decided bottle feeding was time consuming and fiddly, so I first tried her on the milk in a small bowl. For the first and last time in her life Polly decided to let me do things the easy way, she drank straight away. Probably wasn't for my benefit, she probably worked out she could get more down, faster, if she drank that way. From the time she came to me to the time I weaned her, she drank over $700 worth of milk. I suppose she was not prepared to wear the title of 'free donkey' all her life. I had strict instructions to watch her bowel actions for too much, too little, too hard, too soft, so of course she chose not to have any. I was on

238

the phone to the vet every hour or so, 'She hasn't poohed yet, shall I panic?' 'Is it time to panic yet?' 'How long now before I should start panicking?' Aren't vets lovely, long-suffering people? Mine made comforting noises and didn't once indicate he had other more pressing duties.

I decided she should sleep in the house knowing that although donkeys are basically strong, healthy animals, once they become depressed it is very difficult to save them. Actually, I think Pollyanna would have been more depressed staying with her own mother where she would have had to obey. As it was, she got a mother who could be controlled and manipulated any which way she chose. I moved a double mattress out onto the kitchen floor and we slept on it together, waking every two hours to drink and then go outside and walk around the lawn until she answered the call of nature. The book said to feed every two hours for a week or so, then cut out some night feeds so that you ended up with the last feed at night at about midnight and the next first thing in the morning. In between, start lengthening feeds until they are four hours apart. Idiot me thought, 'better to follow nature's way and feed little and often the way a real mother does,' so I made a huge rod for my own back by feeding two hourly

for three months, then started on the reduction.

Is bringing a foal up in the house a good idea? No, never again; next time I move out into the stable if I think it necessary. The problems I came across were many. I couldn't sleep past the two-hour feeding time or Pollyanna would stand up and tread on me to wake me, or, on two occasions, urinate on me to make sure I woke up; quite deliberate, I assure you. That was just before she was moved out onto the verandah at night to sleep one side of the screen door while I slept the other.

I like my bath almost boiling, but for months I had to have tepid water as Polly insisted on coming in and drinking it, so it couldn't be any hotter than her milk. The worst part was that the floor in the bathroom was slippery and on a number of occasions, as she stood drinking, she would gradually do the splits. I would have to leap out in all my glory to stand her up again. I nearly froze to death because I couldn't have the heater on, then turn it off and risk her getting cold.

She had to learn to be a paddock donkey eventually. She pulled things off shelves, opened cupboards, galloped up the passage and then, when I asked her to, refused to repay me. It was like this. She had developed the habit of rushing up the passage and leaping on to my double bed, then off again and biting and kicking the bed before jumping back on to it.

After this went on for weeks I thought, 'Right, you can earn your keep by winning Funniest Home Videos for me,' and asked the chap down the street to come up with his video camera. He set himself up on a stepladder in the corner of the room, Polly galloped down the passage, stopped dead in the doorway, said, 'No way am I going to be exploited,' and from that day on she never jumped on the furniture again. She even threw my camera on the floor and broke it to make sure I didn't have any still photos of her as a baby, walking under the kitchen table, sitting on my knee on the lounge or any of the other 'cute' pics. Like mother, like daughter I guess. I hate having my photo taken too so I suppose I can sympathise... just.

In the mornings, we would go for a walk around the block to buy the paper. This included the local park, where I would let her off her lead to gallop wildly in all directions before coming screaming back to me hee-hawing with joy. The ranger saw us once but agreed there was no law stating donkeys had to be on a lead at all times. In the afternoon at four p.m we would play 'chasey' around the back paddock, as I had observed that was about the time the horses next door played with their foals.

When she got too big to fit in the back of the car I would have to put the trailer on and take her with me when I went visiting so that she could be fed every two hours. She would then lie on the doorstep of the house I was visiting until time to go home again. On the few occasions I couldn't take her with me I hired a baby sitter for her, much to the stunned amusement of the sitter.

This all happened ten years ago. Pollyanna grew up to be an absolute monster in many people's eyes. She hadn't been bitten and kicked at the appropriate times because I don't speak donkey fluently, but we gradually overcame most of her problems and she and I understand each other, even if the rest of the world doesn't know how to take her. Because of her experience of having to be taken everywhere with me as a foal she has no fear of any situation she finds herself in, as long as I am there, and she is absolutely bombproof when in harness. I didn't really want another donkey when I got her, but now I couldn't imagine life without my half-human little donkey.

Helen McIntyre grew up in the early 1940s at Bibra Lake, Western Australia. From the age of eleven she was never without a horse until she married in her thirties and lived in the suburbs. She became involved with donkeys in 1979 when her mother bought a pregnant jenny and gave her the foal which lived on her parents' property. After being widowed in 1990 she purchased a property and became more involved with donkeys, owning them, driving them in harness, finding homes for needy donkeys and being completely besotted by them.

A Vision of Horses and Mules

Marge Piercy

Learn to think like a horse
her trainer had said. She went
into the pasture at noon,
when her horses lay down to sleep
without fear of coyotes,
without fear. They sensed her
but did not mind as she stretched
out beside them with the June
heat's broad strong hand
flattening her into the grass.

But now, she said, I am studying
mules. Her trainer told her
horses forget everything by
and by. Mules never forget.
Carry your intention carefully,
a brimming bowl of water.
Mule skinner, I called her
and from my childhood I saw
a tin of Boraxo my father used
to clean grease from his hands.

Twenty-mule teams crossed
the Death Valley of our bath
room, little black mules along
the bottom of the tin, the driver
in his wagon, the whip cracking
a wicked S in the air. I'm a mule:
stubborn, dragging heavy grudges,
joys and lost friends from the alkaline
mines of my past across the bleak
present to some future use.

Marge Piercy *is the author of
sixteen published novels, including*
He She and It, Three Women *and,
most recently,* The Third Child. *She is
also the author of sixteen collections
of poetry, most recently,* Colors
Passing Through Us. *Her recent
memoir is called* Sleeping with Cats.
*She lives on Cape Cod and is an
editor of the Leapfrog Press.*

Permissions

Marge Piercy, p 3: 'Seven Horses' was published in *A Southern California Anthology*. Vol. XIV, 1997.

Sally Armbrecht, p 232: 'Barn Fire' has been previously published in *Northern Lights*.

Photographs

pix Belinda Morris; px Suzanne Coutanceau; p2 J. Dolce; p3 Ira Wood; p25 (left) Laughlin Cowell (right) Anna Gage; p34 (left) Brenda Coulter (right) Renate Klein; p36, 37 John Coulter; p41 Suzanne Coutanceau; p42 Celeste Croteau; p47 (right) GMK Photographic Excellence; p48 Emilio; p50 Suzanne Coutanceau; p52, 54, 55 Deb Cole; p57 Rodney Cram; p58 Sue Ward; p60 Mervyn Davis; p61 Sue Ward; p69 Darren Kiefel; p72 Annie Coutanceau; p82 Sam and Rita Virduzzo; p88 Francis Cappelletti; p89 Paul T. Sewell; p90 Claire French; p95 Sybil Booker; p96 Michael Azzopardi; p99 (top) Erika Gladhorn (bottom) Leni Meissenburg; p104 P.A. Kant; p114 Tatyana Mamonova and Charlotte Gruwez; p117 Clunies-Ross family; p118 Zbigniew Jaworski; p120 (top) Jenny Barnes Photography (bottom) Andrew McKenna; p121 Cathy Whittingham; p122 Kiersten Coulter; p124 Jenny Barnes Photography; p126, 129 J. Dolce; p130, 131 Troy Elliot; p132,133 Andrew McKenna; p136, 139 Claire Perry; p141 S. Edgecumbe; p142 Cheryl James; p152 Ken Smirk; p155, 157 Andrew McLennan; p159 Tim Bass; p161 O'Connell Photography; p164 Jenny Barnes Photography; p177 (top) J. Dolce; p178 North Central News, St Arnaud; p179 Jo Arblaster; p180 Primrose Hawthorne; p183 Renate Klein; p184 Peter Gower; p189 Cheryl James; p193, 195 Jenny Barnes Photography; p197 (bottom) Tracey Beckler; p202 J. Dolce; p206 Consuelo Rivera; p211 (left) J. Dolce; p215 Greg Smith; p233 Calvert Armbrecht; p235, 236 Nicole Emanuel; p242 Ira Wood.

All other photographs are from the personal collections of individuals named in the text. The publisher acknowledges kind permission to reproduce these photographs.

Other books by Jan Fook

Radical Casework
Professional Expertise (co-author)
Social Work: Critical Theory and Practice
The Reflective Researcher (editor)
Transforming Social Work Practice (co-editor)
Practice and Research in Social Work (co-editor)
Breakthroughs in Practice (co-editor)

Other books by Susan Hawthorne

The Falling Woman
Wild Politics: Feminism, Globalisation and Bio/ diversity
September 11, 2001: Feminist Perspectives (co-editor)
Bird and other writings on epilepsy
Car Maintenance, Explosives and Love and other lesbian writings (co-editor)
The Spinifex Quiz Book
The Language in My Tongue
The Exploding Frangipani: Lesbian Writing from Australia and New Zealand (co-editor)
Moments of Desire: Sex and Sensuality by Australian Feminist Writers (co-editor)
Difference: Writings by Women

Other books by Renate Klein

Radically Speaking: Feminism Reclaimed (co-editor)
Radical Voices (co-editor)
Test- Tube Women (co-editor)
Theories of Women's Studies (co-editor)
RU 486: Misconceptions, Myths and Morals (co-author)
The Ultimate Colonisation: Reproductive and Genetic Engineering
The Exploitation of a Desire
Infertility: Women Speak Out about their Experiences of Reproductive Medicine

Joint books

Cat Tales: The Meaning of Cats in Women's Lives (Jan Fook, Susan Hawthorne and Renate Klein)
A Girl's Best Friend: The Meaning of Dogs in Women's Lives (Jan Fook and Renate Klein)
CyberFeminism: Connectivity, Critique and Creativity (Susan Hawthorne and Renate Klein)
Australia for Women: Travel and Culture (Susan Hawthorne and Renate Klein)
Angels of Power and other reproductive creations (Susan Hawthorne and Renate Klein)

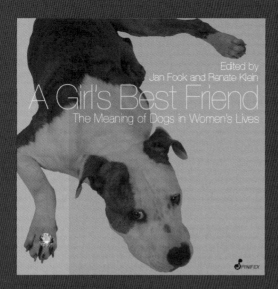

A GIRL'S BEST FRIEND: THE MEANING OF DOGS IN WOMEN'S LIVES

Jan Fook and Renate Klein (eds)

ISBN 1-876756-10-1

Over eighty stories, poems and autobiography, from women and girls about their relationships with dogs. Funny, sad, memorable; readers will laugh and cry as they read this beautifully illustrated book about their best friend.

'Finally, a dog book to recommend unequivocally'
– Debra Adelaide, *Sydney Morning Herald*

'... it is quite possible you won't be able to put this book down'
– Shaunagh O'Connor, *Herald Sun*

'If you are a dog owner, you cannot help but bask in the supreme feeling of justice that these wonderful creatures have finally received the recognition they deserve.'
– *Conscious Living, Summer*

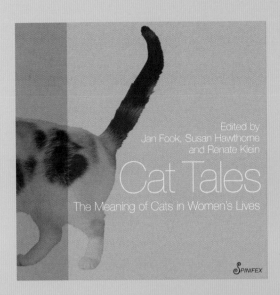

CAT TALES: THE MEANING OF CATS IN WOMEN'S LIVES

Jan Fook, Susan Hawthorne and Renate Klein (eds)

ISBN 1-876756-37-3

Women and cats go back millennia. From ancient Egypt, Assyria and India to the modern world, women's lives are enriched by cats. More than eighty women from many countries and cultures present their stories of feline friendships.

'*Cat Tales* is delightful. It is funny, poignant, thoughtful and sad – and it is a very good book to own… I would recommend this book for all cat lovers – and maybe even the feline-phobic among us. I especially think it would make a great present for those hard-to-buy-for women. It's one of those books you may not think of buying for yourself, but once it's in your collection you will treasure it'.

– Ruth Wykes, *WOW (Women out West)*

'Any cat-loving woman will adore this collection of photographs and stories about women and their beloved cats. There's clever Tiki who travelled one hundred kilometres back to her home after the family moved, only to travel all the way back again. There's Gertrude, much-loved by her owner despite being rather mean and neurotic; and Annapurna, the cat who could not meow. Through their cats, we learn about the women, some saved from loneliness and depression, others heartened and comforted by these miraculous animals. Handsomely designed, this delightful book contains stories, reflections and poems from women all over the world including Marge Piercy and Kerry Greenwood.'

– *Readings Summer Guide 2003.*

If you would like to know more about Spinifex Press,
write for a free catalogue or visit our Web site.

Spinifex Press
PO Box 212, North Melbourne
Victoria 3051, Australia
www.spinifexpress.com.au